Showtime Networks Inc., in association with
Paramount Network Television, Viacom Productions
and Grammnet Productions present

ACT ONE '95
the complete plays

A Festival of New One-Act Plays
April 25 – June 26, 1995

*"The plays seemed too lively, too entertaining, too eager to
please to be the average set of contemporary American theater
work. ...The result is that rare collection of plays, one that,
from first page to last, is a sheer joy to read."*

—BOOKLIST
[Act One '94: A Festival of New One-Act Plays]

Smith and Kraus *Books For Actors*

CONTEMPORARY PLAYWRIGHT COLLECTIONS SERIES

20 One-Acts from 20 Years at the Humana Festival, 1975–1995

Humana Festival '93: The Complete Plays

Humana Festival '94: The Complete Plays

Humana Festival '95: The Complete Plays

Humana Festival '96: The Complete Plays

Humana Festival '97: The Complete Plays

Humana Festival '98: The Complete Plays

Humana Festival '99: The Complete Plays

Women Playwrights: The Best Plays of 1992

Women Playwrights: The Best Plays of 1993

Women Playwrights: The Best Plays of 1994

Women Playwrights: The Best Plays of 1995

Women Playwrights: The Best Plays of 1996

Women Playwrights: The Best Plays of 1997

EST Marathon '94: One-Act Plays

EST Marathon '95: One-Act Plays

EST Marathon '96: One-Act Plays

EST Marathon '97: One-Act Plays

EST Marathon '98: One-Act Plays

Act One Festival '94: One-Act Plays

If you require pre-publication information about upcoming Smith and Kraus books, you may receive our semi-annual catalogue, free of charge, by sending your name and address to *Smith and Kraus Catalogue,4 Lower Mill Road, North Stratford, NH 03590. Or call us at (800) 895-4331, fax (603) 922-3348. WWW.SmithKraus.com.*

ACT ONE '95
the complete plays

Edited by Marisa Smith

Foreword by Risa Bramon Garcia and Jerry Levine

Contemporary Playwrights Series

SK
A Smith and Kraus Book

A Smith and Kraus Book
Published by Smith and Kraus, Inc.
One Main Street, PO Box 127, Lyme, NH 03768

Copyright © 1996 by Smith and Kraus
All rights reserved

Manufactured in the United States of America
Cover and Text Design by Julia Hill

First Edition: January 1996
9 8 7 6 5 4 3 2 1

Library of Congress Cataloguing-in-Publication Data

Act One '95 : the complete plays / edited by Marisa Smith ;
foreword by Risa Bramon Garcia and Jerry Levine.
p. cm. -- (Contemporary playwrights series)
ISBN 1-880399-97-0
1. One-act plays, American. 2. American drama -- 20th century. I. Smith, Marisa. II. Series
IN PROCESS PS627.053 A
812'.04108054--dc20   96-1709
CIP

Contents

Foreword

With our first Festival in 1994, we confirmed our belief that the one-act play is one of the most unique, intriguing and ultimately compelling of all dramatic forms. It has served theatre artists for years as a means to explore the most heightened and intensive conflict in a character's life, an instant that is seized, investigated and changed forever. It allows writers, actors, directors and designers to take great risks in their work and to push the limits of their talents and skills. It provides an absolute experience in the theatre for its creators, performers and audience members alike, bringing everyone together for 30 or so minutes of electric and powerful play.

We are thrilled to have had the opportunity to revisit the one-act with *Act One '95*, our second Festival of new one-act plays. Once again, we set out to provide a theatrical gymnasium in Los Angeles for theatre artists from across the country to come together to create the kind of work on the stage that put *Act One* on the map last spring. With this publication we hope to be able to share the extraordinary power of the one-act with an even wider audience of artists.

In our search for extraordinary one-act plays, we embarked on a six month adventure along with our Artistic Committee of 40 dedicated theatre professionals, reading close to 2,000 pieces, selecting and reading aloud approximately 70 one-acts and work-shopping the most unanimously provocative plays. We had the good fortune to receive about 600 plays that we specifically solicited from emerging and established playwrights alike. We are also delighted to welcome back four of the writers from last year's Festival with new one-acts written and developed for *Act One '95*.

It was our goal last year to do the best theatre we could imagine with a keen eye toward the development of the one-act play into other forms. We knew that there was a logical and natural evolution with the one-act, from the stage to the screen, where an idea, a circumstance, a character, a moment in time would inspire a short film, a series, even a feature film. This year Paramount Network Television, Viacom Productions and Grammnet Productions generously joined Showtime Networks Inc. and The Met Theatre in sponsoring this Festival of 15 new one-act plays, uniting with *Act One* to celebrate the one-act and make a spirited commitment to our work on stage and its future possibilities. Three one-acts are currently being developed by their playwrights into long-form screenplays for Showtime and three more are being developed as series for Paramount Network Television. We are satisfied that the work we do in the theatre is as instantaneous and tenuous as it is meant to be while we strive to find a way to translate its power and capture its brilliance on the screen.

We hope that our efforts and the incredible talents and energies of the artists involved in *Act One* will continue to make a mark on the theatrical landscape of Los Angeles and serve to tighten the bond between the magic of the stage and the power of the screen. We would like to thank all of the directors, actors, designers, stage managers and crew for bringing *Act One '95* to life. Special thanks are extended to Smith and Kraus for their continued vision and dedication in producing this edition; The Met Theatre and our sponsors from their Board of Directors, Alan Vint and Darrell Larson; Co-Producer Kate Baggott and Associate Producer Michael Koopman; Evelyn O'Neill and Suzan Bymel of Bymel/O'Neill Management; Dan Fauci of Paramount Network Television; Kelsey Grammer and Rudy Hornish of Grammnet Productions, and our Executive Producer, Judy Pastore of Showtime Networks Inc., who once again made this all possible. We hope this collection is as exciting, entertaining and beneficial to the reader as was our first edition.

Enjoy!

Risa Bramon Garciá, Producer
Jerry Levine, Producer

A Dead Man's Apartment
by Edward Allan Baker

This work is dedicated to Jim Wargowsky,
in memory of a gentle man.

BIOGRAPHY

Mr. Baker's plays have been produced all over the United States and Canada and include *Dolores, Rosemary with Ginger, North of Providence, Lady of Fadima, Prairie Avenue, Face Divided, The Buffer, The Bride of Olneyville Square, A Public Street Marriage, 27 Benedict Street,* and *In the Spirit* (co-authored with Native American Ensemble Chuka Lokoli). *Dolores* is published in *Best Short Plays 1988–1989,* and was made into a short film that starred Judith Ivey. He is published by Smith and Kraus, Inc., Dramatists Play Service and Applause Theatre Books.

He has authored over a half a dozen screenplays and is currently working on an adaptation for the screen of his play *Rosemary with Ginger* for Showtime, Inc. He's a member of The Ensemble Studio Theatre, The Dramatists Guild, and Writers Guild, East. He resides in northwest Connecticut with his wife Caroline and three children.

AUTHOR'S NOTE

Writing *A Dead Man's Apartment* was great fun for me. I just got out of its way. The writing Master Ray Bradbury said: "Self-consciousness is the enemy of all art, be it acting, writing, painting, or living itself, which is the greatest art of all."

ORIGINAL PRODUCTION

A Dead Man's Apartment was produced by Act One in association with Showtime Networks, Inc., Paramount Network Television, Viacom Productions and Grammnet Productions for Act One '95: A Festival of New One-Act Plays, at The Met Theatre in Los Angeles, CA in May 1995. It was directed by Risa Bramon Garciá with the following cast:

Lonnie	Pruitt Taylor Vince
Valerie Marie	Brittany Murphy
Nickie	Amy Pietz
Al	Jay Thomas

A Dead Man's Apartment was first produced at The Ensemble Studio Theatre Marathon 1995 One-Act Play Festival. It was directed by Ron Stetson (stage manager, Kelly Corona) with the following cast:

Lonnie ....David McConeghey
Valerie Marie ....Alexondra Lee
Nickie..Ilene Kristen
Al ....Bill Cwikowski

CHARACTERS
LONNIE: 38.
NICKIE: 38.
VALERIE MARIE: 17.
AL: mid-40s.

TIME
Noon-ish, Summer, 1994

PLACE
A 2nd floor apartment in Providence

SETTING
A spacious and sparsely-furnished flat with two windows upstage, shades pulled most of the way down. The door is stage-left. A well-worn couch is center. Mismatched kitchen chairs are here and there. A couple of lamps. A table in a corner with soda bottles, pizza boxes, cereal boxes, and doughnut boxes atop it. A phone and phone answering machine are on the floor close to the couch. A suggestion for preshow music—early Joan Armatrading "To the Limit".

A DEAD MAN'S APARTMENT

Preshow music and lights fade to black. Pause. Lights up on Lonnie (38), a balding overweight man clad in workman's overalls. He dashes to the phone machine on the floor. He hits the play-button and hears:

MAN'S VOICE: "You're a dead man."
(Lonnie shakes his head.)
LONNIE: Shit… *(He plays it again.)*
MAN'S VOICE: "You're a dead man."
(Lonnie stands up. Paces, nervously.)
LONNIE: Shit, she's gonna know it's me, Goddamn it! Uh… *(He practices Italianstyle)* You're a dead-a man-ah. *(Doesn't like it. Again, louder.)* You…are…a…dead-a man-a! *(Doesn't like it. Runs and grabs a dish towel from the table. Covers his mouth then does it.)* You're a dead man…
(He likes it. Reaches in his pocket for some change while rehearsing the phrase a few more times. He turns to go for the door when it suddenly opens revealing Nickie (38) in sunglasses, baseball cap, and a hardware-store smock. She looks at him. He looks at her.)
NICKIE: Today's the day, Lonnie. I can't do this anymore. I can't pretend that I believe somethin that I don't cause a the kids yunno, they been in the way an I I don't want to be with you anymore, next to you, callin you or or ironin your shirts or cookin your meals. *(She has backed Lonnie to the couch. She rips off her hat, glasses, and*

smock. Drops her pocketbook.) I'm at a place that is kinda hard to explain but I know it's the end of something and I want to get out before I reach forty, okay? I feel sick inside cause of it every day an an at night I sit on the edge of the bed an I see your shape an I hear you snorin and I grab my Saint Jude Medal and I pray for strength, for help, and I say *"Get me the fuck out of this mess!"* I I say it with tears in my eyes and I say it really pissed off an I say it every night. I I have to say it'd be easier in a way if you hit me an the kids but you never did an you always get your ass outta bed in the mornin to go to work to pay the bills...it's just that um...that I don't feel anything deep for you *and I'm so fuckin' bored I could die, do you understand?!*

(Lonnie stirs to get up. She waves him off.)

NICKIE: Wait wait... *(Beat.)* Where are we goin? I'm afraid and I just want to snap my fingers an go forward five years or back twenty. I for a long time have felt my weddin ring is around my neck an gettin tighter an tighter an...

LONNIE: *(Rises.)* Okay Nickie, I...

NICKIE: *Let me go! Just let me go!* Please say "It's all right, I understand, have a good life, good luck, and good-bye." An then just go. Walk away. No no tears. No anger. No hurt feelings. Just...walk... away...from me...

(He waits. She nods. He rises to where she was standing. She sits on the couch. He begins to get out of his overalls and struggles in doing so.)

LONNIE: *(After a nervous moment.)* I'm...goin to leave you...

NICKIE: *(Waits a beat.)* Uh-huh...and...why are...

LONNIE: Cause I've thought it out an I'm...

NICKIE: You're...

LONNIE: Leavin. I thought it out...

NICKIE: What? That's it?

LONNIE: *(Holds his hand up.)* This isn't as easy for me as as it was for you...

NICKIE: You're right, you're right...

LONNIE: *(Continues.)* Uh...I I want to get out of this before I'm forty an I I'm so sick of your shape...in the in our bed, and it makes me sick inside an you're good with the kids an an cookin an you do get up, you know, in the mornin an uh I uh you you do get up, you know in the mornin... *(Lonnie finally steps out of his overalls in the stage left area revealing him in Bermuda shorts, flowery shirt, black socks and sandals.)* An uh you you never hit me an I'd say that's a good thing an…

NICKIE: *(Suspicious.)* Lonnie…

LONNIE: *(Continuing.)* And if I had a Saint medal, I would scream to its face *"Get me the fuck…"*

NICKIE: *(Stands.)* Lonnie!

(He looks at her.)

NICKIE: Are you havin doubts?

LONNIE: *(Lightens up.)* Oh, oh, you're havin doubts?

NICKIE: *No!* I love you Lonnie!

LONNIE: And I love you Nickie!

(They run into each other's arms and kiss passionately.)

NICKIE: Oh God please don't have doubts…

LONNIE: The way you ended tellin your husband uh, "Say it's all right, I understand, have a good life…"

NICKIE: "…good luck an good-bye and then just go, just leave me, no tears, no…"

LONNIE: It won't happen that way.

NICKIE: It might.

LONNIE: If that happened…

NICKIE: I know it won't be easy but…

LONNIE: If that happened…

NICKIE: But it might if…

LONNIE: If that happened…

NICKIE: If he believes I'm…oh I'm sorry. Finish. Finish. "If that happened…"

LONNIE: If that happened, maybe what we have wouldn't be as deep.

NICKIE: "If that happened, maybe what we have wouldn't be as deep."

LONNIE: You know what I'm sayin?

NICKIE: "If that happened, maybe what we…"

LONNIE: Nickie, there's somethin else…

NICKIE: *(Pulls away from him.)* You're not goin to leave her, are you?

LONNIE: Listen to me. I know that leavin my wife an kids is the right thing to do, shit, I felt that the first time I saw you behind the counter of the hardware store but… *(He takes a breath, holds her steady.)* Somebody wants to take me out.

NICKIE: On a date?

LONNIE: No! Take me out like…kill!

NICKIE: Who would want to kill you?

LONNIE: When I got here today I I saw the light on the machine flashing an...well just listen... *(He gets on his knees. He plays it for her.)*

MAN'S VOICE: "You're a dead man."

(Nickie screams out loud. He plays it again.)

MAN'S VOICE: "You're a dead man."

(Nickie gets on her knees next to Lonnie.)

NICKIE: *(Whispers.)* Who the hell could that be?

LONNIE: *(Whispers.)* Is it your husband?

NICKIE: *(Whispers.)* I...do you think it's your wife?

LONNIE: *(Harsh whisper back.)* How the hell could it be my wife?

NICKIE: Maybe she had someone do it.

LONNIE: Could be the same for you.

NICKIE: "Could be the same for you."

LONNIE: Your husband had someone do it.

NICKIE: "Your husband had..."

LONNIE: *(Stands, upset.)* For Chrissakes Nickie, is it or isn't it?!

NICKIE: *(Hurt.)* Lonnie...that's the first time you ever yelled at me.

LONNIE: I'm sorry. Just a little nervous... Uh, death bothers me.

(She stands and hugs him.)

NICKIE: I don't want nothin to happen to you, oh my God...

LONNIE: I know you don't.

NICKIE: If you die...

LONNIE: You'd die.

NICKIE: *(Beat.)* I don't know, I got kids, hon.

LONNIE: *(Turns away.)* Right-right.

NICKIE: Part a me would die, though.

LONNIE: Yup-yup.

NICKIE: *(Goes to him.)* Would you die if I died?

LONNIE: I got kids too.

NICKIE: That's what I'm sayin.

LONNIE: Same thing, uh part a me would die.

NICKIE: That's what I'm sayin so don't be hurt, okay?

(They embrace warmly.)

LONNIE: Do you think it's your husband?

NICKIE: God, no, it couldn't be because how would he know? *(She moves from Lonnie, thinking.)* Unless...

LONNIE: Unless what?

NICKIE: *(Talking to herself.)* Unless she was so mad at me an decided to tell…

LONNIE: *(Cuts her off.)* Who are you talkin about?!

NICKIE: Valerie!

LONNIE: You told your daughter about us?!
(Nickie goes to the door and swings it open, yells out.)

NICKIE: *Valerie Marie!*
(Lonnie runs to Nickie.)

LONNIE: Wait a minute, wait a minute! *(He closes door.)*

NICKIE: Lonnie, it's all right. Me an her, we're like girlfriends… *(She reopens the door, yells out.)* Get up here!

VALERIE: *(From offstage.)* All right!

LONNIE: *(Closes door.)* This is the same girl who tried to kill herself three times?!

NICKIE: Four if you count the toilet bowl incident but…

LONNIE: *(Blocks door.)* I'm very nervous about this…

NICKIE: *(Gets close to him.)* You love me, don't you?
(He nods.)

NICKIE: Then move from the door, c'mon, we're on a lunch break.
(Sudden knocking at the door. Lonnie tenses up.)

LONNIE: Maybe I'll just leave an you play the message for her without me bein here an that way if…
(Nickie grabs Lonnie's face and kisses him, madly, then yanks him from the door. She throws it open and is face-to-face with Valerie Marie .)

NICKIE: Did you tell your father about me an Lonnie?!

VALERIE: *(Dryly.)* Jesus Christ, Ma, is this him?

LONNIE: *(From across the room.)* Hi.

NICKIE: *(Closes door.)* Lonnie, Valerie. Valerie, Lonnie.
(Valerie is clad in baggy jeans, a flannel shirt over a T-shirt, and a baseball cap worn backwards. She stares at Lonnie.)

VALERIE: You a chef or somethin?

NICKIE: I told you he's a mechanic.

VALERIE: He looks like a chef.

NICKIE: He works on fire trucks.

VALERIE: He looks like a chef.

LONNIE: I work on fire trucks.

NICKIE: *(By the phone machine.)* Get over here, Valerie.

VALERIE: *(Eyes on Lonnie.)* So you're the guy with the "big heart."

NICKIE: Listen to this an tell me who it is.

(Nickie plays message.)
MAN'S VOICE: "You're a dead man."
NICKIE: Is that your father?
VALERIE: I can't tell.
NICKIE: Get on the floor an listen again.
(Valerie does. Message replayed.)
MAN'S VOICE: "You're a dead man."
VALERIE: Ma, I can't tell...
NICKIE: Listen again, closer this time...
(Nickie holds Valerie's head down to the machine.)
MAN'S VOICE: "You're a dead man."
VALERIE: No idea.
(Nickie releases Valerie.)
LONNIE: Uh, forget the message for a sec an let me ask you a question if I can. Did you speak to your father about your mother and I?
VALERIE: Whadda you, retarded?
NICKIE: *(Hits Valerie.)* Watch your mouth!
VALERIE: He asked me a retarded question!
NICKIE: It's not a...
LONNIE: *(Interrupts.)* Okay, okay, so you didn't?
NICKIE: You didn't, right?
VALERIE: *(Stands.)* Me an him don't talk. Don't know how to.
NICKIE: *(To Lonnie.)* It's true. They don't.
VALERIE: Once a year on my birthday he gives me a real weak hug.
NICKIE: Well next year on your birthday you're gonna get a hug from the king-of-hugs, right Lonnie? *(Gestures to Lonnie.)* C'mon, give her a hug, c'mon...
VALERIE: *(Backs away.)* Ma, I don't think so...
(Nickie brings Valerie to Lonnie.)
NICKIE: Hug, hug, feel what a real hug is like.
LONNIE: *(To Valerie.)* It's okay, you don't have to...
NICKIE: C'mon.
VALERIE: Some other time.
LONNIE: Sure.
NICKIE: No, now!
LONNIE: Nickie...
NICKIE: Hug...hug, huh, *hug!*
LONNIE: Okay, all right...
(They hug. Nickie stands back to admire.)

NICKIE: This is soooo nice.

LONNIE: We done?

NICKIE: Huh, Val? Somethin, isn't it?

LONNIE: *(Uncomfortable.)* Okay Val...you can...uh Val?
   (Valerie has tightened her grip on Lonnie.)

NICKIE: You gotta let go Honey, it's not your birthday, c'mon...

LONNIE: C'mon Val, we got other things to uh do so...

NICKIE: *(Pulling at Valerie.)* You gotta let him go... *(More pulling.)*
   Valerie...let...the...man...go!

LONNIE: *(Struggles.)* C'mon Valerie...

NICKIE: *(Steps back.)* Oh Christ! Bang her up against the wall!

LONNIE: I'm not gonna bang her up against the...

NICKIE: God I love you! You're so sensitive...
   *(She kisses Lonnie passionately then tries again to pry Valerie loose
   from Lonnie.)*

NICKIE: Valerie Marie, stop actin like a pit bull an let the man go!
   (Valerie hangs tighter.)

LONNIE: Val? Can you hear us? Can she hear us?

NICKIE: *(Again, backs off.)* Oh I can't believe this. I am so embarrassed.
   Uh I'll be right back.
   (She dashes to the door. Lonnie follows her with Valerie attached to him.)

LONNIE: Where the hell you goin?!

NICKIE: *(At the door, opens it.)* I gotta get my brother... *(She is gone.)*

LONNIE: No! *(He yells out the door.)* I'll bang her up against the wall!
   Nickie! *(Silence. He closes the door.)* Great. *(He moves deeper into the
   flat with Valerie attached to him.)* You want somethin? Doughnut?
   Soda?

VALERIE: *(Muffled.)* Diet?

LONNIE: Yeah.

VALERIE: I hate diet soda.
   (He paces some.)

LONNIE: You really should let go now.

VALERIE: I don't want to.

LONNIE: Why?

VALERIE: I don't know why.

LONNIE: You don't know why?

VALERIE: I don't know why.
   (Lonnie paces around the room with Valerie attached to him.)

LONNIE: Uh okay but just a little thing that kinda bothers me... *(He ambles over to the window and peers out.)* I'm a little nervous today about a lot of things an added to that as of right now is your uncle comin in here an seein you attached to me. I don't think it's how we should first meet, you know what I'm sayin?

VALERIE: *(Suddenly lets him go.)* I'm not stupid!

LONNIE: *(Relieved.)* And I'm not saying you are. You look very stable to me.

(She takes a step closer to him and screams at him, insanely.)

VALERIE: You're just like everybody else! Just like those assholes in school sayin shit like, "Don't fuck, don't smoke, don't wear hats, don't drink and drive!" Don't-don't don't! Meanwhile... *(She pauses, looks at him.)* You listening to me?

(He nods.)

VALERIE: Meanwhile, the TV and magazines are sayin, "Drink! Smoke! Fuck! Drive this car! Image is everything!"

(Valerie is pacing like a maddened animal, fists clenched. Lonnie eyes her.)

VALERIE: I am so sick of it, so so so sick of being pulled an pulled pulled! I am so so sick...of...it!

(She scoops up a bag of Oreo cookies from the table then plops down on the couch. Lonnie inches toward her. She opens a cookie and begins eating the icing, slowly.)

VALERIE: After I quit school I was watchin talk shows like oh probly uh maybe I don't know...ten, twelve a day cause I had the house to myself... *(Eats the cookie.)* Then...I got so fuckin bored at these these assholes on TV that I...*Miss Stupid*...decided I would look an look for stuff my parents had hidden away from me an me *Miss Stupid* found these notebooks a my mother's an I, man, I hit the jackpot, lemme tell ya...*(Leans forward.)* I know all about you.

LONNIE: What do you know a...?

VALERIE: I know about the cyst you had on your...

LONNIE: *(Quickly.)* It was a birthmark.

VALERIE: I know you hate mushrooms. Shellfish. Ham. Chi-chi beans. I know you think your death will come by drowning.

LONNIE: That's changin but um...

VALERIE: I know you cried the time my mother gave you the first back rub you ever had.

LONNIE: *(Worriedly.)* You didn't show your father those notebooks, did you? I mean I don't know you so I have to...

VALERIE: *(Snaps.)* Fuck him! As soon as I got tits we stopped talkin. He's nothin but a shadow who can piss an I don't give him the time of day. *(She gets on the floor next to the machine. She plays the message.)*

MAN'S VOICE: "You're a dead man."

VALERIE: Could be him.

LONNIE: Uh yeah could be him, but listen…

VALERIE: Has reason.

LONNIE: Uh-huh yeah, um…

VALERIE: But I don't know.

LONNIE: But you said he "has reason."

VALERIE: *(Looks up at him.)* Could be him.

LONNIE: Okay okay, lemme ask you this, uh, has he ever…has he ever hurt anyone before?

VALERIE: "Has he ever…has he ever hurt anyone before?"

LONNIE: You know, gettin jealous and hit. Shoot. Beat up.

VALERIE: Have you?

LONNIE: No.

VALERIE: You fuckin whacked your son one time, didn't you?

LONNIE: What? How did you know that?

VALERIE: *(Coyly.)* He told me.

LONNIE: *(Aghast.)* You talked with my son?!

(Door bursts open. Nickie re-enters with Brother Al (45ish) right behind her.)

NICKIE: Oh good, she's off a him!

AL: This him?

NICKIE: Al, Lonnie. Lonnie, Al.

(An exchange of vague nods. Nickie goes to Lonnie.)

NICKIE: No need to be nervous, Lonnie. Al only wants what's good for me.

LONNIE: Good good, that's good.

(Al is a tough-looking man clad in jeans, tight T-shirt that displays his muscles. He wears work boots. He is eating a sandwich and carrying a metal lunch box. He is fixed on Lonnie as Nickie bends to the phone machine.)

NICKIE: Ready Al?

AL: Hit it.

(She does.)

MAN'S VOICE: "You're a dead man."

NICKIE: Did you hear it, Al?

AL: *(Looking at Lonnie.)* I was chewin too loud. Hit it again.

(She does.)

MAN'S VOICE: "You're a dead man."

LONNIE: Boy do I hate hearin that.

AL: Don't blame ya…

NICKIE: What do you think, Al?

AL: I think someone's out to kill him.

NICKIE: No shit, Al, do you know who it is?

AL: I don't give a shit who it is, they're not tryin to kill me… *(Looks at Lonnie.)* But it it'd scare me, I know that.

(Lonnie goes to Nickie, pulls her aside to talk.)

LONNIE: Okay okay then let's…Nickie, let's just back off for today or for a coupla days an then we'll…

NICKIE: *No!* You can't do this to me!

LONNIE: Listen, just until…

NICKIE: No!

LONNIE: …until we let things settle down…

NICKIE: Cause you'll go back to her an probly pick another hardware store to go to an that'll be it!

LONNIE: Calm down, calm down…

(Al snaps his fingers to get Valerie with him and makes to the door.)

AL: Let's go, Nickie…

NICKIE: No! Lonnie, tell Al what you told me that time we was flyin kites…

VALERIE: *(Smugly.)* "I never felt this strong for anybody in my whole life."

NICKIE: *(Stunned.)* How did you know that?

VALERIE: Your notebooks, Ma.

AL: *(Bemusedly.)* You two was flyin kites?

VALERIE: "I want a man to kiss me forever."

NICKIE: *(Goes to Val.)* Two can play this game.

VALERIE: "I want a man to wake me up just to hold me tight."

NICKIE: "I love it when Greg looks at my chest!"

VALERIE: *(Stunned.)* You read my diary?!

NICKIE: "I'd sleep with Larry in two seconds if he asked!"

VALERIE: "I feel so hungry for somethin I can't explain!"

NICKIE: *(Face to face with Val.)* "I wanna scream out *I itch so bad I can't sleep!*"

AL: *Hey! Separate!*

(The girls part quickly. Slight pause.)

LONNIE: *(Finally.)* So look…we're all on a lunch break here an-an…
(He inches his way along the back wall toward the door.) Time's
runnin out so why don't we go back to work an…

AL: *(In Lonnie's way.)* You still thinkin a breakin with your wife tonight?

NICKIE: *(Goes to Lonnie.)* Yes he is! Tell him Lonnie! Say yes-you-are!

LONNIE: Well so much has happened and I…
(Nickie pushes Lonnie up against the wall.)

NICKIE: I need you. I need your life in my life, oh please don't back
from our promises…

AL: Anythin the two of you had is by the boards cause the man is scared
a losin his wife…

LONNIE: Life.

AL: What?

LONNIE: You said "scared a losin his wife" but you meant life.

NICKIE: Oh God Lonnie, are you ascared a losin your wife?

LONNIE: Life!

AL: *(Closes in on Lonnie.)* But if you really loved Nickie, you'd do right
by her, right or wrong?

NICKIE: And he's goin to, right Lonnie?

VALERIE: God Ma, stop slobbering.

AL: Let the man speak.
(All look at Lonnie.)

LONNIE: *(After a beat.)* I do…I do love Nickie. We've had some fun.

AL: Right-right, flyin kites.
*(Lonnie moves to the back of the couch, looks down at Nickie who is
seated.)*

LONNIE: Uh, eating out.

VALERIE: Shitload a that I bet.
(Nickie makes a move to go at Valerie but Lonnie holds her shoulders.)

AL: *(Moves in on Lonnie.)* So basic sneaking around, cheatin, screwin
around with another man's wife, tellin her things you can't tell your
wife an doin things you don't do with your wife an an…
(Lonnie is backing from Al, Al stalks him while speaking.)

AL: You take your wife to the show? Out to eat?

LONNIE: No. I used to.

AL: An your wife's a housewife, right Val?

VALERIE: Yup.

AL: An Nickie she's givin you a a what? A glow kinda in your gut? A feelin that gets you through a day? It makes bein next to your wife uh harder or easier?

LONNIE: Little a both but listen…

AL: No you listen! There are families involved! Kids. Picture albums. Ma-mentoes. In-laws. Bank accounts. Kids. You take your boys fishin?

LONNIE: *(Still backing up.)* What?

AL: Bowlin?

LONNIE: No, I…

AL: Ball games?

LONNIE: Uh no…

AL: Two boys, right? Right, Val?

VALERIE: *(Enjoying this.)* Ten and sixteen.

AL: You go to church?

NICKIE: I love you Lonnie…

LONNIE: *(To Al.)* No I…

VALERIE: *(Right behind Al.)* His son says he listens to tapes um somethin like "unlocking your inner doorknob."

LONNIE: When did you talk to my son?

VALERIE: Last week.

LONNIE: Did you know this Nickie?

NICKIE: *(From the couch.)* I didn't think it would hurt.

LONNIE: We had an agreement not to tell anybody about us!

NICKIE: Lonnie Hon, it's been so nice I couldn't keep it in.

AL: So okay you're listening to tapes. Uh, Val tells me your son says you're moody, sorta lazy, like to smoke grass in the basement.

VALERIE: Can't fix anythin but cars an wanders winda to winda.

AL: No shit?

VALERIE: Plays gospel music real loud and cries.

AL: *(To Lonnie.)* That true?

(Al and Valerie have Lonnie cornered in upstage right corner.)

LONNIE: I don't believe this…

AL: Hey pal, you started this! An I gotta know if you got the insides to go through life with my sista. That fair soundin to you or do you got a problem with me?

NICKIE: Be careful, Lonnie…

(Lonnie backs farther into the corner.)

LONNIE: No, I do have a problem with you. I have a problem now that

I know my son was talked to an an I got a problem with the
surprise of you an an Valerie bein here today an…

VALERIE: Don't forget the death threat.

LONNIE: An that gospel music thing happened one time!

AL: Can't forget someone's on to you.

(Valerie pulls Al to the side to talk with him.)

VALERIE: His son says that he disappears to the fuckin basement when
somethin goes wrong or something like "when he feels cornered."

*(Again Lonnie is trying to inch his way to the door. Nickie notices and
runs to block the doorway.)*

NICKIE: Tell 'em Lonnie that we're goin to a place that'll have no
basement an tell 'em you're gonna change with me an you'll be
different, c'mon, tell 'em…

(Pause. Lonnie is motionless.)

NICKIE: C'mon…tell 'em…

*(Lonnie remains unblinkingly still. Nickie rubs his face in a loving
manner.)*

NICKIE: Okay then, let's tell 'em together, okay? You wanna do that?
Tell 'em together?

*(Lonnie nods, barely. Al and Valerie laugh and move to sit and eat
together. Nickie coaxes Lonnie, pulling him toward Al and Valerie.)*

NICKIE: Nickie and I we…we…

LONNIE: *(Softly.)* Take walks…

NICKIE: Holdin hands an…

LONNIE: An she loves lookin at horses. So we do that…

NICKIE: An we eat…

LONNIE AND NICKIE: Clamcakes…

LONNIE: *(Gaining energy.)* On the rocks a Narragansett…

NICKIE: Not lettin the spray a the waves bother us…and we talk…

LONNIE: To each other…

NICKIE AND LONNIE: Every day…

LONNIE: An then gettin a place hidden away an an the phone an
machine was to have in case one of us couldn't get here…

NICKIE: Cause a some family thing…

LONNIE: We decided to do that…

(Al and Valerie stare at them in quiet disbelief.)

NICKIE: An then we set a date to tell our, which is today an uh…

LONNIE: *(Cuts in.)* An then this message kinda made me look, uh think
at what we intend to do uh real hard an…uh…

(Nickie whispers something to him. Moves behind Valerie and Al.)

LONNIE: Uh…I went with Nickie to her father's grave an I stood there in the rain an watched her cry an bend to smooth the stone with her hand…

(Awkward silence for a beat. Al is waiting.)

NICKIE: An you said…when I came back to the car, you said…

LONNIE: Oh-oh. I said it looked like she was rubbin his face…

NICKIE: *(Leans to Al and Valerie.)* Isn't that nice?

(Nothing from Al and Valerie.)

LONNIE: I felt something for her in a place I never been to before an…

(Lowers his head. He begins to cry, softly.)

VALERIE: You never been to a graveyard?

NICKIE: *(Moved.)* Oh Lonnie… *(She is comforting him.)*

AL: Whoa-whoa is he bawlin?

NICKIE: I told you he was sensitive.

AL: *(To Valerie.)* Is he fuckin bawlin?!

VALERIE: *(Goes to look.)* He's fuckin bawlin.

AL: *(Stands up.)* Don't let me see you bawlin, pal, cause I'll whack you!

NICKIE: Cut it out Al!

AL: An worse than that is a woman goin, "Oh he's so sensitive, I think I'll love him!"

NICKIE: He's all upset cause a that…

(Gestures to phone machine. Lonnie is trying to recover.)

AL: This is it?!

(Nickie is wiping Lonnie's face with a Kleenex.)

NICKIE: Take a breath, Lon-Hon…

AL: *(Pacing.)* This guy is what you want?! So you can go an fly kites an cry together?! This is what blowin my lunch hour is been about?! I thought I was comin to meet a man!

NICKIE: You're not seein the real Lonnie!

(She sits Lonnie down on the couch.)

AL: *(Goes at Lonnie.)* Whadda you goin to do when her son gets outta drug rehab an needs you? Whadda you goin to do when Val here comes screamin to you for answers? You goin to start cryin? You goin to say, "the hell with this," an go back to your wife? You goin to give 'em the wrong answers?!

NICKIE: *(Gets between Al and Lonnie.)* Stop it Al! You don't understand, he's more than what you're gettin today on account a that damn message an…

AL: *(Moves by Nickie.)* Do you think leavin your wife for Nickie is goin to make you smart all of a sudden?

NICKIE: He's not lookin to be smart!

VALERIE: "He's not lookin to be smart!"

(Lonnie is feeling the bombardment as he slouches down on the couch.)

LONNIE: Stop...look...just just...please just...

(Al has had enough. He picks up his lunch box and makes for the door. Nickie runs and stops him before he can exit.)

NICKIE: Listen to me, Al, this is the man I I want an I know you're seein just the outside an an...look at me Al!

(Al does.)

NICKIE: I need him...I'm so afraid of...of turnin into a dried up woman, like Ma, yunno?

AL: *(Points a finger at her.)* Hey!

(He attempts to leave but Nickie swipes his lunch box.)

NICKIE: Look at me Al an I'm askin you to go deep down an an understand why I need Lonnie an...an then, let us go. Let me feel a man's hand on my face again. Look at me Al...

(He does.)

NICKIE: I'm so tired a standin still. I I want the warmth...Lonnie's warmth to move me inside to bein happy.

(She hands him back his lunch box then rejoins Lonnie on the couch. They hold hands. Al takes a full moment to eye the both of them on the couch. He looks straight at Lonnie.)

AL: Is this a dick thing?

LONNIE: What?

AL: This has got to be a dick thing, right?

NICKIE: We haven't even had sex!

AL: *(To Lonnie.)* True?

LONNIE: True.

VALERIE: Wonda if the person who wants to kill ya knows that?

LONNIE: *(To Al.)* All we been doin in here is is kissin on the couch an talkin about uh life an dreamin a bein together, of of another life together!

AL: Oh that sounds like alotta fun...

(Al walks away from them. He is thinking. All wait for his next word. Finally—)

AL: Val, do your thing?

LONNIE: What? What thing?

AL: *(To Valerie.)* Kinda like the shit you did to me last week.

NICKIE: *(Rises from the couch.)* Oh shit…

VALERIE: The uh I-don't-wanna-live-no-more or the-bangin-the-head-up-against-the-wall?

AL: Go with the I-don't-wanna-live-no-more.

(Valerie starts to hyperventilate, getting ready.)

NICKIE: Do your best Lonnie.

LONNIE: Best at what?!

AL: *(Instructs Lonnie.)* Okay so now you're in the parlor…An an say you an Nickie are a "thing" now an an Val comes outta somewhere all upset an has no one else to go to but you…

LONNIE: *(To Nickie.)* Why did you bring them here?!

AL: *(Walking away.)* You can't cash in nothin and get somethin!

LONNIE: What the hell does that mean?!

NICKIE: I love you Lonnie…

LONNIE: Then why are you doin this?!

VALERIE: *(Next to Al.)* Can I start now?

NICKIE: *(Rushes to Lonnie on the couch.)* Listen to me, you can do it. Prove to them we can and will be happy before our lunch break is up.

(Al moves Nickie away from Lonnie just as Valerie jumps on the couch then leans into Lonnie's face.)

VALERIE: I want to die! I can't see any reason to get up anymore!

LONNIE: Nickie, I'm hurtin…

VALERIE: My mother just says, "Do what I say!" An my father says, "Get off the couch I gotta lay down." An every day is the same an I…

LONNIE: Nickie…

VALERIE: Maybe people will feel for me when I'm dead—*the pain of livin will be over*—

LONNIE: Nickie, why can't we just go on the way we been goin?!

NICKIE: *(Goes to Lonnie.)* Lonnie, your face is flushed… *(To Al.)* I never seen that before.

AL: *(Bends to Lonnie.)* Never mind her, what are you goin to say to Val?!

VALERIE: *(Still atop Lonnie.)* A knife in my heart, a rope around my neck…

LONNIE: I have no idea what you're doin!

VALERIE: *(Looks at Al.)* Should I stop?

AL: No, keep goin Val!

NICKIE: Start fightin Lonnie Honey!

VALERIE: I don't wanna live oh stepfather an I need to hear from somebody on why I should, okay?!

LONNIE: *(In her face.)* Well, *fuck you,* okay?!

VALERIE: Gimme a reason oh stepfather for seein the sun come up tammara!

(Lonnie struggles to get off the couch.)

LONNIE: Oh for Chrissakes…

(He turns around to face Valerie who is standing on the couch.)

VALERIE: I-I…look I bit my wrist open an it's bleedin, hurry I'm bleedin bad…

LONNIE: You're not bleedin!

VALERIE: *(Holds out her wrist.)* My blood…it's drippin on your feet, it's gettin…I'm gettin…I'm feelin so so weak…

(She falls into Lonnie's arms. Lonnie lays her down on the couch.)

LONNIE: I don't know what to tell you…I got through it. We all get through it. You do what you have to do and you get through it an yeah yeah most of it sucks but you push on, push on past the beatins and the bein ignored an push past no one there to hold you an you fuckin push on past when you think you don't matta an nothin matters an there's no peace in anybody's fuckin house! For Chrissakes people dyin for gettin laid an other people dyin cause they can't get laid an you kids…you Goddamn kids nowadays… you want all the answers like right away! "Gimme an answer or I'll kill myself!" *Well fuck you!* You don't think we had…we adults had pain when we was growin up?! For Chrissakes *wake the fuck up* an be thankful you got a roof over ya head an food on the table an a bed to wallow over your bullshit in! Be thankful for the malls you hang out in an for the stupid clothes ya wear an the teachers you insult and hate!

(Valerie gets up from the couch to cross the room and is stopped by Lonnie who spins her around to face him. He shakes her.)

LONNIE: Just know that all this will pass, Goddamn it, all…of… this…will…pass!

(Silence. Valerie walks to Nickie.)

VALERIE: *(Looks at Lonnie.)* Oh yeah, I really wanna live now.

LONNIE: *(Turns around to Al.)* Don't you agree? I mean these kids, they gotta be told an I'm sick a them thinkin they can say whatever they want an…

(Al presses down on the machine with his foot.)

MAN'S VOICE: "You're a dead man."
(A slight pause. Lonnie turns to Nickie.)
LONNIE: Nickie, say somethin, tell 'em our love is in this apartment an how much we shared…
VALERIE: Ma, he's the worst one of the whole bunch.
(Lonnie's face drops.)
LONNIE: What? What did you say?
AL: Lon-man, it's all over.
LONNIE: *(Angrily.)* Hey, technically speaking, this is our apartment an I could kick your ass outta here or call the cops!
AL: *(Gets closer to Lonnie.)* I own this building, pal! So, technically speaking, I'm your landlord an I let Nickie use it when she thinks someone like you is the *one* to save her. Shit, I could name five, six guys in the past…
NICKIE: Don't…
AL: I won't honey…
(Nickie crosses to the upstage table to get the picture of Lonnie and her.)
NICKIE: Poor Lonnie… *(She removes the photo.)*
AL: It's all over between you an my sista.
LONNIE: I'm not gonna let this happen.
AL: What are you gonna do?
(Lonnie runs to Nickie and picks her up, holds her in a bear hug.)
LONNIE: Oh God Nickie it's been so nice that no matta what was goin on in my home life, I always knew I had this an you…
AL: Let her go…
NICKIE: *(Struggling.)* Lonnie, let me go…
LONNIE: What we had was fine til…
AL: *(Pulling at Lonnie.)* It's over, let her go!
NICKIE: I I can't breathe…
(Valerie is helping Al to get Lonnie to release Nickie.)
LONNIE: I need you to hold me on Tuesdays an Thursdays an an lets add on Sundays, okay?
AL: *(Pulls harder at Lonnie.)* C'mon, that's enough…let go…
NICKIE: *(Barely audible.)* I…please…Lon…
(Al gets close to Lonnie's ear.)
AL: I killed a man in this apartment!
(Lonnie looks at Nickie. She nods. Lonnie puts Nickie down, releases her.)

AL: A man who was screwin my wife. Name unimportant. I stabbed him beyond repair.

(Nickie is at the table with Valerie touching up her makeup.)

AL: I watched them from the building across the street. I saw him massaging her breasts, the same breasts I kissed when she was seventeen…those were my breasts! His tongue in her ear, that was *my* ear! She was doin it with this bum afta she found out I screwed a friend a hers, which I could not help by the way, I mean I spent so much time fanta-sizin about her that the first time alone with her I…well it was easy to get started cause I had done her so many times in my head but…uh shit, where was I goin with this?

VALERIE: Killin the bum.

NICKIE: "…his tongue in her ear that was my ear…"

AL: Right. So I went nuts. I I came runnin over here and kicked in the door an he turned, saw me, pulled up his fly an ran over to the winda an I…I…

NICKIE: Hurry, Al, hurry…

AL: It happened fast an uh funny the things ya rememba but I rememba he he smelled like her…her smell was all over him…Shall-la-mar… *(Lost for a beat.)* Uh I did my time, my crime-of-passion time, an I a course lost her, a course. She's married now to Paul Morretti…

NICKIE: Morretti of Morretti's pizza…

VALERIE: The one on Pontiac Avenue, that one…

NICKIE: *(Caringly.)* Al, don't drive down there no more, you hear me?

AL: Yeah…I uh…my two kids I don't see no more yunno cut off from that an now I protect Nickie from guys like you Lon-man. All you guys, right? All you guys who wanna be safe with somebody but got nothin but what? Dirty laundry? You can't help her but yunno, I don't blame ya, lookit Nickie, she's beautiful, right? She looks like she's twenty years old for Chrissakes, an an her heart up in her eyes an those teeth, the smile of of niceness…

(Nickie beams. Valerie is bored. Lonnie drained.)

NICKIE: Al Hon, c'mon I don't wanna get fired.

AL: *(Goes to Lonnie.)* But hey, I love the thing about the tape you listen to…the…uh…

VALERIE: "Unlocking your inner doorknob" but c'mon Uncle Al, let's…

AL: *(Cuts her off.)* That's a new one, shit, betta than the mailman who said he and Nickie were lovers in a past life in uh…

NICKIE: Mongolia.

AL: *(Laughs.)* Ain't that a winna! Fuckin Mongolia!

(Al, Nickie and Valerie have a good laugh. When it dies down, they all look to Lonnie alone on the couch. Al goes and sits next to him.)

AL: Cheer up Lonnie, I maybe saved your life cause hey who knows maybe if you and Nickie say got together an one night you an she have a spat an you get to feelin a little homesick an you circle your old house an there's a car in the driveway you recognize an you start to burn inside real hot in the gut an memories from in that house start to surface yunno, holidays, birthdays, monopoly, an you look in the winda an you see her sittin there lookin the best she's looked in years an there's a guy on the couch next to her, an he's smilin an she's smilin... *(Al takes a moment then—)* Are you ready to see somebody goin afta your wife the way you been goin afta Nickie?

LONNIE: *(Pauses a moment.)* No.

VALERIE: *(At the door.)* Good. Can we get outta here now?

NICKIE: *(Goes to Lonnie.)* So I guess this is... *(Stops, looks to Al.)* Hey, what about the "you're a dead man" guy?

AL: Tell her Lonnie.

LONNIE: Uh...it's me. I'm the "you're a dead man" guy.

NICKIE: You threatened your own life?!

LONNIE: I did it to stall the breakin up with my wife cause I wanted to keep things the way they were with me an you...

VALERIE: *(Steps up to Lonnie.)* Well this was fun. Nice to meet ya.

LONNIE: *(Shakes her hand.)* Yeah.

VALERIE: *(Leans into him.)* Don't hit your son no more.

(Lonnie nods, understandingly. Nickie steps up to Lonnie.)

NICKIE: Well Lonnie...no tears...

LONNIE: No uh...anger.

NICKIE: No hurt feelings.

LONNIE: Just good-bye.

NICKIE: Good luck.

(They shake hands. Nickie turns to leave with Valerie.)

NICKIE: Oh Jesus Val, did you remomba to turn the sauce down to low before you...

VALERIE: *(Out the door.)* Yeah yeah afta I heard it bubblin.

NICKIE: *(Exits behind Valerie.)* Your father will have a ca-nip-tion if it's ruined...

AL: It's past lunch, Lon-Man, I don't wanna lose my job. Go home. Tell your wife you lo…

LONNIE: *(Cuts him off.)* Al, don't tell me what I should tell my wife. I know what I should tell my wife.

AL: *(Smiles.)* Now you know. That's somethin, right? *(Gets closer to Lonnie.)* Am I right? Huh? C'mon, am I right? Look at me…

LONNIE: *(Looks at Al, smiles.)* Yeah yeah ya sonofabitch, you're right.

AL: Good. Good.

(Al quickly hugs Lonnie, and cries in his arms. Lonnie comforts him— Al pulls away, he got it out. He proceeds to the door then proclaims—)

AL: I feel good.

(Al exits. Lonnie closes the door then turns back into the room very much a man alive.)

LONNIE: "Now you know. That's something, right?"

(Lights fade as Gospel music is heard coming up and blackout on A Deadman's Apartment.*)*

END OF PLAY

Breast Men

A Comedy in One Act
by Bill Bozzone and Joe DiPietro

Dedicated to Josh Mostel

BIOGRAPHIES

Bill Bozzone plays include *Korea, House Arrest, Rose Cottages, Buck Fever, Saxophone Music,* and *Sonny DeRee's Life Flashes Before His Eyes.* Off Broadway, his work has premiered at the Ensemble Studio Theatre and others. Regionally, his work has been produced by such theaters as the Philadelphia Festival Theatre for New Plays, City Theatre of Pittsburgh, and the Playwrights Lab of Minneapolis. For film, he wrote the screenplay for the 1988 film *Full Moon In Blue Water,* and was co-writer on TNT's *The Last Elephant* which was nominated for a Cable ACE award as Best Movie of 1990. Awards include a National Endowment for the Arts grant, a New York State Foundation for the Arts grant, and a fellowship from the Eugene O'Neill Theatre Center. Bill Bozzone currently lives in Connecticut with his wife, fiction writer Tricia Bauer.

Joe DiPietro wrote the book and lyrics for the musical *I Love You, You're Perfect, Now Change* which broke all box office records at the American Stage Company. His sketch comedy *Love Lemmings* ran Off Broadway at The Village Gate before touring Australia among other places. His play *Over the River and Through the Woods* was selected for the 1994 Eugene O'Neill National Playwright's Conference where it won the Charles MacArthur Fellowship. His farce *The Virgin Weeps* premiered at Sacramento's B Street Theatre, and his comedy *Executive Dance* has been published in *More Ten Minute Plays from Actor's Theatre of Louisville.*

ORIGINAL PRODUCTION

Breast Men was produced by Act One in association with Showtime Networks Inc., Paramount Network Television, Viacom Productions and Grammnet Productions for *Act One '95: A Festival of New One-Act Plays,* at The Met Theatre in Los Angeles, CA in April 1995. It was directed by Josh Mostel with the following cast:

Lloyd ....John C. McGinley
Smart ....Steve Hofvendahl
Gene ....Robert Lessor

Breast Men

A honeymoon cottage somewhere in the Poconos.
The room is set for a romantic evening. Tacky does not even begin to
describe it.
A pink and purple motif. A furry rug. A queen-sized bed with a cupid
bedspread. A basket with fruit, love lotion and condoms. Cheap
champagne. If Martha Stewart saw this room, she would die instantly.
Lloyd enters, wearing shorts and a T-shirt. Looks around, sighs.

LLOYD: God, this is so perfect. Oh! It's better than the brochure even!
Oh, look! (*He goes to fruit basket. Smiles. Pulls out a strip of*
condoms.) They thought of everything! You'd have to be made of
stone not to lose your heart in a place like this.
(*Stuart enters, wearing a bulky cable knit sweater, carrying two bags.*
He looks around, astonished.)
STUART: You've got to be kidding.
LLOYD: Thanks for coming with me, buddy!
STUART: This is somebody's idea of romantic?
LLOYD: I think it's spectacular!
STUART: What kind of sick female came up with this place?
LLOYD: Leave it to you, a man, not to appreciate a love shrine like this!
Oh God, if only Sara was here …
(*Lloyd moves to the phone, dials.*)
STUART: Lloyd, she left you three and a half weeks ago, and since then
you've done nothing but whine and grovel …
LLOYD: (*Into phone.*) Sara, I know you're checking messages!
STUART: Lloyd, don't!
LLOYD: Guess where I am?! Does the name *Love Acres* mean anything to
you? That's right! I came up here without you! Yeah, I came up

with a big, fat waitress I picked up at Stuckey's! She looks just like Sally Struthers in those *Feed the Children* commercials! She's beautiful! I'm lying! It's me and Stuart! You can imagine how much fun that is!

(*Stuart starts to pull the phone away from Lloyd.*)

LLOYD: – call me! I'm dying here!

(*Stuart manages to grab it and hang up.*)

STUART: Lloyd, I will not allow you to do this to yourself! Pull it together! Listen, I know women, I've been through plenty of 'em!

LLOYD: You haven't had a date in eighteen months.

STUART: Hey! That's because I'm choosy! And let me tell ya, a woman's like a bus – you miss one, another comes along in five minutes.

LLOYD: Sara and I used to ride buses all the time.

STUART: Lloyd, I'm trying to be supportive, you're getting to be annoying. Why can't it be like the old days? Remember? No women! We used to sit up all night drinking Peppermint Schnapps and just being buds. Face facts: she's gone, life goes on, get over it! God, it's hot in here! (*Stuart goes to air conditioner, fiddles with it.*)

LLOYD: You know what I miss about Sara? I say this with the utmost respect: her breasts.

STUART: (*Banging on the air conditioner.*) Fucker's not working! (*Stuart goes to phone.*)

LLOYD: I know it's not profound or anything, but they were shaped like balled-up, perfect little kittens. They weren't too big, they weren't too small. I was so happy when I was nuzzled there.

STUART: (*Into phone.*) I'll hold – (*To Lloyd.*) Lloyd look, I know what you're going through. I'm a breast man! But you can't let a couple of mammary glands run your life –

LLOYD: Yes, I can –

STUART: Then you're nothing but a simpering nipple worshipper … (*Into phone.*) No, not you, sir. Look, we're in cottage … (*Stuart looks over to Lloyd.*)

LLOYD: Cupid II.

STUART: (*Into phone.*) We're in the Cupid II and the air conditioner won't turn on. Can you make it quick? Okay, thanks. (*He hangs up.*)

LLOYD: Why don't you take off your sweater if you're hot?

STUART: Who said I'm hot?

LLOYD: How can you not be hot? It's gotta be ninety-five degrees in here. (*Lloyd peels off his shirt.*)
STUART: We're firemen, Lloyd. To a fireman ninety-five degrees isn't that hot.
LLOYD: You're not a fireman. You're a dispatcher.
STUART: Hey, don't go down that road!
LLOYD: I just think it's important to be clear who fights the fires and who sits in the cage and talks on the phone ...
STUART: Hey! Who do you think is responsible for everything? Like the night you were driving and you couldn't find City Hall. Who had the entire map of Bayonne committed to mind?
LLOYD: By the time you got us there, it was burnt to the ground.
STUART: At least you got there. You made an appearance.
LLOYD: Fine. Now would you please take that sweater off. It's July – in the Poconos.
STUART: Why are you so obsessed with me and my sweater? It's my lucky sweater! You got a problem with that?
LLOYD: You know, I had a lucky sweater. Sara took it. She probably gave it to her new boyfriend. I followed them. He weighs over 300 pounds. A 300-pound man is stretching out my lucky sweater! (*A beat.*) I'm sorry. I don't mean to continuously talk about my wife. My ex-wife. She's gone, dammit. It's only been three and a half weeks. And those have been the best three and a half weeks of my life.
STUART: There you go!
LLOYD: What am I saying? I wish I were dead. We should have gone hunting. You could have shot me. My life is over! I need a hug.
STUART: No hugging!
LLOYD: But I need one!
STUART: Lloyd, get a grip! We're in Cupid II. There will be no hugging this weekend.
LLOYD: You know what I even did for that woman: I even wrote her a poem – me! It was like – like giving birth! I don't suppose you want to hear it?
STUART: No Lloyd, I'd hate to.
LLOYD: Okay, here goes. It's to the tune of *Gilligan's Island.*
    Just sit right back and you'll hear a tale
    A tale of this crazy guy
    Who met the woman of his dreams

My oh my oh my
The girl was a mighty poem of love
Her breasts were firm as mountains
And every time I held her tight
We erupted like love fountains.

STUART: Good poem, Lloyd. If someone wrote that for me, I'd be theirs.

LLOYD: Thanks, buddy. Hey, but you're more than my buddy: we're the two musketeers!

(*They gesture.*)

LLOYD: I love you coming on this trip with me. I love you going in half with me.

STUART: Half? I'm going in half?

LLOYD: Well, sure. I just thought it was understood. (*A beat.*)

STUART: Well – fine. Okay. One shipmate throwing a life preserver to his best amigo. I'll write you a check because I know if I were in trouble, you'd write me an even bigger check.

LLOYD: Damn right, buddy! Hey, c'mon! We're here to have a good time no matter how awful my life is! No more moping! Put on your swim trunks! Let's cruise the pool! (*Lloyd thrusts off his shorts.*)

STUART: No! Uh, swimming – no, I, uh – not possible.

LLOYD: C'mon, we'll sit pool-side, meet some babes, show off our chests –

STUART: No swimming. Lloyd – we've got to talk.

LLOYD: I'll talk about anything but Sara.

STUART: Fine.

LLOYD: God I miss her! The way she would eat a cheeseburger – she'd wolf it down in one bite, no chewing! The woman was a saint!

STUART: Listen, I know you're going through a really bad time right now –

LLOYD: Yes, I am.

STUART: And I sympathize. But there are worse problems in the world to have, much worse, and I have one of them now.

LLOYD: What're you talking about?

STUART: Okay, I didn't want to mention this back home, cause I wanted your full attention. Here goes – I need an operation. I have a terrible medical problem.

LLOYD: Sara once had a terrible medical problem …

STUART: Could we please get off of Sara?! I have a terrible medical problem.

LLOYD: Oh my God …

STUART: I need an operation. And it costs about five grand. And firemen don't make that kind of money.

LLOYD: You're not a fireman. You don't even have the red hat.

STUART: Look, I need an operation! Can I have the money or not?

LLOYD: What's the matter?

STUART: I – I can't reveal that. It's personal.

LLOYD: We're the two musketeers.

(*They gesture.*)

LLOYD: How personal can it be?

STUART: Look, it's private and I just need you to trust me.

LLOYD: I told you about my swollen testicle.

STUART: I know, and I love you for that, but this is – even more personal. This surgery, our medical insurance doesn't cover it. It's considered – cosmetic.

LLOYD: Like a nose job?

STUART: It's not exactly a nose job. It's what the doctors call a suction-assisted lipectomy – or a gynocostomy.

LLOYD: Sounds like a woman thing –

STUART: Me? A woman thing? Right! That's a laugh! You're fucking out of your mind! C'mon, punch me in the stomach as hard as you can!

(*Lloyd prepares to.*)

STUART: No, forget it! Okay, it's a condition that affects men – the more manly, the more it affects them – and it involves a swelling of the pectoral area to unnatural, mammalian proportions.

LLOYD: Help me out, Stu, in English.

STUART: I've grown breasts. (*Pause.*)

LLOYD: I didn't hear ya.

STUART: You know, breasts.

LLOYD: That's not funny. I'm very vulnerable right now, and you're playing jokes.

STUART: It's no joke. My doctor says it's a common condition but I'm not so sure I didn't get it from some nutty chick I dumped who was secretly into voodoo.

LLOYD: (*After a moment.*) You have breasts. (*Pause.*) So how come I don't see them?

STUART: They're not huge, and, well, the sweater is hiding them.

(*A beat. Lloyd stares.*)

LLOYD: Well, let me see 'em.

STUART: I rather you didn't.

LLOYD: Then let me feel them.

STUART: That's not going to happen.

LLOYD: You're full of shit.

STUART: Lloyd, if you had breasts, would you show them to me?

LLOYD: We're the two musketeers.

(*They gesture.*)

LLOYD: – if I had breasts, you could wallow between them.

STUART: Lloyd, as my sidekick, I'm asking you to trust me and give me the money!

LLOYD: You know what I think this is? I think this is you attempting to divert all the attention –

STUART: What?

LLOYD: My heart is in two, on the floor, I'm a melted pile of agony, and you come in here, trying to steal my thunder –

STUART: Look, Lloyd, lots of men get divorced, not lots of men grow breasts!

LLOYD: You do not have breasts!

(*Lloyd lunges for Stuart and feels his chest. Stuart tries to stop him, but it is too late. A frozen moment, as Lloyd has his hands on his buddy's chest. Lloyd quickly reels back. Stuart steps away, very embarrassed.*)

LLOYD: Oh my God ...

STUART: Happy now?

LLOYD: Those are – those are –

STUART: So – now will you lend me the cash?

LLOYD: How can you talk of money at a time like this? You have breasts. Breasts! It's just so amazing ...

STUART: So you now understand the severity of the problem. Write me a check.

LLOYD: Well – ya know, I, uh, I could do that. But something like this doesn't come along every day.

STUART: What're you talking about?

LLOYD: – well, I've always been curious about breasts. I'm a breast man, too! And I have a lot of questions – questions that I'm too embarrassed to ever ask a real woman.

STUART: You want to ask me questions?

(*Lloyd nods.*)

STUART: Then you'll give me the money?

LLOYD: Absolutely.

STUART: I feel like a prostitute, but go ahead, ask your questions.

LLOYD: Okay – okay – this is exciting. All of a sudden, I miss Sara a lot less.

STUART: Ask!

LLOYD: Okay. Do you wear a brassiere?

STUART: No, but I do wear an elastic support garment.

LLOYD: That's a brassiere!

STUART: Next question!

LLOYD: All right. (*Beat.*) When you rub them, do you get a warm, glowy sensation?

STUART: I have no idea. I haven't tried.

LLOYD: No time like the present.

STUART: I'm not gonna try it in front of you!

LLOYD: Stuart, come on. We're as close as any two guys can be. We've seen each other in the basest of situations – naked, humping, puking.

(*A beat. Stuart softly rubs one of his breasts.*)

STUART: Yeah, it feels nice.

LLOYD: You want me to do the other one?

STUART: Get the fuck away from me!

LLOYD: I'm outta line! You're right, I'm sorry. How does whipped cream feel on'em?

STUART: That's it! Questions are over! The check!

LLOYD: Look, this is an awful, awful problem. And of course I'll give you the money – well, I would, if I had it.

STUART: You don't have it?

LLOYD: Sara took our checkbook.

STUART: Then why'd you toy with me like that?

LLOYD: I saw an opening and I went for it. I'm a guy.

(*Stuart angrily advances towards him.*)

LLOYD: But hey, I'm gonna help you get the money!

STUART: How?

LLOYD: Top of my head – we sell your story to television.

STUART: What?!

LLOYD: Just hear me out. We go on *Oprah*. *My Best Buddy Has Breasts*. You cry like a baby. We run over to Richard Bey. You're wearing a halter top. The audience goes nuts! TV movies, porno flicks, Broadway! We make a mint! You can have all the operations you want! Sara crawls back to me on her hands and knees, but at this point, who needs her?! Who needs that little … !

(*Stuart breaks down. A beat. Lloyd looks at his broken friend.*)

STUART: Lloyd look – we're not going on television. The last thing in the world I want is for anyone else to know about this.

LLOYD: Okay, pisano, okay. Right now, you're the only person in the world who means anything to me. Nothing will ever come between us. I want you to know that.

(*A beat. They exchange a smile. Stuart takes off his sweater. He is wearing a T-shirt. A pair of small-ish breasts peek through.*)

STUART: There you go. No secrets.

(*Lloyd looks at him for a moment. Then he starts to cry.*)

LLOYD: My God, my brain is on overload! I'm here in this fabulous love nest I was supposed to be sharing with my beloved Sara. I should be working on my third orgasm as we speak. Instead, my wife's gone, my money's gone, I'm a broken shell of a man, and my best friend has breasts.

STUART: Hey, we're the two musketeers –

(*They gesture, Lloyd still sobbing.*)

STUART: – we'll pull through this! How about tonight, it's just you and me.

LLOYD: Really?

STUART: Yeah, why don't you run out and rent a movie – a guy movie! –

LLOYD: I love guy movies!

STUART: Yeah, like *Lethal Weapon!* And pick up a bunch of guy stuff!

LLOYD: Yeah, guy stuff!

(*Stuart leads Lloyd to the door.*)

STUART: And we'll just be here for each other, we'll get through it, we'll do what we have to, wives or no wives, breasts or no breasts! We're a tag team!

LLOYD: You're right, you're right! Who needs women, dammit! We're men! All we need is men! Men, men and more men!

(*Lloyd exits. Stuart closes the door, he fans himself – he is feeling the heat. He removes his pants, then flips on the radio. He quickly comes upon Nat King Cole's 'Unforgettable.' He catches his reflection in a mirror. He stops, looks – he begins to appreciate his body. After a few moments, front door swings open. Gene enters.*)

GENE: (*Gleefully.*) Am I interrupting?!

(*Stuart screams, grabs his sweater and quickly holds it in front of him to cover up.*)

GENE: What's the matter with you, pal? You're shrieking like a woman!

STUART: You're in the wrong cabin!

GENE: This Cupid II? I'm here to fix the air conditioner.

STUART: So you just walked right in? You scared the shit outta me!

GENE: Sorry about that. But you know, whenever I get a job at *Love Acres* – see, a lot of the couples come here and go right at it, so they leave the door open. So I like to just accidentally burst in and see if I catch any sweaty brouhaha going on. Hey, I'm not a pervert or nothing, it's basically the only perk of my job. (*Beat.*) What are you doing?

STUART: What?

GENE: Covering yourself up. You spill something disgusting on your shirt?

STUART: Could you just fix the air conditioner, please?

GENE: Sure, sure. It's amazing, ya know, cause my wife does just what you just did every time I walk in the room and she don't have no top. I don't know what it is, I mean I've seen her naked breasts like eight million times and all of a sudden, unless we're in the sweaty throes of love-making ecstasy, she don't want me to see the merchandise.

Which kind of disappoints me, cause I'm a breast man. Oh, yeah. Which is amazing when you think about it cause you know what they're made of? Fat. Nothing but fat. They're just two mounds of fat. If they were anywhere else on a woman's body, you'd be repelled.

So I'm watching the pay-per-view the other night – Miss LaToya Jackson starring in *Breast-A-Thon '95* for only nine-ninety-five. You get ninety-five women – at first very classy, they're dancing, they're wearing feathers, then five minutes later, they're all naked and it's raining. Nine-ninety-five, I was thoroughly entertained.

So the wife comes in and sees the *Breast-A-Thon '95* and she says, get this, she says, "You know something, they're all fake!" And I say, "Hey, they coulda bought them in Caldor's and they're gonna take 'em off right after the show." Who cares? I'm thoroughly entertained.

Then of course, she's gotta ask for the one-hundredth-thousandth time, "So why do ya like breasts so much?" And I say, "I don't know. I mean, I like cars, too, and I have no idea why. I mean, they're like this ton of metal with wheels, and I just love'em! Breasts and cars, I just love'em! Hell, I guess if I ever saw a Corvette with breasts, I'd go bananas. (*Bangs on the air conditioner.*) Piece of shit!

So you know what my overall theory on breast attraction is?

STUART: Could you just fix the fucking air conditioner!

GENE: Yeah, yeah, yeah. My theory: You're a little kid, the woman you'll always love most, your mother, gives you the milk of life from the shrine that is her breasts. Then all of a sudden, they take away the breasts, but that's okay, cause you're distracted by other things – toys, school, baseball – things like that. Then all of a sudden you hit like fourteen and you say "Hey wait a minute! What happened to those breasts?!" And you think, "Well, I ain't going near my mother's again! That's sick!"

Remember that Jane Russell? She used to wear that bra, made'em look like weapons. That wasn't part of my theory. That was just an extra thought.

So you spend the rest of your life going after every pair you see. Why? Cause they compel. They have the power. The power that is life. The power that is woman. That's what makes'em beautiful. That's why I like to look. (*Gene turns on the air conditioner. It starts right up.*) All better. So you here with your wife?

STUART: Ah yeah, sure.

GENE: Well enjoy your beautiful lady and her beautiful breasts in the cool air of ...

(*Lloyd enters carrying a bag.*)

LLOYD: Hey buddy, ya miss me! (*Lloyd stops, sees Gene.*)

GENE: Oh, so it's like that. Hey, doesn't bother me. A man's gotta go in the direction of his erection – that's my motto. Still – do yourself a favor, boys – every once in a while, for God's sake – look at a breast! (*Gene exits.*)

LLOYD: Who was that?

STUART: The air conditioning guy.

LLOYD: The air conditioning guy's here and you're flouncing around in your little briefs?

STUART: It's sweltering. What're you talking about? So what did you get?

LLOYD: Stuff. Guy stuff. (*Lloyd goes into the bag.*) I got a six-pack of Bud, I got a deck of cards, I got some skanky cigars ... I also rented a movie ...

STUART: You get *Lethal Weapon?*

LLOYD: Better. *The Towering Inferno.*

STUART: Get the fuck outta here.

LLOYD: I know. It's *our* movie. How long has it been? We were two teenage boys, watching an all-star cast get burned to a crisp. We both wept when Robert Wagner got roasted. This movie changed our lives.

STUART: (*Stuart looks in bag.*) Why'd you get whipped cream?

LLOYD: Did I buy whipped cream?

(*Stuart holds it up.*)

LLOYD: For the ice cream. I thought we'd have sundaes.

STUART: (*Looks in bag.*) You didn't buy ice cream.

LLOYD: Oh. Well – maybe we could just dab a little on your breasts …

STUART: Would you stop acting so fucking weird!

LLOYD: I'm not acting weird! Okay, maybe a little, I'm sorry, but …

STUART: We're guys, Lloyd. Let's please start acting like guys, all right?

LLOYD: Yes, sure, fuckin' A.

STUART: What else you buy? (*Stuart digs through.*) Candles, a Yanni tape, Brut aftershave, a piece of brie … This is like your basic woman seduction kit! There are no women – (*Realizes.*) Wait a minute …

LLOYD: All right! So big deal! Look when I was out, there were couples everywhere – except for me! The loneliness hit me like a sledge-hammer! I'm a man, I need a woman, dammit! You're the closest thing right now!

STUART: Jesus Christ on a stick!

LLOYD: Okay, so I'm attracted to my best buddy, actually just part of my best buddy, but it's a big part! Look, I get along with you better than anybody else on the face of this earth! I love you, man, and you have breasts!

(*They both stop, realizing. They look down at Stuart's breasts.*)

LLOYD: – there's something about them. I don't know what it is –

STUART: They're the power that is life. They're the power that is woman. That's why they compel.

LLOYD: Shakespeare?

STUART: The air conditioning guy.

LLOYD: (*Accusingly.*) Oh, so you and him talked a lot.

STUART: I always knew they were powerful. But I never knew they were this powerful. They can turn any man into some whimpering, obedient slave.

LLOYD: You're full of shit!

STUART: Get me a glass of water.

LLOYD: Okay. (*Lloyd goes for the water.*)

STUART: God, this is such a mindfuck! I mean, I've never believed there was anything so special about me that people should stop and take notice. And now, I have breasts. They're such a responsibility. Can you imagine if they fell into the wrong hands?

LLOYD: Well, what if they fell into the right hands?
(*Stuart looks at him.*)

LLOYD: All I'm saying is – maybe they aren't a curse. Maybe they're a blessing.

STUART: What're you talking about?

LLOYD: I'm talking about maybe you should keep'em.

STUART: Are you kidding? I'd be the target for every sick fucking guy walking around out there.

LLOYD: Unless …

STUART: Unless what?
(*Lloyd pops 'The Towering Inferno' into the VCR. We hear people screaming.*)

LLOYD: Unless – we take care of each other, like the old days, before Sara. Nothing weird – two men, one with breasts, one without – there's nothing more beautiful, or more manly, than two men watching each other's backs.

STUART: Like Paul Newman and Steve McQueen in *The Towering Inferno.*

LLOYD: Exactly. You quit your job, go to cooking school, I'll support us. All I ask is a hot meal at night and a quick feel, nothing weird, every now and then.

STUART: The old days – we really were happy then, weren't we?

LLOYD: Yeah, and now look at us – (*Lloyd extends to him a slip of paper.*)

STUART: What's this?

LLOYD: My poem.

STUART: Your *Gilligan's Island* poem?

LLOYD: It's for you.

STUART: But you wrote this for Sara?

LLOYD: Sara's gone. You're here. (*A long beat.*)

STUART: "Just sit right back and you'll hear a tale

A tale of a crazy guy … "
(*Stuart puts his arm around Lloyd. Stuart pauses.*)
"Who met the woman of his dreams
My oh my oh … "
(*Stuart's hand moves towards Lloyd's breast.*)
" … my.
The mate was a … "
Lloyd, isn't this kind of sick?

LLOYD: Just because it's sick, doesn't mean it's wrong.
(*A beat.*)

STUART: "Just sit right back and you'll hear a … "
(*The phone rings. They freeze for a moment.*)
"Just sit right back and you'll hear a … "
(*Lloyd goes for a breast. Phone rings again.*)
"Just sit right back and you'll … "
(*Phone rings again. Stuart finally grabs it.*)

STUART: (*Into phone.*) Hello! … Yes, hello. Lloyd? …
(*Lloyd gestures that he's not here.*)

STUART: He's not here. Yes, I see … uh-huh … I will pass along that
message. Yes. (*Hangs up.*)

LLOYD: Who was it?

STUART: Lloyd, before I tell you who it was …

LLOYD: It was Sara, wasn't it?

STUART: Yes, it was. And before I tell you what she wanted …

LLOYD: She wants me back, doesn't she?

STUART: Yes, she does. But before you make that decision, I must tell
you something. I'm very fragile right now. I'm a lonely, desperate
guy. How can I even call myself a guy? I'm a dispatcher. I'm on the
phone all day, I make coffee for the firemen, I'm like a woman!
(*Holding up the poem.*) The only thing I have in my life right now
is this! "Just sit right back and you'll hear a … "

LLOYD: Well if you need me, I'll be with Sara.
(*Lloyd snatches the poem from Stuart.*)

STUART: So you're leaving?

LLOYD: Hey, good thing! Whoa, I mean I almost touched those things
on your chest!

STUART: You told me they were beautiful a few minutes ago.

LLOYD: Stuart, as one guy to another I shouldn't even have to remind
you of this. They were beautiful a few minutes ago. But right now

I got a woman named Sara who I am proudly going to go crawling back to.

(*Stuart moves away. A beat.*)

LLOYD: C'mon buddy, say something.

STUART: I don't know what to say? You walk in here with your Brut aftershave and your Yanni tape and your *Towering Inferno* and you play me like a violin. And now you tell me you're leaving?

LLOYD: Yep.

STUART: Well then, fine. Fine, fine, fine!

LLOYD: Stuart, calm down.

STUART: Don't patronize me, you fucking – man! These breasts are the best things that ever happened to me – my one-way ticket to the top! Sure, you thought you were calling the shots there. Ha! For the first time, you were listening to me! Dancing to *my* music. Remember that song, that great song, Helen Reddy used to sing. "I am woman, hear me roar, I'm really angry and I'm really fantastic." I'd sing that song right now if I remembered how it went!

One thing I've learned today, my flat-chested friend: men are weak and I plan to take full advantage. Damn right! I'm gonna use'em! I'm gonna use'em to convince Captain Stubby to make me a real fireman! One quick feel and these babies are gonna get me on that truck. I have breasts, Lloyd, love'em or get the hell out of my way!

LLOYD: Okay Stuart, I think this is fucked up, but in a really positive way. Right now, I gotta go find my woman. Just remember, whatever happens – we're both men.

(*Lloyd exits. Stuart takes his sweater off and goes to the mirror. He takes another look at himself. Gene enters.*)

GENE: Hey, you boys flustered me so much I forgot my …

(*Sees Stuart, who can't retrieve the sweater in time.*)

GENE: Oh my God! You've got breasts! That's the sickest thing I've ever … You're a sideshow! You're a freak! You should be wiped from the face of the earth!

(*Gene's eyes are fixated on Stuart's breasts.*)

STUART: Get me a glass of water.

GENE: Okay.

(*The lights fade.*)

END OF PLAY

Affections Of An Alleycat
by Wil Calhoun

BIOGRAPHY

Wil's work has been produced Off Broadway at New York's Circle Repertory Company, The Empty Space Theatre in Seattle, The Company of Angels Theatre in Los Angeles, The Buffalo Theatre in Chicago and The Kennedy Center in Washington, DC. His production of *Call It Clover* was seen last year at the Act One Festival. Wil lives and works in Los Angeles.

AUTHOR'S NOTE

As far as I'm concerned, there are plays I *need* to write and there are plays I *want* to write. The ones I *need* to write sort of inhabit me and I am driven to write them. Which is very fortunate because I'm not terribly disciplined and frankly, I'd rather take a nap.

Affections Of An Alleycat was a play I *wanted* to write. I've got a drawer full of plays I want to write. *Alleycat* is the only one that ends with "End of Play" and under normal circumstances I would call it a miracle. But there is an explanation.

I found Arliss Howard's portrayal of Eddie so compelling in *Call It Clover* (produced by Act One '94) that I *needed* to keep that character alive. The notion for *Affections Of An Alleycat* was conceived with Arliss' reaction to this couplet in *Call It Clover:*

SANDY: Perry says you like to buy whores, Eddie.

EDDIE: That ain't true!

It would take me ten pages to describe what I saw Arliss do in that moment. Hell, I wrote a play about it.

I didn't want to write a play about Eddie and a prostitute. I wanted to write a play about Eddie desperately trying to win the love and affection of a woman who is emotionally unavailable. And she happens to be a prostitute.

I had seen Susan Barnes performance in Edward Allan Baker's terrific play *Rosemary With Ginger*. I *needed* to write something for Susan. I *needed,* in a very selfish way, to see her work in one of my plays. So I wrote Denise with Susan Barnes in mind. Much of the depth of character that Denise has came from my conversations with Susan. She knew who I wanted to write and she helped me keep her safe. Much of the strength and humor of Denise came from Susan Barnes. Her performance was something very special.

Risa Bramon Garciá had directed *Call It Clover* and once I decided to write *Alleycat,* I knew I *needed* her to direct it. I knew I *needed* her to go through this process with me. I never figured she'd make me write so many drafts, though. Just when I thought I was getting close (and I could take a nap), she'd say something smart and unravel the whole thing. She kept making me make it better. Eventually, much to my delight (and chagrin), she came to know this play and these characters more fully than I did. She brought out levels that I didn't even know existed in the play.

Affections Of An Alleycat would not exist if not for Arliss, Susan and Risa. It's as much their play as it is mine. I *wanted* to write it. But I *needed* them there with me. And that's how I managed to get to "End of Play."

By the way. There's nothing in Denise's room. It's just Denise's room.

ORIGINAL PRODUCTION

Affections Of An Alleycat was produced by Act One in association with Showtime Networks Inc., Paramount Network Television, Viacom Productions and Grammnet Productions for *Act One '95: A Festival Of New One-Act Plays,* at The Met Theatre in Los Angeles, CA in April 1995. It was directed by Risa Bramon Garciá with the following cast:

Denise...Susan Barnes
Eddie..Arliss Howard

Affections Of An Alleycat

The play takes place in the living room of a small house in New Orleans. The place has an old and faded look but it's picked up and about as neat as it gets.

We see the living room and kitchen area. There is a door upstage leading to the rest of the house. In the living room there is a day bed decorated with many pillows and an afghan neatly draped across the foot. There is a worn easy chair. There is a small Formica table with two chairs placed under a window stage left, close to the kitchen. The small kitchen area consists of a sink, refrigerator and stove.

A cigarette is smoldering in an ashtray as the lights go up. Denise, a woman in her 40s, enters from the upstage door. She is dressed in a light, sleeveless cotton dress and has a wet washcloth draped around her neck to combat the heat in the room.

She goes to the kitchen counter, takes a pull from her cigarette and stubs it out. She wets the wash rag again, wrings it out and places it back on her neck. She takes a shallow bowl from the sink and opens the refrigerator and pulls out a carton of milk. She fills the bowl with milk, walks over to her little table and sets the bowl down. She pulls out one of the chairs, kneels on it and peers out through the window.

DENISE: Butch! Kitty, kitty, kitty, kitty, kitty. (*Beat.*) Butch! Kitty, kitty, kitty, kitty, kitty. (*Beat. Denise spins on the chair and sits at the table. She pushes the bowl closer to the window. Frustrated, angry and upset about her missing cat.*) Starve then, ya shit for brains cat.

(*A knock on the door. Denise gets up and goes to the door, slides the chain lock free and cracks it open a bit. It is Eddie. He carries a grocery bag with him.*)

EDDIE: Hey.

DENISE: Hey.

(*Eddie enters the room. Denise walks out the front door.*)

EDDIE: Where you headed?

DENISE: (*Re-entering.*) You see Butch outside?

(*Eddie crosses to the kitchen area and sets the grocery bag down on the counter.*)

EDDIE: He get loose again?

DENISE: Lookit this shit. (*Denise crosses to the window and pulls back the curtain.*) Lookit.

(*She pushes the lower right corner showing Eddie where the screen has been torn.*)

EDDIE: Damn, Denise. Butch did that?

DENISE: Last night when I was sleepin'. Pushed it right out the fat sonofabitch.

EDDIE: He ain't much of an inside cat, is he?

DENISE: (*Holding out her arm.*) Look here.

(*Denise shows Eddie the inside of her left arm.*)

EDDIE: Skeeta bites?

DENISE: Comin' in through the goddamn … (*Motions toward screen.*) Woke up this morning, *clouds* of the little bastards flyin' around. Fed on me all night.

EDDIE: Quit scratchin' at 'em.

DENISE: I can't help it.

EDDIE: You got some Calamine lotion?

DENISE: What's that?

(*Eddie begins a cross to the upstage door.*)

EDDIE: If ya gotta ask then ya ain't got it. What about rubbin' alcohol? Ya got any of that?

DENISE: (*Sharply.*) Wait a minute. Where you goin'?

EDDIE: Bathroom. For the alcohol.

DENISE: Here. Come see.

(*Eddie moves away from the door. Denise opens a cupboard and retrieves a bottle of hydrogen peroxide. She hands it to Eddie.*)

DENISE: What about peroxide?

EDDIE: That'll do. (*Re: the cupboard.*) Funny place for it.

(*Denise goes to the table and sits. Looks anxiously out the window. Eddie rips a couple of paper towels from a roll.*)

DENISE: I keep it in there for Butch. Scratches and things. (*Beat.*) Ain't a breeze in sight is there?

EDDIE: Prolly get a shower this afternoon.

DENISE: That don't help. Just make it stickier.

(*Eddie walks over to the table and sits. He begins daubing the peroxide on Denise's arm.*)

EDDIE: Sting?

DENISE: Feels good. Nice and cool. Christ. I oughta take a bath in it.

EDDIE: This'll take the itch out. You keep scratchin' at 'em, you're liable to get 'em infected.

DENISE: (*Worried glance at screen.*) I wonder where he's got to? He don't usually stay gone so long.

(*Eddie continues daubing Denise's arm.*)

EDDIE: I don't understand why ya put up with that cat. He's alla time runnin' off. Pisses on the floor. Kinda ugly too, Denise. Whatcha oughta do, get yourself one a them little birds.

DENISE: (*Defensive.*) He's ugly 'cause he fights alla time.

EDDIE: From the looks of him, he ain't too good at it.

DENISE: No. Gets tore up every other day. Keep havin' to get his goddamn head drained 'causa infections.

EDDIE: What's he got the red ass about?

DENISE: He just don't like other cats.

EDDIE: Prolly don't like bein' a cat himself's what it is. You know? That's why other cats piss him off so bad. Every time he sees one, it reminds him of bein' a cat so naturally, he runs over there, tries to kick its ass. Whatcha think?

DENISE: I think he's just a mean son of a bitch don't care 'bout nothin' but fightin' and fuckin's what I think.

EDDIE: I don't know. They's a lotta people act like that too.

(*Eddie gets up and throws the paper towel in the trash. He reaches into the grocery bag and takes out a carton of milk, placing it in the refrigerator. Denise is distracted, still glancing out the window.*)

EDDIE: Know what I'm sayin'? Like all that killin' 'n violence you see in the paper, the TV 'n shit … I think a big percent of the time it just comes down to a man not likin' the looks of somebody. No bigger reason that that.

DENISE: (*Pretty uninterested.*) That right?

EDDIE: Yeah. I mean like – okay, well, like this. Let's say a man breaks in, gonna rob somebody's house. Most times, the fella gettin' robbed ain't gonna do nothin' 'bout it. He ain't gotta gun or nothin'. He's scared, see. Says, "Here. Take my car, while you're at it." Gives him the keys, whatever …

DENISE: Fuck that. I'd blow his sorry nuts off.

EDDIE: Well, that's you. I'm sayin' a big percent of some people, they just want the man to go away. So they ain't about to 'cause the man no problems. Give him coffee and pie if he'd just go away. But what's the man do seven, eight, nine times outta ten? Boom! He'll shoot the fella dead anyways. You know why, I think?

DENISE: 'Cause he's a mean sonofabitch don't care 'bout nothin' but fightin' …

EDDIE: No, no, no. Listen. 'Cause when it comes right down to it, he don't like bein' a person. Don't even like lookin' at 'em. Like I was sayin' 'bout Butch, see?

DENISE: Well, why don't he just shoot himself in his silly fuckin' head then and do us all a favor?

EDDIE: (*Shrug.*) Be nice wouldn't it?

(*Denise rises from the table and walks toward the front door again. She opens it and stands at the screen door looking out.*)

DENISE: You didn't see him out in the road, didja?

EDDIE: You gonna let that cat worry you to death, ain't ya? Them little birdies, now, they quiet. Just some cheep, cheep, cheepin'. No trouble to feed hardly. My little niece got her a blue parakeet. She lets it go in the house, it'll fly around for awhile and then go set right on her finger. Takes it outside even and it don't fly off! Just sets on her finger. (*Demonstrating.*) Like that.

DENISE: Why? It's ignorant or somethin'?

EDDIE: No, see, 'cause it's trained like that.

DENISE: I ain't much for birds.

EDDIE: Pretty to look at, too.

DENISE: I'm scared of birds. Them ugly little feet with all them claws on 'em … (*Shivers.*) Ugh!

EDDIE: Oh. Well then …

(*Denise notices the grocery bag and crosses over to Eddie.*)

DENISE: What's all this shit?

EDDIE: For you.

DENISE: What?

(*Eddie pulls out a carton of Virginia Slims, hands them to Denise.*)

EDDIE: Here.

DENISE: Fuck is this, Eddie? What're you doin'?

EDDIE: You said pick you up some smokes.

DENISE: A *pack* of smokes I said. I ain't payin' ya for no goddamn *carton!*

EDDIE: Don't worry about it.

(*Eddie takes out a carton of eggs and some luncheon meat and puts them in the refrigerator. He turns to Denise.*)

EDDIE: *'Fraida birds* ... I knew this woman once, she was 'fraida *flowers.* B'lieve that shit? You ever hear of somethin' like that?

DENISE: (*Off groceries.*) Wait, wait, wait a second, Eddie. What're you doin'?

EDDIE: Well, uh, you remember we was talkin' the other evenin' and you was sayin' how you wish you didn't eat so much junk food but you was always too tired to go to the store for groceries? 'Member?

DENISE: No.

EDDIE: Last time I was over, Denise, and you said you was feelin' sick from one of them Time Saver Burritos.

DENISE: Oooo. God yeah. Stay away from them things. Like goddamn stomach grenades.

EDDIE: You remember though, right?

(*Beat. Denise just looks at him.*)

EDDIE: (*Frustrated.*) We stood right there by the door ...

DENISE: Well if you say so, I mean what the hell difference does it make?

EDDIE: (*Edgy, getting angry.*) No difference. Never mind. It don't make no difference.

DENISE: Whatcha gettin' mad at me for?

EDDIE: I ain't mad, Denise, I'm just sayin' I was in the store buyin' your smokes and I remembered what you said. So I picked up some things.

DENISE: I never asked you to.

EDDIE: (*Frustrated with her.*) I know you did not goddamn ask me to do it. I just thought I'd, you know, it'd be like a surprise or somethin'. Like it'd be ... funny ... or somethin' ... maybe. All right?

(*Denise turns and makes a bee line toward a chair by the day bed. She picks up her purse and digs for her pocketbook.*)

EDDIE: (*Knowing what she's up to.*) Shit, Denise ...

DENISE: I'm gonna pay ya for them groceries.

EDDIE: No, that's not ... C'mon now ...

(*Denise pulls some bills from her pocketbook and holds them out for Eddie.*)

(*Overlap dialogue.*)

DENISE: Here.

EDDIE: Put your money away ...

DENISE: Then take them groceries home when you leave.

EDDIE: No, now, I got 'em for you.

DENISE: I can pay for my own goddamn groceries. I got money.

EDDIE: I know you got money. That ain't the point.

DENISE: Well then what is the point other than maybe you lost your damn mind?

EDDIE: I just wanted to. That's all. No more reason than that.

DENISE: It don't make no sense.

(*End overlapped dialogue.*)

EDDIE: (*Boiling calm.*) Right. It don't. I wanted to do it. I thought it would be a nice thing to do for ya. But ya took it the wrong goddamn … Let's just shut up about it. All right?

(*Beat. Denise smiles at him. Pokes him with her finger. Eddie swats her finger away like a pouting child.*)

DENISE: Aw, what? What? Now you got your lip all hangin' out.

(*She pokes him again. Eddie tries to stay mad but can't. He struggles trying to maintain a stern face.*)

EDDIE: Cut it out, Denise.

DENISE: Ahhhhhh, look at you. You can't stay mad. You just like Audley Ranson's big yella dog. I seen Audley kick that mutt right in the teeth and the dog acts like he gave him biscuits for breakfast.

EDDIE: Audley's a drunkard and a wife beater and ain't got no business ownin' a dog.

DENISE: Audley's all right. Don't take it out on him.

EDDIE: (*Mumbling.*) Trash is what he is …

DENISE: (*Opening carton of smokes.*) I used to buy 'em like this 'cause it's economical. But it made me smoke more. (*Denise moves toward the counter. Peers into the bag. Reaches in.*) What else you got in there?

(*She pulls out a can of beer. A "Tall-Boy." Denise hands the beer to Eddie, knowing it's for him. Eddie turns and opens a cupboard, knowing where the glasses are. Denise reaches in the bag again and pulls out a nice steak.*)

DENISE: Damn, Eddie.

(*Eddie opens his beer. He's warming up again. Takes the steak from Denise.*)

EDDIE: Yeah, now with this, whatcha do, take you a little fork, jab some holes all on the top. Rub some black pepper and garlic all on it. Maybe put somma that Tony's on. Rub it in real good so's it gets in the little fork holes. Broil it up, eat what you want with maybe a little 'tater, you know? Save what you can't eat 'n make sandwiches. Eat on that goddamn thing all week.

(*Eddie puts it in the refrigerator. Denise looks in the bag again. She pulls out a box of Pop Tarts.*)

DENISE: Pop Tarts.

EDDIE: You like those, right? Know how I know? Saw a box in your garbage.

(*Denise opens the box and tears into a packet. She crosses to the table with her Pop Tart and sits. She breaks little bits off and pops them into her mouth.*)

DENISE: Jillie's the one got me started on these things. Every mornin' I'd get up, "What ya want for breakfast, Jillie?" "Pop Tarts!" she says. Like I didn't fuckin' know.

(*Eddie is putting away the rest of the groceries and pours his beer.*)

EDDIE: Hey. She anywhere's close to Galveston?

DENISE: Huh?

(*Eddie moves over and sits with her. Just as he sits, Denise take the little bowl of milk from the table and walks to the refrigerator. She puts the milk inside, turns and heads for the day bed.*)

EDDIE: Your daughter, right? Didn't you say she was in Texas?

DENISE: Yeah. Texas.

(*Denise sits on the bed. She slips out of her shoes and puts them neatly by the bed. She lies down and absently unbuttons a couple of buttons on her dress. Eddie watches and shifts a little in his seat.*)

EDDIE: See 'cause I had me a job haulin' pipe once. Galveston and back, Galveston and back, Galveston ...

(*Denise opens a drawer on the end table and takes out a little pipe and a Baggie with dope in it. She prepares to load her pipe. Eddie watches her.*)

EDDIE: Best job I ever had. Pay was pretty good. I liked it 'cause you could do a lot of thinkin', you know? Drivin' like that. Nobody around, you kinda get in your head. Ideas and things. I'd still be drivin' but the speedometer was broke on the truck 'n I got stopped outside Gonzalez one night comin' home. Boss man let me go 'cause 'a the ticket. He went 'n hired his fat ass brother-in-law next day. That dumb sum 'bitch couldn't pour piss out of a boot if the instructions was on the heel. Ain't that some shit? If I was union, I'da had him by the short 'n curlies, wouldn't I?

DENISE: Yeah. And if a frog had wings he wouldn't bump his ass so much. 'Sides, if it was a union job, he'da hired his dumbass brother-in-law in the first place.

(*Beat. Denise has her pipe cleaned and is loading her dope. Eddie looks at her. He's uncomfortable with the dope smoking but trying not to show it.*)

EDDIE: Yeah. Yeah, I reckon that's true.

(*Denise takes a hit, holds the smoke in, frowns thoughtfully and blows it out.*)

DENISE: Scared of flowers? Why the fuck would anybody be scared of flowers?

EDDIE: Huh? Oh. Uh … 'Fraid they'd bite her she said.

DENISE: *Bite* her? What kinda idiot thinks flowers could bite?

EDDIE: It ain't that she's dumb. It's somethin' in her head. Psychological, see? I figure maybe she got tangled up in a rose bush or somethin' when she was little. Somethin' like that. Little kids can get things stuck in their heads – some bad experience or somethin' – mess with 'em their whole lives. The littlest things. You'd be surprised.

DENISE: Check out ole Sigmund Froin over here. Got that psycho shit down, don't ya?

EDDIE: No. I don't know nothin' 'bout it really. Just shit I pick up. People talkin' on the news … pick up a magazine, somethin'.

(*Beat. Denise fires up the lighter and takes another hit. Eddie looks away. Denise grins. She begins teasing Eddie. She screws up her face, playfully.*)

DENISE: Dope fiend!

(*Eddie smiles and shakes his head, trying to ignore her.*)

DENISE: She's a – *dope fiend!* Huh Eddie? Ooooooo! A druuuug addict!

(*Eddie tries to blow her off.*)

EDDIE: Smoke all that shit you want, don't bother me.

(*Denise flicks her lighter over the pipe, still teasing Eddie.*)

DENISE: Ooooooo! Hope I don't – O.D.!

(*Eddie waves the smoke away.*)

EDDIE: Go ahead'n laugh, then. I ain't sayin' no more about it 'cept that shit is dangerous and will mess with your head. Now that's all's I got to say.

DENISE: Look at you gettin' all righteous. 'Course it fucks with my head. Why you think I smoke it?

EDDIE: I don't mean like that. It like, can damage your brains and shit.

DENISE: How the fuck do you know?

EDDIE: I just do.

DENISE: Oh, I know. From the egg on TV, huh? (*Mocking.*) "This is your brains on drugs. Any questions?" Yeah. Can I have my brains with some hash browns and hot sausage? (*She reaches over to the night stand and puts her Baggie back in. At the same time, she pulls out a packet of rubbers. Chuckling.*) Hoooo, I'm a funny bitch, huh, Eddie?

(*Denise tears off one of the rubbers and tosses it in Eddie's direction. Eddie glances at the rubber but doesn't move to get it. Denise unbuttons her dress, opening it in the front. She takes the wash rag from around her neck and wipes her body with it.*)

DENISE: You know anything 'bout cars?

EDDIE: Little bit.

DENISE: I got somethin' leakin'.

EDDIE: Front or back?

DENISE: From the middle but like, more toward the front. I seen it yesterday mornin' backin' out. Big spot on the gravel 'bout like this. (*She indicates a circle with her hands.*)

EDDIE: Oil prolly.

DENISE: No. It ain't black like oil. Looks more red.

EDDIE: Transmission fluid.

DENISE: Trans ... ? Fuck! I spend more money on that raggedy piece of shit. Good money after bad, goddamnit!

EDDIE: You want I'll take a look at it.

DENISE: Just put a brand new set of tires on the sonuvabitch ... two-hundred somethin' dollars ...

EDDIE: Might just be a little hose ... steerin' hose or something' ...

DENISE: (*Irritated.*) Hose? You just said it was transmission.

EDDIE: *Fluid,* yeah. But that could be comin' from anywhere.

DENISE: Well, goddamn, Eddie, scare the shit out of me next time.

EDDIE: I'll check it out before I leave.

DENISE: No. I gotta man works on it for me.

EDDIE: I got some tools in my truck ...

DENISE: (*Sharply.*) No! I said I got somebody already works on it. I don't want you fuckin' with it.

EDDIE: (*Edgy again.*) All right. Fine then. You the one asked me did I know about cars. Give the man your money ... unless ya'll got some other kinda *arrangement* ... where he kinda takes it out in *trade,* well then I guess I can unnerstand that ...

DENISE: Hey!

EDDIE: ... wouldn't wanna cut into a slice of somethin' that ain't mine ...

DENISE: Hey, lemme tell you somethin' ...

EDDIE: Don't want to get in the way of everybody's *business* affairs ...

(Denise takes a pillow from the bed and throws it at Eddie. She gets up from the bed, rushes at Eddie and pushes him toward the door, almost knocking him down.)

DENISE: *(Furious.) Out!* Get out!

EDDIE: God*damn*, Denise ... !

(Pushes Eddie again.)

DENISE: Get the fuck out! Go on! I mean it Eddie, cut a trail! Go talk your trash someplace else, ya little piss ant!

EDDIE: What the hell's the matter with you?

DENISE: Goddamn smart ass ...

(Denise kicks at Eddie but misses.)

EDDIE: Whoa now! Denise! Damn. Hold on. Hold on!

(She tries another kick but misses.)

DENISE: Stand still, damn ya!

EDDIE: Denise! Denise! Stop now. All right? I'm sorry. I didn't mean nothin' by it. I'm sorry, okay?

(Denise glares at him but at least she's not trying to attack him anymore.)

EDDIE: Damn, girl. What the hell's the matter with you?

DENISE: I don't need you in here talkin' to me like that. You don't like it, take it someplace else. Go find you some ignorant slit don't know no better 'cause it ain't welcome here. Unnerstand?

EDDIE: All right. All right, Denise. I'm sorry. Let's not get all ... you know, hot under the collar'n shit. I mean ... damn.

(Beat. Denise goes to the kitchen table. She takes a pack of cigarettes from the new carton. She picks up the rubber and looks at Eddie. She flips the rubber to him. Eddie looks at the rubber in his hand. Closes it in his fist. Denise crosses to the bed and sits. She motions him over.)

DENISE: C'mon then. Let's go.

(Eddie crosses over to her. She pulls him over and positions him between her legs. She begins unbuckling his belt. Eddie stands there, allowing her to do it. He reaches out and slips his hand inside her dress, cupping her breast. Denise doesn't react. She unzips Eddie's pants and pulls his shirttail out. Eddie takes his hand from Denise's breast

and touches her hair. Denise takes the rubber from Eddie's hand and opens the packet. She tugs on his pants. They don't come down easily.)

DENISE: (*Impatient.*) You gonna help me out here, or what?

(*Eddie backs off a little and looks at Denise.*)

DENISE: (*More impatience.*) What?

EDDIE: Nothin'. I like lookin' at ya.

DENISE: (*Mumbles.*) Jesus Christ. (*She takes the rubber from the package.*) Here.

(*Eddie doesn't take it.*)

DENISE: Put it on!

(*Eddie leans in quickly and kisses Denise on the mouth. Denise recoils backward. Quickly wiping her mouth with the back of her hand.*)

DENISE: Goddamnit!

EDDIE: (*Disgusted with her reaction.*) Yeah, wipe it off, wipe it off …

DENISE: Are you out of your fuckin' …

EDDIE: I guess I am, ain't I? (*Angry.*) I don't unnerstand, Denise. I mean you do … Man walks in, asks for a *blow job,* that's okay. But if I just wanna … Ahhhhh, shit! *Shit!*

(*Denise picks up the rubber.*)

DENISE: Man wants a blow job, he puts this on. My mouth don't touch nothin'. You want kissin', get yourself a girlfriend. I mean it, Eddie. You can't behave yourself, don't come here no more. All right? Now come on. Let's get this done.

(*Denise slips the dress down below her shoulders, lies back down on the bed and begins raising the bottom of the dress up. Eddie just stares at her.*)

DENISE: C'mon. Let's go.

(*Eddie doesn't move. He continues looking at her. Denise is out of patience. She jumps from the bed and angrily begins buttoning up her dress.*)

DENISE: (*Pissed.*) Goddamnit. You call me up on a Sunday afternoon when I got about ten jillion other things to do and you stand there poutin' and fartin' around wastin' my goddamn time. Go get your nut someplace else 'cause I ain't got the patience for it.

EDDIE: What else you got to do today?

DENISE: None of your goddamn business is what I got to do today.

EDDIE: You're so busy, how come you said I could come over.

DENISE: 'Cause I figured you'd come over, do your thing and be outta here inside of fifteen minutes and what the *fuck* am I standing here explainin' myself to you for?

EDDIE: That ain't what I said, Denise. I didn't say nothin' 'bout a screw. I just asked 'could I come by. That's all's I said.

DENISE: No, you said ...

EDDIE: I said could I come by the house for a visit. That's all's I said.
(*A beat.*)

DENISE: Get the fuck – So, like, you didn't have it in your mind whatsoever to come by for a little Christmas, right? You was just ... this was a *social* call, huh, Eddie?

EDDIE: Yeah. Yeah, maybe it was, Denise.

DENISE: So, you standin' over there two seconds ago with your hand on my titty ... that was just us socializin'? Passin' some time?

EDDIE: (*With humor.*) Well, it was just settin' there wasn't it? You the one started takin' your clothes off the minute I walk in. I didn't ask you to but if it's out there then, yeah, I'm gonna touch it, I guess.
(*Denise walks over close to Eddie.*)

DENISE: Oh well, shit. I shoulda set out some crackers or somethin'. Baked a goddamn cake. I hope I didn't hurt your feelin's or nothin'. I didn't know what was on your mind.
(*Denise reaches out and cups Eddie's crotch, feeling it.*)

DENISE: Whoop! Maybe I did, huh?
(*Eddie bats her hand away. It's not funny anymore.*)

EDDIE: Why you gotta be such a hard ass alla time, Denise?

DENISE: (*Tired of this.*) Do you wanna fuck?

EDDIE: Don't ... *damn* ...

DENISE: Do you wanna fuck?

EDDIE: Cut it out, Denise, it sounds goddamn terrible ...

DENISE: Do you wanna fuck?

EDDIE: No! I don't ... I don't know, I just thought maybe we could ...

DENISE: What? Maybe we could what?

EDDIE: I don't know. Somethin' different, maybe.

DENISE: Somethin' different?

EDDIE: Yeah. You know ...

DENISE: No. No, I *don't* fuckin' know. Would you please tell me so we can do it and I can go on about my business?

EDDIE: Somethin' ... special kinda.

DENISE: (*Exasperated.*) I'm gonna fuckin' ... It is too *hot* in here to be assin' around like this, Eddie, now would you fuckin' *tell* me! I'm sure it ain't nothin' I never heard of. Long as it ain't some sick kinda shit ...

EDDIE: No, no, no. Nothin' like that.

DENISE: Well what then?

EDDIE: I was thinkin' maybe we could go in there.

(*Eddie points to the upstage door.*)

DENISE: My bedroom?

EDDIE: Yeah.

(*Denise dismisses the thought. She brushes by Eddie.*)

DENISE: Take off, Eddie. I gotta go find my cat.

EDDIE: Fuck the goddamn cat ...

DENISE: No. Fuck *you!*

(*As Denise brushes by him, Eddie reaches for her.*)

EDDIE: Hey ... Hey! Don't walk away from me like that.

(*Denise knocks his hand away.*)

DENISE: Keep them grubby fuckin' hands offa me.

EDDIE: Denise ...

DENISE: Get on outta here. Go on. Go on.

EDDIE: Listen at that. You know what it sounds like sometimes, Denise, when you talk to me? If somebody was passin' in the street they'd think you was talkin' to a dog. (*Beat.*) I ain't a dog. All right? I treat you with respect. I don't imagine them other fuckheads treat you like I do.

DENISE: No. You the nicest fuckhead of the bunch.

EDDIE: (*Angry.*) Damn! I don't even know why I bother with your tired ass. So goddamn ornery your goddamn *cat* tears out the window to get away from ya.

(*This hits Denise where she lives. Eddie turns to the door. Denise grabs a broom that's leaning by the door and hits him with it.*)

EDDIE: (*Shocked.*) Oh! Damn, Denise!

(*Denise is furious. She tries to take another swipe at him.*)

DENISE: You son of a bitch!

(*Eddie grabs the other end of the broom and they start a tug of war with it.*)

(*Overlapped dialogue.*)

EDDIE: Let it go, let it go, Denise!

DENISE: Who the hell are you to come in here and talk to me like that?

EDDIE: Turn it aloose I said!

DENISE: I ain't turnin' it loose, I'm gonna knock your stupid fuckin' brains out with it!

EDDIE: Ya damn near did already, now let go of it, Denise!

DENISE: You let go! You got no right! No right, ya hear me?! Talkin' 'bout my cat. You don't know nothin' 'bout it!

EDDIE: Well, I'm sorry I said it then. Now leggo the broom!

DENISE: Take it back!

EDDIE: Leggo the broom!

DENISE: Take it back!

EDDIE: Leggo the goddamn broom!

(*End overlapped dialogue.*)

(*Eddie tugs hard and Denise loses her grip on the broom. She rushes to the kitchen and fumbles around for something to hit Eddie with. Eddie sees what she's up to and rushes in right behind her. She gets close to a knife.*)

EDDIE: Oh, shit! Shit, shit, shit …

(*He gets her hand clear of the knife so Denise picks up the nearest object. A plastic spatula. She tries to hit him with it.*)

EDDIE: Whoa, now! Whoa –

DENISE: – fuckin' kill ya, ya worm –

(*Eddie manages to grab Denise's wrist and twist it behind her back.*)

DENISE: Ow!

EDDIE: Well, calm down, Denise. I don't wanna hurt ya! I don't wanna –

(*Denise struggles against him, causing Eddie to tweak her arm a little more.*)

DENISE: Ow, ow, ow! Goddamnit!

EDDIE: I ain't twistin' that hard. Just – be still and it won't hurt. (*Despairing.*) Oh Lord. Lord look at this. Look at this.

DENISE: Lemme go! It hurts!

EDDIE: Well – be still I said.

(*Eddie pins her against the kitchen counter, restricting her movement.*)

DENISE: Leggo! Leggo!

EDDIE: Well. Shit. I don't know. I'm kinda 'fraid to. You gotta calm down some. I don't know what you're gonna do, actin' all crazy.

DENISE: (*Crying hard.*) You … you piece of shit! Why'd you say that? Why'd you say that about Butch? It ain't true!

(*Denise makes a quick move to get away but Eddie moves with her, still keeping her pinned against the kitchen counter.*)

EDDIE: Whoa, now. I know. I know. Denise. I didn't mean to, I swear to God. (*Beat.*) I tell ya, this whole thing turned out wrong. I come over, I thought maybe we could just have ourselves a nice little visit ya know? Now, look a here at this. Ain't this some shit?

DENISE: Well maybe ... maybe we still could, you know?

EDDIE: No. No, I b'lieve that plan's pretty much gone south.

DENISE: No, now listen. I'll tell you what. You just let go and we'll start off again. Okay? I'll take care of ya real good, Eddie. Real good just like you like.

(*Beat. Eddie considers this.*)

EDDIE: I don't know. I don't know.

DENISE: C'mon now, Eddie. Whatever you wanta do, okay? I'll take care of it.

(*Beat. Eddie looks at the upstage door.*)

EDDIE: In your room, then.

DENISE: No! No fuckin' chance.

EDDIE: You said whatever I want. That's what I want.

DENISE: Not that. I don't take work in there. It's the same for everybody.

EDDIE: Well maybe I don't want it to be like everybody else today, all right?

DENISE: That is *my* room I toldja! I'd drop dead before I let a prick like you in there!

(*Eddie turns her and forces Denise toward the bedroom door.*)

EDDIE: Is that right? Is that right?! Well let's go see then. Let's go see what's so goddamn special 'bout that room in there.

(*Denise rushes upstage and tries blocking the door with her body.*)

(*Overlapping dialogue.*)

DENISE: What the hell difference does it make where we do it ... ?!

EDDIE: That's what I wanna know ... !

DENISE: Out here then ...

EDDIE: I don't want it out here no more! I toldja!

DENISE: I don't want none of you stinkin' sonsabitches in there! You hear me?!

EDDIE: I ain't like them, I said! Don't you put me in the same pack as them!

DENISE: Yes you are! Just like them.

EDDIE: No!

DENISE: Worse than them.

EDDIE: I ain't listenin' to that!

DENISE: Ten times worse 'cause you're so fuckin' *stupid!*

EDDIE: I ain't listenin'! I ain't listenin', Denise!
(*End overlapping dialogue.*)
DENISE: You're the only motherfucker I know sticks his dick in me'n thinks it *means* somethin'! If that ain't stupid …
(*Eddie makes a rush for the door and tries to shove Denise away. There is a struggle as Eddie tries to get to the doorknob.*)
EDDIE: Oh, Christ will you please just *shut up!!*
DENISE: Eddie! Eddie! If you open that door, if you step foot in that room, I'll burn the fucking house to the ground. I swear to God I'll burn it to the ground! Don't make me have to burn my house down, Eddie.
(*Eddie looks at her. They hold on each other a beat. Eddie suddenly throws her off. She sits heavily on the floor.*)
EDDIE: Burn the son of a bitch then.
(*Eddie shoves at the door. Denise springs to her feet, screaming but Eddie is already inside and has locked the door behind him.*)
DENISE: No! No! No! Get out! Get outta there! Nooooooo!
EDDIE: (*Offstage.*) Okay now, let's see what we got! Oh yeah, looka here. Look where I'm at, Denise! I'm in the magic goddamn kingdom ain't I?!
(*Denise covers her ears. Furious, and helpless, she runs to the day bed and starts ripping it up, pulling sheets and pillows off, pounding on the mattress. Eddie's voice adds to her fury and frustration.*)
EDDIE: (*Offstage.*) Denise's goddamn room! Oh, yeah. This is special! Why, I don't believe I ever seen nothin' like it in my life! It's a goddamn honest to God honor and privilege, Denise, I swear to God. What a wonder to behold.
(*Denise tries to lift the mattress off the bed. It's too heavy and she collapses onto it, exhausted and crying in defeat.*)
EDDIE: (*Offstage.*) Oh yeah! Looka here at what we got! Why there's four walls! Can you imagine?! We got us a window and curtains. A goddamn lamp! Lorda mercy, what a lamp it is! We got us a bed with some pillas. Oh, don't they look special! Are these special pillas, Denise? Why I never did see such …
(*Eddie stops. The only sound we hear now is Denise crying quietly on the bed. We hold a long beat. The door to Denise's room opens slowly. Eddie walks out. He looks at Denise and slowly closes the door. A moment then:*)
EDDIE: I didn't touch nothin'.

(*Denise sits up and looks at him, her eyes filled with hate. Silently, she rises and goes to the kitchen sink. She wets a clean washcloth, wrings it out and wipes her face.*)

EDDIE: I just stepped inside there, I didn't really ...

DENISE: Shut up!

(*She crosses to the kitchen table and sits. She picks up the remains of her Pop Tart, breaks off a piece and pops it in her mouth. As she chews, something deep within her breaks. She cries now, not out of anger, but softly, from a place of unimaginable pain. Eddie can barely look at her.*)

EDDIE: Jesus Christ. Jesus Christ, Denise. I'm sorry.

(*Eddie walks slowly toward the door.*)

DENISE: (*Quietly.*) Where the hell is my goddamn cat?

(*Eddie freezes. Beat.*)

EDDIE: What?

DENISE: I shoulda never brought him home. Shoulda left him where I found him, freezin' in the rain. Every time I turn around, I gotta go get him sewed up or drained or some shit. What do I get out of it? Huh? I reached out the other night, just to pet him on the head and he tried to scratch me! What the hell kinda cat is that?

EDDIE: What the *fuck* do you want him to do, Denise?! He's an alley cat! That's all in the world he is. Just a goddamn alley cat! Jesus Christ! I shouldn'a gone in your room like that. I shouldn'a done that. It's the wrongest thing I ever did, but Jesus, if you'da just ... *talked* to me, Denise, one time like a goddamn human bein' ...

(*Eddie suddenly lashes out in frustration. He slaps at the door. Kicks at objects scattered on the floor.*)

DENISE: Stop it! Stop! What do you *want?!* What the hell do you *want* from me?!

EDDIE: I wanta know why you treat me like a horse's ass! I wanta know did you ever think for a minute that I might be better company than a goddamn *cat?!* (*Beat.*) Just seems like it could be nice, ya know? Seems like maybe it could be. (*Long beat.*)

DENISE: You gotta fondness for me, Eddie?

EDDIE: I guess I do. Don't make no sense, maybe but that's how it is. (*Beat.*) You know that house right behind yours? I put the roof on that house. Up there workin' ... I could look right down inta your backyard. I seen ya back there rakin' up pine needles. Rakin' 'em up in little piles. Musta been about a hunnert little piles. You was wearin' green tennis shoes. Had your hair pulled back in one a them ponytails. Looked like a kid. Couldn't take my goddamn eyes offa ya. Watched ya cut off some sweet olive branches. Put 'em in a plastic ice cream bucket, didn't ya? I kept waitin' for ya to look up so I could wave or somethin', but ya never did. I was makin' all kinda racket and ya never looked up once. Just kept on about your business. I asked the fella owned the house did he know you. Man started laughin' 'n talkin' all kinda shit. Didn't matter to me 'cause I'd already made up my mind to meet ya. I'da liked to done it natural, ya know, get to know you like a regular person but I couldn't figure out how. So I started comin' here like this. I thought maybe ... I dunno. You know what's crazy? I prolly just imagined it, but the first time I was with ya, I kept thinkin' your hair smelled like that sweet olive. Ain't that some shit? (*Beat.*) I wish I'da called out to ya on the roof that day.

DENISE: Wouldn'a made no difference, Eddie.

EDDIE: Maybe not, I guess.

DENISE: Listen, Eddie. Listen to me, okay? Whatever it is you want, I ain't got it. I'm sorry, but there ain't nothin' for ya here, Eddie. I promise ya that. (*Beat.*)

EDDIE: All right then. There it is, I guess.

DENISE: There it is.

(*Eddie crosses to the door.*)

DENISE: Listen, Eddie. It might – might be best if you didn't come 'round here no more, okay?

EDDIE: Yeah. I'd 'bout worked that one out myself. (*Eddie opens the door. He pauses and looks back at her.*) Hope your cat comes back, Denise.

DENISE: I don't care if he does or not. (*Beat.*)

EDDIE: Suit yourself. (*Eddie exits.*)

(*Music comes up slowly. Denise rises from the table and goes to the refrigerator. She takes the bowl of milk out and crosses back to the table. She sets the milk down near the window, sits, lights a cigarette, peers out through the screen and waits for Butch. Lights fade.*)

END OF PLAY

Gladiator
by Richard Caliban

BIOGRAPHY

Richard Caliban is artistic director and co-founder of the critically acclaimed Cucaracha Theatre in New York, where he has written and directed many of his plays since 1985, including *Homo Sapien Shuffle* (at the Public Theatre), *A Vast Wreck, Famine Plays* and *Rodents & Radios*. He also directed the Outer Critics Circle Award and Obie Award winning En Garde Arts production of Mac Wellman's *Crowbar* at the Victory Theatre as well as other Wellman plays at the Berkshire Theatre Festival, and in Budapest, Hungary. Caliban was the recipient of a Rockefeller Foundation grant from the Back Alley Theater for the production of his play, *Suburban Romance*. And he has directed for The Young Playwright's Festival at Playwright's Horizons and the Public Theatre. In the spring of 1996 Caliban will direct a feature length film of his most recent play, *Budd*.

AUTHOR'S NOTE

Gladiator was first workshopped at Cucaracha Theatre in New York. Many thanks to all the artists who have worked on the play – especially Jerry Levine, whose contributions greatly improved the script; and Martin Donovan, who first created the role of Bill.

CHARACTERS

In order of appearance.
PETER, black, journalist, early 30s.
JOE, prison guard.
BILL, convict, 30s.

SETTING

The play takes place in a small visiting room at a federal penitentiary.

ORIGINAL PRODUCTION

Gladiator was produced by Act One in association with Showtime Networks Inc., Paramount Network Television, Viacom Productions and Grammnet Productions for *Act One '95: A Festival of New One-Act Plays*, at The Met Theatre in Los Angeles, CA in May 1995. It was directed by Jerry Levine with the following cast:

Peter	Jeff Williams
Bill	Jeff Kober
Guard	Mark Burnham

Gladiator

In black we hear a montage of prison sounds: men yelling, doors and gates slamming, buzzers, etc. This grows louder and louder, crescendoing in one final reverberating slam.
Federal penitentiary: a small room with a table and two chairs. Peter stands at the table. He is black, neatly dressed, in his early thirties and has with him a briefcase, thermos and tape recorder.
He turns on the recorder and speaks into it.

PETER: Okay, this will be Findlay. Bill Findlay. Life sentence for murder. (*Turns off the recorder and pours himself a cup of coffee from the thermos. Joe, a guard, enters with Bill, whose hands and feet are cuffed. Joe carries a night stick. Bill is in his late thirties. His hair is gray. His skin, bloodless and taut. He moves with tight deliberateness, a sense of restrained violence.*)

PETER: Hello, Mr. Findlay. Thanks for consenting to the interview. I appreciate it. I was hoping we could be left alone, but apparently that's not possible.

JOE: It's either me or a plate glass window in the regular visiting room.

PETER: Right. And your name is … ?

JOE: Joe.

PETER: Hi, Joe, how are you? Listen, I wonder if you could do me a favor, Joe. I wonder if you could unlock him just for the interview.

JOE: Unlock him? No sir, I can't do that.

PETER: No, but Joe, I'm saying just his hands, you know? That's all. And if you're standing right here I don't see …

JOE: I said I can't do that. He stays just as he is while he's in this room and that is standard procedure at this facility.

PETER: All right. I'm not going to argue it. You have your reasons, I guess. Anyway, I'm sorry we have to meet under these conditions, Mr. Findlay, but I do prefer this to a plate glass window, unless you'd be more comfortable. Mr. Findlay?

(*Bill is staring fixedly, straight ahead.*)

PETER: Mr. Findlay, would you rather ... sit ... stand?

(*Bill does not move for a long moment. He then moves to the chair and sits.*)

PETER: Okay, good. Terrific. Cigarette?

(*Offers him a fresh, opened pack of cigarettes. Bill glances at it but does not respond. Peter leaves the pack by him.*)

PETER: I first want to explain a little about what I'm after. As I mentioned in my letter, I'm speaking to a number of convicts all across the country and of course any part of our conversation I might use in the book would of course be submitted to you for approval. I'm interested in the psychology of survival: what keeps people going in impossible situations: inmates with life sentences, terminal patients and so forth. I'm going to turn this on now and ask you some questions. Joe? Is it possible for you to stand a little ways off? Just a little so Mr. Findlay can at least feel more ...

JOE: Don't push your luck, kid.

PETER: I beg your pardon?

JOE: I'm stayin' right where I am.

PETER: First of all, mister, I would appreciate you not calling me kid, all right? And furthermore, I don't see that it's necessary for you to stand right over him like that.

JOE: I'm sorry, sir, but this inmate is my responsibility and I'm standin' right here where I'm standin'.

PETER: Mr. Findlay, can you speak freely with him standing right there?

JOE: Don't you be askin' him, cause he ain't got nothin' to do with it.

PETER: I know what goes on in prison, Mr. Findlay, and I wouldn't want you to hold back from any fear of retribution from something you might say. Shall I speak to the warden? I will. I don't mind.

(*Bill remains impassive, revealing nothing.*)

PETER: Well, all right then. If it doesn't bother you it doesn't bother me. (*Turns on the recorder.*) Let me get a little history first if I may. How long have you been in prison, Mr. Findlay?

(*Bill does not respond for a long moment. He speaks slowly, with difficulty.*)

BILL: I read that ... that article you sent.

PETER: Oh. Well good. I'm glad. How did you like it?

BILL: This book ... that's what this book is?

PETER: Writing the article made me realize there was a book in it, yes. What did you think?

BILL: It was ... ignorant.

PETER: Oh really? How so?

BILL: Outside ... You're ... outside. You don't ... know shit.

PETER: Well, that's fair enough. But then, that's why I'm here, Mr. Findlay. I'm hoping you can enlighten me. And that's why I chose you, by the way. I could see from your letter you were a man who ... well ... you're not exactly the average convict. You're apparently very well read. I was much impressed. And you seemed to have some strong feelings about your situation here. Anyway, time is limited so shall we get on with it? How long have you been in prison?

(*Bill thinks a long moment then rises.*)

PETER: Mr. Findlay? Is there something wrong?

JOE: (*To Bill.*) You finished?

(*Bill nods. Joe leads him to the door.*)

PETER: Mr. Findlay, am I to assume I'm too ignorant for you to waste your time on? It will be your words that will appear in the book. Your words, Mr. Findlay. Not mine.

(*Bill stops.*)

PETER: It's your chance to speak. I'm giving you your chance to speak. To be understood.

(*Bill stands with his back to us a long moment, then returns to the table and sits.*)

PETER: Thank you.

(*Bill takes a cigarette from the pack on the table. Peter pushes his lighter over to him. He lights the cigarette and pockets the lighter.*)

PETER: All right then. How long have you been in prison?

BILL: What's that matter?

PETER: Well, just so I have a better understanding of your situation, that's all.

(*Bill stares at him long and hard, with something like grim amusement in his eyes.*)

PETER: Give me a shot, Mr. Findlay. I may surprise you.

BILL: I've been on the outside ... one year and four months ... since I was fifteen.

PETER: And how old are you now?

BILL: Just spent ... six years ... in the hole. My hair was ... black when I went in.

PETER: So you haven't been doing much talking lately.

(*Bill does not respond.*)

PETER: Why were you in solitary?

BILL: Why?

PETER: Why were you sent to solitary? What did you do? What was the reason?

BILL: The reason ... is me. I'm the reason.

PETER: Go on. Take your time.

BILL: The point ... of prison ... is to ... is to break you.

PETER: In what way?

BILL: Break you. How else ... do you say it? Like ... like when a man is dying – there's a moment when he ... gives up ... lets go of his life. You can feel it in his ... in his body. You ... you've never put a knife in a man.

PETER: No. I'm afraid I haven't.

BILL: That's what prison is. It wants you to be dead while you're still alive. If you let it ... if you break ... if you crawl ...

PETER: Then what?

(*Bill takes a drag of his cigarette. He has finished his thought.*)

PETER: Are you afraid of death, Mr. Findlay?

BILL: I am ... indifferent.

PETER: Even violent death?

BILL: I assume ... I have always assumed my death will be violent.

PETER: Why? Why would you assume a violent death?

BILL: That's the way it is. In here.

PETER: Everyone dies a violent death?

BILL: No. Not everyone. But I ... I will be carried out of here on my shield, I fucking promise you that.

PETER: But how do these other men survive? How do they get by?

BILL: I don't know.

PETER: How do you think?

BILL: How do *you* think?

PETER: I'm interviewing you, Mr. Findlay. Okay. All right. Let me ask you – do you feel you're here unjustly?

BILL: I'm trained to be here. I grew up here. Only thing I ever did on the outside was a rob a store. I'm not a criminal, man. I'm a professional convict.

PETER: But you did commit murder?

(*Bill slowly turns to Peter and stares through him with a look of deep, long-hardened contempt.*)

BILL: Murder is common in prison. A prison like this.

PETER: Has it been common for you? Has murder been common for you?

BILL: Listen to me, man – I live here. I'm not visiting. I live here. Every day. Only thing I can do is fight.

PETER: So you feel there is a certain … a certain justice to murder?

BILL: It don't have nothin' to do with justice.

PETER: What does it have to do with?

BILL: I've been tellin' you.

PETER: Yes, but … All right – what about right and wrong – in the larger sense? Mr. Findlay?

BILL: Listen, man, it's your first night in here, you're eighteen years old – a lifer comes into your cell – he's checked out – he don't give a fuck about nothin' – and he tells you to get down on your knees and suck his cock. What are you gonna do? You gonna talk him out of it?

PETER: I'd try. What would you do?

BILL: What I *did* was had a knife at that son of a bitch's throat in one second and had him on his knees suckin' my cock. It was either that or kill him. One or the other. If I don't I spend the rest of my life gettin' gang fucked and crawlin' on the floor lickin' up spit.

PETER: You have to be tougher than the next guy.

BILL: We're not asocial in here, we're intensely social. We're hyper-social. The way a pack of wolves is. I have to be willing to kill a man for what you on the outside would consider something insignificant. You can't avoid shit in here. It's in your face every day. You have to have moral strength in here – moral strength.

PETER: Is moral strength the ability to intimidate or kill?

BILL: Moral strength is the determination not to let another man make you crawl, motherfucker!

PETER: I seem to have hit a nerve.

BILL: Don't fuck with me, asshole.

PETER: You can call me Peter, Mr. Findlay. Only my friends call me asshole.

BILL: If you were on the inside.

PETER: If I were on the inside – what?

BILL: We smell weakness in here like a shark smells blood. I know what you'd be if you were in my skin, sonny boy.

PETER: Because I don't have what you call moral strength?

BILL: Lookin' down at me.

PETER: I'm not agreeing with you, Mr. Findlay, but I'm not looking down at you. I happen to know a little about growing up in a tough environment myself. I didn't exactly grow up in the suburbs, all right? I understand you better than you think.

BILL: You don't understand shit, nigger.

(*Peter tenses a moment, lets it go.*)

BILL: You got blood in your body. I got rage.

PETER: Rage at what?

BILL: The most intimate moments I have ever had in my life with another human being were when I was slippin' a knife into 'em. I have never held a human being ... never been held ... Never. My body ... will not allow it.

PETER: Why not?

BILL: But don't think I don't know what I am. I know. Fucking waste of life. I know. I'm in the inferno, man. I'm in the pit. So don't you be lookin' over the edge at me like some motherfuckin' tourist!

PETER: Why a waste? Why get up in the morning if it's all a waste? What are you looking for, Mr. Findlay? – revenge, justification, forgiveness? What are you living for?

BILL: My face, man – look at my face. When I sleep at night there's motherfuckers that come down on me with chisels and hammers and they pound away and put vice grips on my temples and suck the blood out till I don't even look like a human any more. They peel my skin off and sew on leather, they pry my heart out and make it stone. Jesus – what do you think I live for? I live not to be broken. I live to wake up in the morning and spit in their goddamn, motherfucking faces!

PETER: Even if it's exactly that attitude that's kept you in prison all these years?

(*Bill gets up.*)

PETER: Mr. Findlay?

JOE: (*To Bill.*) You finished?

(*Bill nods and goes to the door where he waits as Joe unlocks it.*)

PETER: All right, Mr. Findlay, but let me just tell you something –
between you and me, and this is off the record – (*Turns off the
recorder.*) I think you're full of shit.
(*Bill stops in the doorway.*)
PETER: I don't believe the only choices open to you are violence versus
losing your soul or your dignity or whatever you want to call it –
being broken. You're in a tough situation all right, I don't deny
that. But this moral strength kill or be killed bullshit of yours is
exactly what's put you there. There are other ways, Mr. Findlay.
And your way is ultimately that of a coward. That's my two cents.
For what it's worth. Thanks for the interview.
(*Begins packing his things. Bill, who has been standing with his back
to us, slowly turns around, a broad smile on his face.*)
JOE: You comin' or goin'? Make up your mind.
PETER: Is there something else, Mr. Findlay?
BILL: Yeah. Let's ... let's talk. I get a little ... wound up. I'm ... I'm
okay. Let's talk.
PETER: Fine with me.
(*Bill stands at the table as Joe locks the door again.*)
BILL: That coffee?
PETER: Yes. Would you like some?
BILL: Oh man, been a long time since I had coffee from the outside.
PETER: Here. Careful, it's hot.
(*Bill takes the cup of coffee.*)
BILL: Joe. How 'bout you?
(*Bill suddenly throws the coffee in Joe's face, grabs his club and jabs
him in the gut with it, doubling him over and sending him to the
floor. He clubs him several times in the ribs and then turns on Peter.*)
BILL: On the floor.
(*Peter quickly lies down on the floor. Bill crouches to the side of him
holding the club over his head. Joe is on the floor, cursing and groaning
in pain.*)
BILL: Joe. You look over at me, Joe. Toss the keys over here or I'll waste
this motherfucker.
(*Joe groans in pain.*)
BILL: You hear me, Joe!?
JOE: Go ahead, waste the prick.
(*Bill gives Peter a shot in the ribs.*)
PETER: Ohhhh ... !

(Bill gives him another.)

PETER: Shit ... !

BILL: I'll crack his fuckin' head open, man. Gimme the keys.

(Peter tries to cover his head.)

PETER: Please ...

JOE: You're fuckin' up big time. *(Tosses the keys on the floor.)*

BILL: Now you crawl your ass over to the door.

(As Joe crawls to the door Bill grabs the keys and begins unlocking himself.)

BILL: Now what you're gonna do is go and get me a gun. You don't have a gun back here in two minutes and this kid's dead.

JOE: You're in deep shit, Billy boy.

BILL: Yeah, that's right. I am.

(Joe opens the door and crawls out. Bill finishes unlocking himself and pushes the table up against the door. Outside, an alarm sounds. Bill pulls Peter's hands behind his back and begins to handcuff him.)

PETER: What are you doing?

BILL: Shut up.

(He pulls Peter to his feet. There is a knock at the door.)

BILL: Joe?

JOE: *(Off.)* Yeah.

BILL: Got the gun?

JOE: *(Off.)* Yeah, I got it.

(Bill gets behind Peter and holds the club tightly across his throat.)

BILL: Okay. You push the door open about an inch. Nice and slow. I see a hand or anything else comin' through there I break his neck. Now push, nice and slow.

(The door is pushed open a crack.)

BILL: That's enough. Now stick the gun on the table, butt end first. Nice and slow.

(A hand gun appears through the door opening and is set down on the table. Bill then pushes the table against the door, shutting it, and picks up the gun.)

BILL: Now listen to me, Joe. I want an armored car, one of them big Wells Fargo type jobs, bulletproof glass, the whole deal. I want it out by the front gate.

JOE: We ain't got nothin' like that.

BILL: Well I guess you better find one. And I don't want anybody near this door until you do. I'll waste this pussy. You know I will, Joe.

JOE: Anything you say, Billy boy.

(*Bill listens at the door as Joe's footsteps fade away down the hall.*)

PETER: Even if they get you an armored car what good's it going to do you? They'll follow you everywhere you go.

BILL: Everywhere *we* go.

PETER: Shit. I think my ribs are broken. Come on. You're in enough trouble. Just let me out of here.

BILL: Out?? You just got in, fish bait, you just got in.

(*Bill pushes Peter into the chair that he himself sat in.*)

BILL: Yeah. You're in the pit now. You leaned your ass just a little too far over and you fell right in the pit. You ain't no tourist now, motherfucker.

PETER: I never came here as a tourist. I ...

(*Bill turns on the tape recorder and straddles the chair Peter formerly sat in.*)

BILL: What are you now?

PETER: What do you mean?

BILL: What are you now, man?

PETER: I don't know. I don't know what you want me to say.

BILL: You're a convict. Just like a me. A convict.

PETER: All right, fine, I'm a convict.

BILL: Except you ain't gonna last very long around here lookin' like a scared-ass punk.

PETER: Well, that's what I am. I can't help it.

BILL: You're gonna have to learn to make your eyes go dead, man. You're gonna have to look at me like I was a wall or a piece of furniture – something of no consequence whatsoever. Come on, lemme see.

PETER: I can't.

BILL: Yeah you can.

PETER: I really can't.

BILL: Do it.

(*Peter tries to deaden his face.*)

BILL: Oh no. No, see – you're fakin' it, man. You won't last two seconds in here like that. We'll eat you alive. We'll cut your fuckin' heart out.

PETER: That's the best I can do.

BILL: No man, you gotta do better than that. Now let's see it. (*Slaps him.*)

PETER: I can't.

BILL: I wanna see a killer inside there. Now come on! (*Slaps him again.*)

PETER: I'm not a killer.

BILL: Well maybe you're gonna have to be, motherfucker. (*Gets close, almost whispers.*) Yeah. That's right. You could end up dead.

PETER: You need me to get out of here.

BILL: I don't need nothin'.

PETER: Then let me go. Please.

BILL: Don't beg, man. Beggin'll get you killed for sure.

JOE: (*Off.*) Bill. Hey, Bill.

BILL: What.

JOE: (*Off.*) Warden wants to talk with you.

BILL: Tell him I'm busy. You got that car comin'?

JOE: (*Off.*) I'm gonna come up to the door. I'm bringin' the warden with me.

BILL: That's fine. You do that and I'll light this punk's hair on fire. I told you, shithead, no one comes near this door till you got that car. Now go on back and get that fuckin' car here! (*He listens at the door. Turns to Peter.*) You scared?

PETER: Yes. Of course I'm scared.

BILL: What are you scared of?

PETER: Dying. I don't want to die. Like this.

BILL: You think maybe I'm gonna kill you?

PETER: I don't want to get shot by some goddamn guard while you're trying to escape.

BILL: I'd say that'd be the least of your worries.

PETER: But what if they can't get you an armored car? I mean, what if they really can't? What are you going to do?

BILL: I guess I'll have to shoot off one of your fingers and toss it out the door. Maybe that'll encourage 'em a little. Maybe it won't.

PETER: Jesus ... Look ... I'm asking you – I'm not begging – I'm asking you as one human being to another: Don't do this. Just ... don't. Let me walk out of here.

BILL: Man, I hate it when you talk like a scared-ass punk. It makes me want to put a bullet right down your fuckin' throat.

PETER: I don't know what you want from me!

BILL: Lookin' down at me. All you smug little candy-asses think you know the score. Lookin' down at me.

PETER: I'm not looking ...

BILL: Coulda been a nice polite fella. Stayed outta trouble. Been out years ago. Have a job, family. Real simple.

PETER: I never said it was simple.

BILL: Other choices? that what you said, man? Other choices? Yeah, I got choices. We all got choices in here, don't we, Pete. (*Suddenly puts the gun to Peter's temple. Softly, closing his eyes.*) I could kill you so easy right now.

(*Cocks the gun. We wait, hearing only the sound of their breathing. Finally, Bill uncocks the gun.*)

BILL: Get down on your knees and crawl, motherfucker.

PETER: What ... ?

BILL: On your knees and crawl.

PETER: What will that prove? You've got a gun. I'm defenseless.

(*Bill unlocks one of his cuffs and tosses him the gun.*)

PETER: What are you doing?

(*Bill takes the club and stands on the other side of the room. The door is between them.*)

BILL: Okay, punk.

PETER: Okay, what? Can I go? Are you letting me go?

BILL: This is it. You kill or you crawl.

PETER: Wait a minute ...

BILL: Get down on your knees and crawl over here.

PETER: Now wait a minute ... You drop that club or I'll shoot you.

BILL: Do it, punk. Do it!

PETER: I'm walking out that door.

BILL: You're gettin' down on your knees or I'm breaking your fucking skull.

PETER: I don't want to shoot you.

BILL: You kill or you crawl.

PETER: I don't want to shoot you.

BILL: Come on, punk, come on.

PETER: I will if I have to.

BILL: Come on!

PETER: Believe me.

BILL: *Come on!!*

PETER: I'm not playing any stupid fucking games with you!!

BILL: (*Insane.*) *This ain't no game — this is my fuckin' life!* (*Suddenly quiet.*) Now come on. Do something. Make a move. Take a step. One step.

PETER: Don't make me.

BILL: One step.

PETER: No!

BILL: You kill or you crawl.

PETER: No!

BILL: Come on, motherfucker. Come on! *Come on!!*

PETER: I'll kill you!

BILL: That'a boy – let's see it – come on!

PETER: I swear to God!

BILL: You're full of shit!

PETER: You move and I'll kill you!

BILL: You got three, motherfucker – *one!*

PETER: I'll kill you Goddammit!

BILL: Come on, punk, come on!

PETER: I'll blow your fucking head off!!

BILL: *Two.* Come on, man – *Come on!!*

PETER: *I'll blow your fucking head off!!!*

BILL: *Three!!*

(*Bill raises the club, Peter suddenly walks right under it, dropping the gun, and tightly embraces him. Bill almost brings the club down on his head but checks his swing. He stands awkwardly, not returning the embrace. He slowly crumbles to the floor, Peter still holding him. Peter finally releases him, goes to the door and walks out.*

Bill picks up the gun, points it into his mouth and pulls the trigger. It clicks. He pulls the trigger again – and again and again and again. The gun won't fire. His body drains, goes limp. He weeps.

The door is suddenly kicked open, sending the table flying. Joe stands there pointing a shotgun at Bill.

The montage of prison sounds slowly builds in volume as Bill slowly picks himself up off the floor, unhurriedly, with deliberate indifference, and stands.

As the prison sounds build to a climax we see the hardness, the resistance return to Bill's face and body.

He spits. Blackout.)

END OF PLAY

After All

by Vincent Canby

BIOGRAPHY

Born in Chicago in 1924, Vincent has been working in newspapers all his life. *The New York Times* Film Critic from 1969-93 and their Sunday Drama Critic in 1994, he has been the *Times'* Senior Daily Drama Critic since December 1994. Vincent has written two novels published by Knopf: *Living Quarters* and *Unnatural Scenery.* His first full length play was produced at Ensemble Studio Theatre in New York in the late 1970s. *The Old Flag* was also widely produced regionally and then done by Herbert Berghof at his studio in New York in 1989.

ORIGINAL PRODUCTION

After All was produced by Act One in association with Showtime Networks Inc., Paramount Network Television, Viacom Productions and Grammnet Productions for *Act One '95: A Festival of New One-Act Plays*, at The Met Theatre in Los Angeles, CA in May 1995. It was directed by Roxanne Messina Captor with the following cast:

Katharine...Barbara Tarbuck
Henry...Hal Linden

THE CHARACTERS
HENRY
KATHARINE

TIME
The present.

PLACE
New York City

SETTING

A portion of a richly furnished master bedroom in a Manhattan townhouse. At stage center is a king-sized bed, with night tables on each side. On Katharine's table, right, are a reading lamp, telephone, books, cigarettes, ash tray, hearing aid, bottles of medication. On Henry's table are a reading lamp, telephone, books, magazines, a large, old-fashioned alarm clock, a well-used spiral memo-book and pencil, a Rolodex address file. The door, upstage right, leads to the bathrooms.

After All

As lights come up we find Katharine sitting in bed, right, propped up by pillows. Katharine, a very, very old but still aristocratic woman, wears a satin bed-jacket trimmed in marabou and, around her head, a matching turban from which a few curls of thin white hair seem to escape. She sits with her hands resting palms-down on the blanket, looking straight ahead. She sighs several times with increasing volume.
Henry, who is also very ancient, enters from the bathroom. He wears natty, monogrammed silk pajamas. He walks erect but slowly, as must someone who has to be very sure of his footing. Katharine watches his snail's progress with impatience. He makes his way to her, puts his face to hers in a gesture that, many years ago, was a kiss, then resumes his deliberate walk around the foot of the bed up to his side where, with the manner of a lord who has just walked his estate, he gets in.

HENRY: (*Very loud.*) I could hear you sighing in the bathroom, even with the door closed.

KATHARINE: (*Very loud.*) I've never known anyone who took so much time at night. What do you do in there?

HENRY: (*Very loud.*) I massage my gums. I count my teeth.

(*Once in bed, Henry adopts the same position as Katharine, sitting nearly bolt upright against the pillows, hands on the blanket, looking straight ahead.*)

KATHARINE: (*Sighs again. Very loud.*) Now what do we do?

HENRY: (*Very loud.*) Wait. As always.

(*Pause.*)

KATHARINE: (*Very loud.*) I've never been very good at waiting. You know that.

HENRY: (*Very loud.*) It's time you learned.

KATHARINE: (*Very loud.*) I certainly am not going to sit around like this for the rest of my life.

HENRY: (*In ordinary voice.*) Then read.

KATHARINE: (*Almost screaming.*) What did you say?

HENRY: (*Turns to look at her, very loud.*) For heaven's sake, Katharine, if you want to talk, please use your power pack.

(*Katharine reaches over to her night table, picks up her hearing aid and puts it on.*)

HENRY: (*When Katharine is fully wired. Ordinary voice.*) You can read.

KATHARINE: There's nothing I want to read anymore.

HENRY: That's a bad sign ... disinterest in contemporary affairs. You've always kept up.

KATHARINE: I'm going to have a last cigarette.

(*She picks up her cigarettes, her lighter and an ashtray. Hands the lighter to Henry, who turns away in disgust. Unsurprised, she lights her own cigarette. She grasps the cigarette from below, between her thumb and forefinger, her elbow resting on the blanket, so that when she takes a puff she must go to it, as if it were a hookah, leaning forward each time.*)

HENRY: I've asked you not to smoke in bed.

(*She inhales a long, satisfying drag. He turns and furiously scribbles something on his memo pad.*)

KATHARINE: What are you doing now? Making a note to tell Dr. Douglas I'm smoking again?

HENRY: Making a note to myself about purchasing a fire extinguisher.

(*He finishes the note, turns to stare at her as if he expected her to burst into flames at any minute.*)

KATHARINE: Well, I thought it was a very nice party. Very impressive.

HENRY: Impressive, yes. The other, no.

KATHARINE: Nice.

HENRY: I don't like your using that word. It's a mannerism. You say something is *nice* to avoid having to make a commitment ... *I* am going to read.

(*Picking up the book is not easy. It's on the far side of the night table. The book (Tallyrand) is big and heavy. Not until he has successfully retrieved it does Katharine speak.*)

KATHARINE: The light will keep me awake.

HENRY: *I* am not going to lose interest.

KATHARINE: I thought the party was very ... very ... I think it was ... unique.

HENRY: To the extent that you and I can celebrate a seventy-fifth wedding anniversary only once in our lives, yes. It was unique.

KATHARINE: Celebrate?

HENRY: Yes.

KATHARINE: Did my ears deceive me or did you say *celebrate?*

HENRY: Your ears can't deceive you. They are worn out.

KATHARINE: You have a very curious way of celebrating: being rude to everybody ... having a coughing fit as soon as anyone mentioned my name.

HENRY: The telegram from the President was completely inadequate.

KATHARINE: (*Laughs.*) He probably didn't even see it. Some secretary sent it out, most likely.

HENRY: He hardly mentioned you.

KATHARINE: It was addressed to the two of us.

HENRY: He made no reference to Chinese war relief, to the Trieste settlement, or even to the Potsdam conference. Harry would never have forgotten.

KATHARINE: Harry is dead.

HENRY: "Advisor to twelve presidents" ... that's what the *Times* said. When the chips are down, you can count on the *Times*.

KATHARINE: What time is it?

HENRY: Eleven-thirty-five.

KATHARINE: We missed the Channel Seven news. I wanted to see how we looked.

HENRY: Probably presented as *human interest*, sandwiched between Wimbledon and the weather. I would have hoped that by this time your vanity would be satisfied.

KATHARINE: I thought the interviewer asked extremely boring questions.

HENRY: Do you always have to talk about being the first woman in the State Assembly to wear trousers?

KATHARINE: Slacks.

HENRY: At best, it's a very small milestone.

KATHARINE: She never once brought up the subject of sex. All things considered we were very avant-garde about sex in our day.

HENRY: The public is not interested in the sex lives of old people.

KATHARINE: Not in what we do now ... what we did then.

HENRY: It embarrasses them to think we had any sex lives at all.

KATHARINE: Now they call it Open Marriage.

HENRY: More labels. I'm fed up.

KATHARINE: Oh dear ... Is this going to be one of your "I must make a change" nights?

HENRY: I want a divorce.

KATHARINE: It is ... (*Cheerfully.*) You "simply can't go on like this ... "

HENRY: No, I can't.

KATHARINE: Henry, consider your age. It should tell you something.

HENRY: That I should pay more attention to my private life. Do I disturb you?

KATHARINE: You haven't disturbed me in a very long time.

HENRY: You are being unpleasant again.

KATHARINE: I've always been frank with you. I can't change now.

HENRY: When I look back over our life together ... When I look back over our life ...
(*Pause.*)

KATHARINE: Well, what ... ?

HENRY: I can't remember it. It has disappeared.

KATHARINE: Nonsense. You have the memory of a steel trap.

HENRY: A mind.

KATHARINE: A mind what?

HENRY: A mind like a steel trap. A memory like an elephant's.

KATHARINE: Don't brag, Henry. I understand but other people wouldn't.
(*She pushes back the blanket, opens a drawer in her night table and removes a pair of men's heavy wool sweat socks, which, with some difficulty, she puts on. Henry watches her without pleasure.*)

HENRY: I don't like old people any more. I don't like you.

KATHARINE: Why does everyone say that age mellows a personality? More often it exaggerates a person's defects. Yours, for example ... Your abiding self-interest.

HENRY: *My* abiding self-interest? Who was the one who left me with four children while you went off to Stanford to finish your law degree? I was the one who stayed home.

KATHARINE: (*Laughs.*) Yes, you did. You stayed home in Geneva, in Paris, in London, in Washington ... with people to take care of the children, who were away at school most of the time. And don't forget Joanna whatsername, the one-time Swedish beauty. If I hadn't been away at Stanford at the time, you would have insisted on an immediate divorce to marry her. Then where would we be now?

HENRY: When was all that?

KATHARINE: Nineteen-twenty … the year William came down with polio.

HENRY: I wonder if he would have turned out better than the others.

KATHARINE: He was a natural-born leader, like you.

HENRY: He was eight years old when he died. How can you say he was a natural-born leader? He wasn't around long enough to lead anybody.

KATHARINE: In school he was the leader in all his activities. He was the youngest Boy Scout in the entire history of scouting.

HENRY: That was Jimmy, not William.

KATHARINE: Are you sure?

HENRY: I can't be sure, but I think so.

KATHARINE: Maybe you're right. I don't remember William that clearly. I can say that to you. I couldn't say it to anyone else.

HENRY: Jimmy didn't look well tonight.

KATHARINE: He's started to fail.

HENRY: It's the drinking.

KATHARINE: He's not drinking now.

HENRY: That's what he says.

KATHARINE: He didn't have a drink all evening. Not even champagne.

HENRY: He drinks at the Yale Club. He comes into town, takes a room for the weekend, orders several quarts of whatever it is he drinks, and stays drunk for three days. That's what Mary told me.

KATHARINE: Why didn't she tell me?

HENRY: She knows that you don't like her … that you'd blame her.

KATHARINE: Well I do. Jimmy never drank until he married her. That's not a coincidence.

HENRY: When he was arrested in the park with that little girl, she could have left him. She didn't.

KATHARINE: (*Laughs.*) Because of the children, she said … Jimmy's money had nothing to do with it.

HENRY: They've raised good children …

KATHARINE: Babbit's … they're all as conventional as Mary. Stuffy is a nice word for them. I would call them tight-assed.

HENRY: Well, their children's children aren't … musicians, tap-dancers, poets, tour guides … and the one who lives in that commune in Hawaii, where they eat fish and pineapples. (*Laughs.*)

KATHARINE: That's the poet. There's also one in jail in Amsterdam.

HENRY: Were there any here tonight?

KATHARINE: The red-headed girl … Ellen's granddaughter.

HENRY: The one who was pregnant?

KATHARINE: She's an architect.

HENRY: Who's her husband?

KATHARINE: She's not married. She's the only sensible one in the lot.

HENRY: I don't try to keep that generation straight any more. A great-grandchild is a distant relative, though the relationship is vertical.

KATHARINE: Seventeen.

HENRY: What?

KATHARINE: We have seventeen great-grandchildren.

HENRY: That's information I haven't time for.

KATHARINE: And several of them are of an age for great-great-grandchildren.

HENRY: They can't be stopped. Spawning, like salmon.

KATHARINE: They're sweet when they're small.

HENRY: Where's Margaret Sanger? Doesn't anyone practice birth control any more?

KATHARINE: Margaret Sanger is dead.

HENRY: Abortion is legal.

KATHARINE: I would never ask any daughter of mine to go through an abortion. A man can never understand how a woman is emotionally damaged by a terminated pregnancy. I never really recovered from mine.

HENRY: You had the best doctors in Switzerland.

KATHARINE: For the first one, not the second.

HENRY: You had only one abortion.

KATHARINE: The second was the one I didn't tell you about at the time. You don't want to remember.

HENRY: Oh, yes … the hack politician from Brooklyn. The Irish mick who was indicted …

KATHARINE: He was never convicted … He did have charm, a way with words. You could never understand a demonstrative love like that.

HENRY: He loved you so much he almost killed you, sending you off to that gypsy in Coney Island …

KATHARINE: I could hear the roller-coasters and the music of the merry-go-round ... did I ever tell you?

HENRY: On more than one occasion.

KATHARINE: I was butchered.

HENRY: It was early in the pregnancy.

KATHARINE: I was still butchered.

HENRY: A good thing, too ... If it had lived, it would have gone on to have children, and those children children ... Today we'd be awash in distant relatives. My left leg has gone to sleep.

KATHARINE: Shake it.

(*We see Henry attempting to shake the leg under the blanket.*)

HENRY: It's tingling in an unpleasant way ... the entire leg.

(*Katharine starts to get out of bed.*)

KATHARINE: I'll massage it for you ...

HENRY: Stay in bed, *please!* (*Laughs.*) I'd be dead before you could reach me.

KATHARINE: I'm as agile as you are.

HENRY: If I have a stroke, I pray that it will be a massive one. I don't want to go gradually, by installments, like Jack.

KATHARINE: Imagine, only sixty-four and he looks older than we do.

HENRY: Jack really shouldn't try to talk in public. At least, not until he recovers the use of the muscles in the left side of his face. The small children were laughing at him tonight.

KATHARINE: That's hardly *in public.* It was just family. If one can't make a spectacle of oneself *en famille,* where can one?

HENRY: Louise should keep him at home.

KATHARINE: He wants to go out.

HENRY: I had no interest in seeing him tonight ... looking at that twisted mouth ... that desperate pleading in his eyes ... (*Henry imitates his son's grotesque manner.*) "I ... woooould ... like ... to sit ... downnnn." He's ridiculous.

KATHARINE: He reminds you of your failures as a father. That's why you don't like to see him.

HENRY: Sometimes I wish you'd never gone to Vienna. Analysis made you into a very noisy woman.

KATHARINE: It saved our marriage at a difficult juncture.

HENRY: *Your* difficult juncture, not mine. *I* didn't discover Sapphic love and seek to become its high priestess and chief publicist.

KATHARINE: I'm not ashamed of that time ...

HENRY: I'm only saying that Jack's strokes are his failures, not mine.

KATHARINE: As Jack's father you identify with him, though, I must say, not in any healthy way. You are quite neurotic, really. (*Pause.*)

HENRY: These are the Golden Years ... I'm not terminally ill. I'm terminally well.

KATHARINE: We are alive.

HENRY: For us, that was never enough.

KATHARINE: We've always worked for others.

HENRY: *I* did. You were always so busy getting elected, you never had time for others.

KATHARINE: I wasn't named Woman of The Year in nineteen ... nineteen ...

HENRY: Nineteen-thirty-eight ... the year of the Anschluss ...

KATHARINE: I wasn't named Woman of The Year because of the clubs I belonged to.

HENRY: No, but you might have found a cure for cancer with the money you spent on your campaigns, many of which you lost.

KATHARINE: I went ahead that others might follow.

HENRY: (*Considers her words.*) That makes no sense whatsoever.

KATHARINE: *The Daily News.*

HENRY: What about the *Daily News?*

KATHARINE: I'm saying that's what the *Daily News* wrote.

HENRY: It's slipping ... the *Daily News.*

KATHARINE: In your estimation, everything is always slipping ...

HENRY: It is.

KATHARINE: Except you ...

HENRY: Cissy Patterson ...

KATHARINE: (*Another small triumph.*) Cissy Patterson is dead!

HENRY: (*Angrily.*) I know she's dead. She would never have published such drivel.

KATHARINE: They're *all* dead!

HENRY: Except you and me. That's why I want a divorce. Now.

KATHARINE: I won't stop you ... but I do think it's a waste of time.

HENRY: (*Laughs.*) The incomparable Katharine ... divorced, at last. It will be a major defeat. I won't enhance your reputation to have been divorced by me.

KATHARINE: On the contrary ... I'll be *Woman Alone!* I always have been anyway. (*Cheerfully.*) It will do me good to strike out on my own again … buy my own little flat … entertain. Small dinner parties, never more than six or eight, so that everyone can talk to everyone else. Intelligent conversation, that's what I long for … (*Pause, as they both pursue private thoughts.*)

HENRY: (*Obviously referring to something he's been saying in an interior dialogue. Decisively.*) … and not many men would say that!

KATHARINE: Say what? You haven't said anything.

HENRY: I haven't accomplished all that I might …

KATHARINE: Oh, Henry … not at this hour.

HENRY: This evening during Jimmy's boring toasts I was thinking of all the other things I might have been. Don't you have regrets?

KATHARINE: Not often.

HENRY: I've always dealt with power, never with people.

KATHARINE: You live on power.

HENRY: I want to become a doctor!

KATHARINE: Now?

HENRY: Yes.

KATHARINE: Go to medical school?

HENRY: Johns Hopkins …

KATHARINE: Then intern … ?

HENRY: Of course … Can there be any greater satisfaction than ministering to the sick?

KATHARINE: You could become an orderly.

HENRY: I wouldn't specialize. The medical profession puts far too much emphasis on specialization these days.

KATHARINE: Medical school is four years. Then two years in a residency …

HENRY: I know.

KATHARINE: Henry … when you began your practice, you'd be one hundred and two.

HENRY: (*Furiously.*) Ahah! I knew I couldn't count on your support. I want a divorce!

KATHARINE: Whatever you say.

HENRY: I'm trying to be far-sighted. It's not likely that both of us will live to be a hundred. One of us, perhaps. I see no point in our staying together just for the record books.

KATHARINE: The children need us.

HENRY: The children are old. Look at them. They are other people now.

KATHARINE: We never had much time for them when they were young.

It's our good fortune to be able to take care of them in their twilight years.

HENRY: Spoiling them. You're not only senile, you're sentimental.

KATHARINE: Jimmy with his drinking ... Jack with his strokes ... (*Thinks, starts to giggle.*) You're right ... He does look ridiculous ...

HENRY: (*Repeating his imitation of the partially paralyzed Jack.*) "I ... wooooould ... like ... to sit ... downnnnn."

(*They both giggle and laugh happily. After a few moments the laughter dwindles away. Pause.*)

KATHARINE: And we shouldn't forget poor Ellen.

HENRY: No.

KATHARINE: Those manic-depressive cycles are becoming shorter all the time.

HENRY: (*Triumphantly.*) *You* don't remember!

KATHARINE: I do remember ...

HENRY: Ellen ... dead on the floor of your bathroom at the Blackstone Hotel in Chicago ... you off counting convention votes for Roosevelt. "Help me Mama" written in lipstick on the mirror ...

KATHARINE: I remember. I put it out of my mind.

HENRY: Nobody mentioned *that* tonight.

KATHARINE: She couldn't go to you for help. You were in New Delhi.

HENRY: Chungking.

KATHARINE: Poor, poor Ellen. I often put her out of my mind.

HENRY: That's typical of a certain kind of woman. Working for a better world while her own house falls to ruin. There's nothing more heedless than a Radcliffe girl on fire for a cause.

KATHARINE: I did my part when people called it socialism ... the N-R-A, the C-C-C, the W-P-A, the T-V-A. For a new kind of government, a new kind of language.

HENRY: Alphabet soup.

KATHARINE: Those were exciting days. The future was limitless then.

HENRY: (*Glances at her with disgust.*) How can you say such a thing? Not one of those programs was a success. They were all stop-gap measures. Hare-brained schemes. They would have bankrupted the country if it hadn't been for the war. The war pulled Franklin's irons out of the fire. Even he knew that. Hasn't time taught you anything?

KATHARINE: Not to listen when you talk like this.

HENRY: It used to grieve me that you were jealous. Now I find it tedious.

KATHARINE: Jealous? Of what?

HENRY: When he named me Special Envoy.

KATHARINE: (*Pause.*) You refuse to retain the unpleasant memories, don't you? (*Patiently.*) Henry, the reason Franklin appointed you Special Envoy was to get you out of the house ... not that you weren't uniquely qualified ... (*Laughs.*) but that was an unexpected dividend ... I did so love Warm Springs. I'm sorry.

HENRY: You have your memories ... I have mine. I'm pleased to admit that I've always been honorable.

KATHARINE: You're no better than I am.

HENRY: I am a man.

KATHARINE: So you can equivocate?

HENRY: So I can now have a divorce.

KATHARINE: Oh, Henry, I'm not up to a scandal ...

HENRY: Scandal be damned!

KATHARINE: People telephoning. Walter Winchell writing dreadful things. Westbrook Pegler too ...

HENRY: They're all dead.

KATHARINE: (*Sighs.*) Then call Burton Johnson. Right now.

HENRY: I will. I'll see him in the morning and we'll start action as soon as possible ...

(*Henry fumbles through his Rolodex looking for the number. Katharine watches unimpressed. He finds the number and dials.*)

HENRY: (*To Katharine as he waits for the call to be picked up.*) At a certain point a person must act. I haven't been taking the initiative the way I used to. I've let things slide ... If I were you, Katharine, I'd get some legal advice.

KATHARINE: You forget ... I *am* a lawyer. You're making a fool of yourself.

HENRY: I'll be generous in the settlement. You'll never have to worry about money.

KATHARINE: (*Appalled.*) It's my money ... at least half of it!

HENRY: (*Speaking into the telephone.*) Burton? Henry ... Yes, I'm all right ... No, Katharine's fine ... Yes, it *is* late, I know. I apologize for calling at this hour, but ... but ... yes ... well ... yes ... well, that *is* why I called ... Yes, yes ... right ... Of course, of course ... You're going to Los Angeles tomorrow? For how long? ... Yes, yes

... I'll ring you on the twenty-eighth ... (*Makes a note on his memo pad.*) We'll have lunch ... Of course, of course ... Have a good trip ... And Katharine sends *her* love to *you* ... Thank you ... Good-bye. (*Hangs up the receiver.*) Burton is going to Los Angeles tomorrow. Hush-hush business of some sort.

(*Pause.*)

KATHARINE: Henry? I think I can sleep now ...

(*Katharine turns off her light.*)

HENRY: I don't like sleeping on my back like this. I don't close my eyes for five minutes in any one night.

KATHARINE: It's your idea. Dr. Douglas thinks it's silly.

(*Henry turns off his light.*)

HENRY: Either one of us could break a rib at any minute.

KATHARINE: But we haven't ...

HENRY: It used to be that when one broke a rib, one was bound round with adhesive tape. They don't do that any more. There's a new school. They force you to sleep on your back. We must get into the habit.

KATHARINE: I'm not sure I can. (*Takes off her hearing aid.*) I've removed my power pack.

(*Pause.*)

HENRY: I thought nature would take care of things as we got older ... make our minds tired, so that we wouldn't attempt to hang on ... so that, as our bodies disintegrated, we wouldn't care ... or, at least not notice ...

(*Katharine drifts into sleep. She wheezes with regularity. Henry waits for his sleep to come.*)

HENRY: I care ... I notice ... (*He dozes for a moment, then awakes with a jolt.*) ... I ... hang ... on ...

(*Henry falls asleep. As we hear his breathing, the lights dim to Blackout.*)

END OF PLAY

Leon and Joey
by Keith Huff

BIOGRAPHY

Keith's play *Nightlight* was first performed in Chicago and garnered three Joseph Jefferson Award Citation Wing Recommendations including one for Outstanding New Work. *Nightlight* was workshopped at The Minneapolis Playwrights' Center Midwest PlayLabs and received its professional premiere at The Eureka Theatre Company in San Francisco. His plays *Birdsend* and *Mud People* were both developed at the Eugene O'Neill Theatre Center's National Playwrights Conference. *Birdsend* premiered at the Cricket Theatre in Minneapolis, was produced at Studio Arena Theatre in Buffalo and Art and Work Ensemble in New York City and earned Keith an Illinois Arts Council Playwriting Fellowship. It has since been produced by Artists Repertory Theatre in Oregon; Theatre By Design in Chicago; and Fourth of July Creek Productions in Los Angeles. For *Birdsend* Keith was awarded a playwriting grant from the Pilgrim Project in New York. *Mud People* received a production workshop at the East Coast Arts Theatre in New Rochelle and was included in Florida Studio Theatre's National Playwrights Festival of New Plays. It then received concurrent productions at the International City Theatre in Long Beach, California, and at the Woolly Mammoth Theatre in Washington, DC. For *Mud People* Keith was awarded the Cunningham Prize for Playwriting and his second Illinois Arts Council Fellowship for Playwriting. In addition, *Mud People* won seven Drama-Logue Awards, including one for Best New Writing. *Dog Stories,* a prizewinner in the Drury College One-Act Play Competition, was produced in New York City as part of the Love Creek Annual Short Play Festival and went on to be included in the Best-Of-The-Fest Weekend. *Dog Stories* was then selected as the winner of the John Gassner Playwriting Award, and was produced by Phoenix Theatre in Chicago's Off-Off Loop Theatre Festival. It has since been produced in the University of Iowa's Spring Play Festival; by the Public Trust Theatre Company at the Organic Theatre in Chicago; by Eye-of-the-Storm Theatre in Minneapolis; and as part of the Key West Theatre Festival. For *Dog Stories* Keith was awarded a $15,000 Berrilla Kerr Award. Other plays include *Harry's Way, The Actor, The Chances of Surviving Death, A Steady Rain* and *Pitchman.* His screenplay *The Man In the Window* was optioned for production by True Pictures. His stage play *Crossing the Line* was commissioned by the New York Shakespeare Festival. Additionally, Keith was commissioned to do story development for *Bokchoy Variations,* a new opera that premiered at Minnesota Opera, directed by Eric Simonson. Keith is a frequent collaborator with director Mark Hunter. Their fifth project together, *A Greater Good,* was recently produced in New York by the Miranda Theatre Company. Keith lives in Chicago with his wife, Georgette.

AUTHOR'S NOTE

Many years ago, with a handful of friends, I cofounded a theatre company in Chicago called The Blueprint Theatre Group. We came up with this name because we believed a written script is simply that: a blueprint; the vision in it incomplete until fleshed out by actors, directors, designers and audiences. I still believe this to be true. The script of *Leon and Joey* that appears in this collection is barely half the story of what appears on stage. For that reason, I'd like to thank those who helped bring this tale of magic and human imagination to life. I want to thank Paul McCrane for his inspired direction; Mary O'Sullivan for her spirited assistance; Ben Meyerson for convincingly recapturing innocence (and for the déjà vu); Annie O'Sullivan for an inner light that outshines adversity; Wayne Péré for taking the plunge on such short notice; Barry Del Sherman for daring to give a wood-nymph soul; Risa, Jerry, Kate, Michael and Judy for believing in the play's magic; and most of all, my wife, Georgette, for her support, encouragement and unflappable willingness to let imagination make of our lives whatever it will.

CHARACTERS
LEON, a simple man with a complicated fantasy life
JOEY, his brother
MO-BILLY, a wood-nymph*
GINA, a deformed woman**
*Mo-Billy may be a puppet or a live actor; whichever, it is crucial that he have something of the fantastic about him.
**latex masking should be used to suggest Gina's facial deformation.

ORIGINAL PRODUCTION
Leon and Joey was produced by Act One in association with Showtime Networks Inc., Paramount Network Television, Viacom Productions and Grammnet Productions for *Act One '95: A Festival of New One-Act Plays*, at The Met Theatre in Los Angeles, CA in April 1995. It was directed by Paul McCrane with the following cast:

Leon ....Ben Meyerson
Joey ....Wayne Péré
Mo-Billy ....Barry Sherman
Gina ....Anne O'Sullivan

THE TIME:
The present – and variations thereon.

THE PLACE
Locations alternate among: Leon and Joey's house in southeastern Wisconsin; the woods nearby; and an Italian restaurant in a nearby city

THE SET
A bare stage with simple properties that allows smooth transition from one scene to the next. Essentials are called for in the text. Variations in lighting and music should create atmosphere and carry the weight of scene transitions – not walls or flats.

Leon And Joey

Joey, frothing with shaving cream, glares hatefully at bathroom mirror while Leon happily sets the table for breakfast. As music crescendos, Joey punches the mirror. A huge, echoing crash. Blackout.

SCENE 1

Lights up on Leon dropping flower petals into a bowl of oatmeal, humming 'Guess I'll Go Eat Worms.' He wears an apron. Joey bursts in, his hand bleeding. Joey snatches apron from Leon, wraps hand with it.

JOEY: I'm gonna kill myself, Leon.

LEON: You always say that, Joey.

JOEY: This time I mean it.

LEON: Mo-Billy eats eight flowers a day, Joey. Petunias, bluebells, marigolds. Roses if he can get 'em. He even eats dandelions, even though they got somewhat of a peed-on taste to 'em. Guess why. Give up?

JOEY: Leon, I could care less why your imaginary wood-nymph friend eats flowers.

LEON: Mo-Billy isn't imaginary, Joey.

JOEY: Then why does nobody see him but you?

LEON: (*Stumped.*) He's anti-social?

JOEY: Before I do this, I'm gonna find someone to take over my place.

LEON: You should eat more flowers, Joey.

JOEY: You got your retard disability check. Plenty for two to live on. I'll find you somebody. You're not too particular about looks, maybe even a girl, Lee.

LEON: A girly?

JOEY: (*Hits Leon.*) I'll make it look accidental. Insurance money, you two can take a honeymoon to Hawaii, maybe even open that burrito stand we always wanted.

LEON: Girls make me nervous, Joey.

JOEY: The world needs the female principle, Leon. Woman, she's got this cleansing aura disintegrates bullshit as she walks. You walk hand-in-hand with that, you do better than most.

LEON: But, Joey –

JOEY: This is not open to debate. I find you a friend, I'm history. This is a decided thing.

(*Blackout.*)

SCENE 2

Mo-Billy's Secluded Retreat in the Woods. Late night, woods. Crickets, hooting owl, moonlight through leaves. Leon enters with flashlight, whistles secret whistle softly. Mo-Billy appears eating flowers. Leon sits, takes a flower. They look out into the woods as they eat.

LEON: Know what Joey said, Mo-Billy?

MO-BILLY: Now how would I know that? Am I a mind reader? I read eyes. I read foreheads. 'Less I got the man himself open-eyed and face fronta me, how'm I s'posed to read him? Answer is "I can't." (*Eats flower.*)

LEON: He's gonna kill himself.

MO-BILLY: Brave man. Tried to kill myself a lotta times, Lee-boy.

LEON: Did you, Mo-Billy?

MO-BILLY: Half-assed it. Hung myself with a rope from a steeple in Plattville, Wisconsin. The year was 1946. First the steeple broke. Then the rope broke. Church come tumbling down top of me thundera God. I strolled off, not a scratch, bump nor diddly squat of a bruise on me. Little dazed but none the worse for it, knock wood. (*Sound of woodblock as he taps his head.*) None the better.

LEON: No?

MO-BILLY: Man needs a more appropriate means of suicide. If he's serious.

LEON: Joey's serious all right.

MO-BILLY: That case, I advise an elephant gun to the uvula. Hollow you out like a scoop to a pumpkin. But you gotta be brave to suck buckshot through 3 feet of steel. Conquering human nature ain't cake.

LEON: I don't want Joey to die, Mo-Billy.

MO-BILLY: Did you suggest eating a flower or two?

LEON: Yeah.

MO-BILLY: Begonias are just the thing for depression.

LEON: He thinks you're my imaginary friend.

MO-BILLY: Well, if his mind's that dead-set and he won't take the cure, there's not much you or anybody can do. (*Beat, singing.*) Nobody likes me. Everybody hates me. Guess I'll go eat worms. Long sleemy, slimy ones. Gross greemy, grimy ones. Guess I'll go eat – (*Stops abruptly.*) Ever eat worms, Leon?

LEON: No.

MO-BILLY: I advise against it.

(*Crossfade to:*)

SCENE 3

An Italian Restaurant. Red-checkered tablecloth, candle, Italian restaurant music. Joey and Gina seated.

JOEY: I've read of instances – documented cases in medical journals, mind you, in which – and this I tell you not to spoil your meal but by way of making the case that all of nature, though ostensibly freakish, is essentially natural – instances in which there has been cannibalism in the womb. Yes, babies have been born with an extra set of skin. An extra mouth in place of a navel. Having devoured the other, sucked up the other's life-blood, babies have been born with stomachs full of picked-clean bone. As if – What's your name?

GINA: Gina.

JOEY: As if, Gina, the one ingested the other one whole. Only remnant we see of the dark battle are the tips of five tiny fingers protruding out the forehead. And you thought the womb was a safe place. How's the calamari?

GINA: Good.

JOEY: They make it with canola oil.

GINA: Do they?

JOEY: Very low in saturated fat.

GINA: Is it?

JOEY: The lowest. (*Dipping and eating.*) Leon and me are twins. Not identical twins. Nor are we fraternal. We are, as our mother hatched this predicament, of one egg. What transpired between Leon and me in the womb, I have no way of knowing. The result? Leon got the goodness. I got the evil. I am the evil twin Joe. Joey if you prefer. I answer to both though not always politely. But enough about Leon and me, uh, what was your name, again? Lisa?

GINA: Gina.

JOEY: Gina, right. God. (*Pounds head.*) Gina, Gina, Gina. (*With a laugh.*) What about you, Gina?

GINA: I had a fairly uneventful childhood. Dad abusive, Mom abused. Dad cheats, Mom goes insane. Usual turn of events.

JOEY: Sure.

GINA: I eventually left home and was raped at college while I was handing out leaflets in front of the student union. Um … I believe in love and solidarity. I despise money and competitive hatreds. I believe in a kingdom of social justice. I despise man's inhumanity toward man. I believe in a classless fraternity on earth. I despise inequality. I believe in communal rationality and self-sacrificial austerity. I despise human egotism, man's competitive pulse and his lust for waste. In spite of the fact that I believe wholeheartedly in forgiveness, my comrades at the university urged me to identify the rapist. For the sake of the raped of the future.

JOEY: Did you?

GINA: (*Nods.*) He was released from prison three months later due to overcrowding. He found me, raped me again and poured lime on my face. I felt sorry for myself for a long time.

JOEY: Which, needless to say, goes without saying.

GINA: After unsuccessfully practicing witchcraft for 2 years, I placed the ad in the personals you called on. I lost sight in one eye, but not my hope. I don't dwell on the past. I lost my beauty, but not my utopian drive. There's always the future. In the future I see the resplendent sunburst of the messianic.

JOEY: That's easy for you to say. You still have plastic surgery as an option.

GINA: I've had plastic surgery.

JOEY: And still you're –

GINA: Ugly.

JOEY: I didn't say ugly. Did I say ugly?

GINA: I have to wait 15 to 20 years for more scar tissue to build up before the doctors can do anything else.

JOEY: Which in and of itself is reason for hope. Me, conversely, can I have plastic surgery performed on my ugly soul in 15 years? 20 years? Ever?

GINA: Hope can be transformative.

JOEY: That's debatable. It can, perhaps, when and if one has a glimmer of hope to begin with. I, however, am darkness through and through. It rears its ugly head at me daily in the mirror. I know the ugly face of impossibility. I see it every day when I shave. Which is why, on occasion, this occasion for instance, I appear in pubic unshaven.

GINA: I don't think you're ugly or evil, Joey. I think you're a good person deep down. And if you're not too particular ... I mean, if my looks don't disgust you too much ... well ... I'm having a good time. I wouldn't mind going out with you again.

JOEY: Whatta you, dense? Not me. My brother.

GINA: Your brother?

JOEY: My brother Leon.

GINA: You answered my ad for him?

JOEY: What, my looks, you think I gotta go hunting up desperate, ugly women in the personals?

GINA: (*Hurt, leaving.*) Thanks everlastingly for the lovely meal.

JOEY: Whoa one horsy minute, Gina. You eat like a garbage truck, shoo me the blow-off, you pay.

(*Gina throws $20 and turns to leave. Joey stops her – their consequent tug and pull on the dance floor inadvertently becomes a dance.*)

JOEY: Hey, Gina. Wait. At least meet him.

GINA: After you humiliate me like this? You're poop that's been stepped in. On top of that, you're vain.

JOEY: Look, reason I said nothing, my brother, Leon, he's a good guy. He's short a few bricks, but nonetheless I do not fix him up with any syphilitic-ridden scumbag out the stinkfinger pages of Miss Lonely Hearts.

(*Gina starts to leave. Joey spins her back to the table, grabs napkin and shows her.*)

JOEY: Gina, wait. I got a checklist. Lookit. 45 minutes you kept me waiting I etched it out on my napkin. Lookit that: Every qualification dotted by a blot of shrimp dip. You passed with flying colors. You're the one.

(*Joey dips Gina. They are very close.*)

JOEY: Look, you're not particular, he's not particular. I need someone to take care of him after I kill myself.

GINA: After you what?

JOEY: A formality. Just meet him, okay?
(*Gina looks at Joey, obviously in love with him. The lights fade to black.*)

SCENE 4

Leon and Joey's House. Joey singing to himself, setting table. Leon enters, sits. Joey serves Leon oatmeal with a flourish. Leon eats. Joey sits, smiling. Leon looks up.

JOEY: So?
LEON: So what, Joe?
JOEY: How was it?
LEON: Fine.
JOEY: Fine? Just fine?!
LEON: Are we talking about oatmeal, Joey?
JOEY: (*Swats Leon.*) The girl, numskull.
LEON: What girl, Joey?
JOEY: The girl. Gina.
LEON: (*Looks around, beat.*) Who's Gina, Joey?
JOEY: The girl you slept with last night, dimwit.
LEON: You put a girl in my bed?
JOEY: We're gonna do this, Leon, you gotta show some initiative. I promised Ma on her deathbed I'd take care of you. How'm I supposed to 86 myself you don't cooperate?
LEON: You were gone out late, Joey. I was scared alone. I took a extra medication. You know how I sleep when I take a extra medication.
JOEY: You're a real ladies' man, Leon. Christ, I had to wine and dine this one for two hours to hook her.
LEON: She was a hooker?
JOEY: (*Hits Leon.*) Shame you let this one get away. She was nice. Ugly but nice. She had this glow from down deep.
LEON: Women scare me, Joey. They're so beautiful I get my nervous stomach like I gotta go pee and throw up both the same time.
(*Gina enters in Joey's bathrobe, towel wrapped turban-like around her wet hair.*)
GINA: (*To Leon with a kiss.*) Morning, Leon. (*Sits.*) What's for breakfast?
(*Leon, nervous and sick, runs out.*)
GINA: Mmmmm. Haven't had oatmeal in ages. Any coffee?

JOEY: Sure. (*Pours coffee.*) So. How'd things go last night?

GINA: Wonderfully, thank you.

JOEY: We thought you left.

GINA: I didn't.

JOEY: Bouncy-bouncy?

GINA: Pardon me?

JOEY: Way Leon talked he didn't know you were in his bed at all.

GINA: Leon's reticence is entirely understandable, Joseph. When spiritual communion enables two souls to transcend the temporal confines of mere sexuality, talking about it is virtually impossible. I'll look after Leon, now. Don't you have something to do?
(*Beat. Joey exits. Leon re-enters.*)

LEON: Hi.

GINA: Hi.

LEON: Sorry, I ran out like that.

GINA: I'm used to it.

LEON: I got a nervous stomach.

GINA: I have that effect on people.

LEON: You're Gina?
(*Gina nods.*)

LEON: What happened to your face?

GINA: Lime.

LEON: Fruit juice?

GINA: Calcium oxide.

LEON: Were you really in my bed last night?

GINA: I slept on the floor.

LEON: I sleep like a rock. (*Beat.*) You like him, don't you?
(*Gina looks away.*)

LEON: He's not a bad guy, Joey. He just doesn't have any vocation. He's got a problem with sugar, too, I noticed. And he never eats enough flowers. Maybe exercise'd make a difference. Or good luck. Or psychotherapy. (*Beat.*) I could help you.

GINA: (*Leaving.*) I better go.

LEON: I'll just tell him what I see.

GINA: Do that he'll run off and toss his cookies, too.

LEON: What I really see. How I see your eyes so open-brown and deep, I could disappear inside them, fall forever slow like flight.

GINA: Stop it.

LEON: And how your voice gurgles in my chest like warm bath water.
(*Gina laughs.*)

LEON: And how your laugh tingles the hair at the back of my neck.

GINA: Don't make fun.

LEON: And how your skin breathes warmth like fresh bread from the oven.

(*Gina tries not to smile.*)

LEON: And your smile is a candlelit window on a lightless night.

GINA: You can't make him see what's not there.

LEON: It's what anyone would see if he'd just close his eyes and look at you. Mo-Billy says it's the only way to travel.

GINA: How?

LEON: Eyes closed. Close our eyes, we go all over, me and Mo-Billy. Venice last night, Elysian Fields night before.

GINA: Elysian Fields isn't a real place.

LEON: It is while me and Mo-Billy are there. They got all-you-can-eat grapes big as ping-pong balls fresh off the vine.

GINA: (*Amused.*) Do they?

LEON: One in your mouth, it's like an explosion of ice cold Kool-Aid. Mo-Billy made us leave because I was laughing so much I was disturbing the peace. Grapes ferment on the vine in Elysian Fields. I can't handle liquor too well.

GINA: Who's Mo-Billy?

LEON: My best friend. Beside Joey. Joey doesn't believe in Mo-Billy. Mo-Billy told me that's precisely the kinda skepticism that, in a different world, coulda spelled the untimely demise of Tinkerbell. (*Beat.*) He said you were nice.

GINA: Joey did?

LEON: He said you have this glow from down deep.

GINA: He did not. Did he?

LEON: Just this morning. Listen, you two'd make a great couple. Joey's dark. You're light. Mo-Billy says put the two together, dark doesn't have a chance in –

(*Shot!*)

LEON: Joey … ?

(*Blackout.*)

SCENE 5

Mo-Billy's Secluded Retreat in the Woods. Mo-Billy, Leon eating flowers.

MO-BILLY: Dead? Don't fret, Lee-boy. When I was last in analysis with

Sigmund Freud, Siggy told me in his Vistful Wiennese way: "Mo-Billy, in my considered opinion I have found little that is good about human beings as a whole. In my experience most of them are trash." The year was 1915. Or thereabouts. My Wiennese is rusty. That's a rough translation. Still and all, if I had a choice between suicide and the girl, I'd take the girl hands down.

LEON: 1915 was before you were born, Mo-Billy, wasn't it?

MO-BILLY: Yes, Leon, it was. But in the expended days of my youth I had a time machine. Went everywhere. Which only goes to show you: a man's world view depends very much upon where and not where he stops or don't stop while traveling through time.

LEON: Do you still have that time machine, Mo-Billy?

MO-BILLY: Donated it for scrap metal during the Good War.

LEON: I wish I could travel through time. I miss Joey so much.

MO-BILLY: Tripping through time and space can be a dangerously discombobulating business, Lee-Boy.

LEON: I don't care. If I could go back I'd change everything.

MO-BILLY: Well, the machine may be long gone, but the technology remains. (*Taps head: a woodblock sound.*) When you've traveled extensively through time the technology stays with you always. Where to? Gimme your head, I'll send you.

LEON: Really?

MO-BILLY: Name your destination.

LEON: Yesterday morning. Breakfast.

(*Mo-Billy presses his hands upon both sides of Leon's head. We hear reverse track music, gradually louder.*)

LEON: Something's happening, Mo-Billy! I can feel it!

MO-BILLY: Let it happen!

(*Music very loud. Lights sputter and Blackout.*)

SCENE 6

Leon and Joey's House. Joey singing to himself, setting table. Leon enters, sits. Joey serves Leon oatmeal with a flourish. Leon eats. Joey sits, smiling. Leon looks up.

JOEY: So?

LEON: So what, Joe?

JOEY: How was it?

LEON: Fine.

JOEY: Fine? Just fine?!

LEON: Are we talking about oatmeal, Joey?

JOEY: (*Swats Leon.*) The girl, numskull.

LEON: Oh, the girl. Gina, you mean.

JOEY: Yes, Gina. So?

LEON: She slept on the floor.

JOEY: You're a real ladies' man, Leon. We're gonna do this, you gotta show some initiative. I promised Ma on her deathbed I'd take care of you. How'm I supposed to 86 myself you don't cooperate?

LEON: Gina's not interested in me, Joey. Gina's in love with you.

JOEY: What?

LEON: It's you she loves.

JOEY: She told you this?

LEON: You can tell just by looking at her.

JOEY: Yeah, right.

LEON: You told me yourself, you thought she's nice.

JOEY: I never said that.

LEON: You told me she has this glow from down deep.

JOEY: When did I say this?

LEON: Yesterday.

JOEY: I met her for the first time last night, moron!

LEON: I know but Mo-Billy, he sent me back in time to change things.

JOEY: The wood-nymph again!

LEON: Don't kill yourself, Joey. You'll see.

    (*Gina enters in Joey's bathrobe, towel wrapped turban-like around her wet hair.*)

GINA: (*To Leon with a kiss.*) Morning, Leon. (*Sits.*) What's for breakfast? (*Leon runs out.*)

GINA: Mmmmm. Haven't had oatmeal in ages. Any coffee?

JOEY: Sure. (*Pours coffee.*) So. How'd things go last night?

GINA: Wonderfully, thank you.

JOEY: We thought you left.

GINA: I didn't.

JOEY: Bouncy-bouncy?

GINA: Pardon me?

JOEY: Way Leon talked he didn't know you were in his bed at all.

GINA: Leon's reticence is entirely understandable, Joseph. When spiritual communion enables two souls to transcend the temporal confines of mere sexuality, talking about it is virtually impossible. I'll look after Leon, now. Don't you have something to do?

(Beat. Joey exits. Leon re-enters concealing something in robe pocket.)
LEON: Hi.
GINA: Hi.
LEON: Sorry, I ran out like that.
GINA: I'm used to it.
LEON: I had to get Joey's gun.
GINA: He's not serious about killing himself.
LEON: Oh, yeah. *(Beat.)* You like him, don't you?
   (Gina looks away.)
LEON: Tell him.
GINA: *(Leaving.)* I better go.
LEON: Know what Joey told me? He sees a glow from deep inside you.
GINA: *(Turning back.)* Joey told you that?
LEON: Yesterday at breakfast.
GINA: I just met him for the first time last night.
LEON: I've got this friend Mo-Billy, he used to travel through time. And
   even though he donated his time machine for scrap metal during
   the Good War he put his hands on my head and there was this
   music and he sent me back because Joey killed himself yesterday.
   So I took Joey's gun and now if I can get you two together,
   everything'll work out just fine.
GINA: God, you really are retarded.
LEON: You don't remember because Mo-Billy sent me back from
   tomorrow. Joey really needs someone like you. He's all dark and
   you're all light, and Mo-Billy says put the two together and dark
   doesn't have a chance in –
   (Shot!)
LEON: He couldn't. He wouldn't. Joey!?
   (Blackout.)

SCENE 7
*Mo-Billy's Secluded Retreat in the Woods. Leon enters breathlessly
with flashlight. Mo-Billy eating flowers.*

LEON: I need you to send me back in time, Mo-Billy!
MO-BILLY: Back in time?
LEON: Joey killed himself, again! I forgot my dad's shotgun in the attic!
MO-BILLY: There's an efficient way to go.
LEON: Can you send me?!
MO-BILLY: Fact-o-the matter is –

LEON: You donated your time machine for scrap metal during the Good War!

MO-BILLY: You are turning into one expert of a mind-reader, Leon.

LEON: Can you do it again?!

MO-BILLY: Again?!

LEON: You sent me yesterday!

MO-BILLY: I did?

LEON: You don't remember because it was the present when you sent me! Now the present is the future and yesterday is today and today is tomorrow and … ! I'm confused, Mo-Billy.

MO-BILLY: Exactly the reason I gave up time-travel to begin with. Never did particularly enjoy being discombobulated.

LEON: All I know, I gotta go back and save Joey!

MO-BILLY: Second chance, same outcome? Seems fate's dead set against it.

LEON: Send me anyway!

MO-BILLY: Well, seeing I already sent you, seems I got no choice in the matter, do I? Gimme your head and let's get skipping.
(*Mo-Billy presses Leon's head as before. Reverse track music again as lights sputter and Blackout.*)

SCENE 8
Leon and Joey's House. Joey and Leon at breakfast as before. Gina enters in Joey's bathrobe, towel wrapped turban-like around her wet hair. Joey and Gina's initial interchange thick with déjà vu.

GINA: (*To Leon, with a kiss.*) Morning, Leon. (*Sits.*) What's for breakfast?
(*Leon runs out.*)

GINA: Mmmmm. Haven't had oatmeal in ages.
(*Joey pours coffee.*)

GINA: Any … coffee?

JOEY: (*Realizing he's already pouring.*) Sure.
(*Joey and Gina look at one another, confused, connecting in a way they never have – as if they've done this all before.*)

JOEY: So. How'd things go last night?

GINA: Wonderfully, thank you.

JOEY: We thought you …

GINA: I didn't.

JOEY: … left.
(*Beat. This is weird.*)

JOEY: Bouncy-bouncy?

GINA: Pardon me?

JOEY: Way Leon talked he didn't know you were in his ...

JOEY AND GINA: ... bed at all.

GINA: Leon's reticence is entirely understandable, Joseph. When spiritual communion enables two souls to transcend the temporal confines of mere sexuality, talking about it is ...

GINA AND JOEY: ... virtually impossible.

(*Déjà vu again. Gina and Joey take a double beat to shake it off. Joey begins to exit.*)

GINA: I'll look after Leon, now. Don't you have something to ... do?

(*Beat. Joey halts, looks back and, shaking off that strange sensation, exits. Leon re-enters concealing handgun in robe pocket as well as shotgun under his robe.*)

LEON: Got 'em both this time.

JOEY: (*Offstage.*) Leon!!

LEON: (*Inadvertently brandishing guns.*) Now, Gina, you march in there and tell Joey how you feel about him before he finds something else to kill himself with!

JOEY: (*Entering angrily.*) Have you been messing in my things?

LEON: (*Badly concealing shotgun and handgun.*) No. (*Drops gun.*) I don't want you to kill yourself, Joey!

GINA: (*To Joey.*) You're not really going to do it.

JOEY: (*To Gina.*) Please. This is a family matter. (*To Leon.*) Gimme the gun, Leon.

LEON: But she loves you, Joey! And you love her!

JOEY: (*To Gina.*) From the mouths of retards.

LEON: Close your eyes and see, Joey! She's beautiful! You need her!

JOEY: (*To Gina.*) He gets like this, give him a double-dose of his medication. (*Advancing on Leon.*) That don't work, a swift crack in the head does wonders.

LEON: (*Backing away.*) I traveled through time twice to save you! You can't do it again! I won't let you!

JOEY: Just gimme one of the guns.

LEON: This story's gonna have a happy ending if it kills me!

JOEY: Have it your way, little brother.

(*Joey bolts after Leon. They wrestle. A shot! Leon falls to the floor.*)

JOEY: Leon?

LEON: I'm bleeding, Joe. Joey?

JOEY: Oh, Christ. I killed him. (*To Gina.*) Do you know first aid?

(*Gina, calmly kneeling, removes towel from hair, presses it to Leon's chest.*)

GINA: (*To Joey.*) Do you have any candles?

JOEY: (*Runs off in a panic, stops short.*) For a gunshot wound?!

GINA: I know what I'm doing. Get one.

(*Joey runs out. Leon fades fast.*)

LEON: (*Weakly.*) Am I dying, Gina?

(*Joey enters with candle. Music begins as lights change and Gina begins to perform a ritualized dance.*)

GINA: (*To Joey.*) Light it.

(*Joey lights candle. Gina positions Leon's body on floor and circles with candle around him.*)

GINA: (*To Leon.*) Leon, concentrate on the light. Don't let go of the light.

(*Gina performs a dance, perhaps a song, around Leon's rapidly expiring body.*)

JOEY: He's bleeding to death and you do a candlelight hootchie-cootchie dance?!

(*Gina goes to Joey, touches her palm to his lips to silence him.*)

GINA: (*With great authority.*) I know what I'm doing.

(*Gina's ceremonial song/dance continues. Music swells, lights fluctuate, something is most definitely happening. Gina concludes by blowing out the candle at Joey, the expiring smoke puffing into his face. The music ends and lights return to normal. Joey approaches Leon cautiously. He kneels down and feels for a pulse.*)

JOEY: Oh, great. You know what you're doing and he's dead.

(*Leon's voice echoes over PA system.*)

LEON: (*Over PA.*) I'm not dead, Joey.

JOEY: (*Frightened, looking around.*) Leon?

GINA: (*Unable to hear Leon.*) Can you hear him?

JOEY: Can't you?

(*Gina shakes her head "no."*)

LEON: (*Over PA.*) Of course, she can't, Joey. I'm in here.

JOEY: In where?

GINA: Leon is inside you, now. You two are now one as you should have been from the beginning. Courtesy of the Tibetan Soul Meld. (*Exhausted, sits.*) Whew.

JOEY: You put that retard inside me!?

LEON: (*Over PA.*) God, it's dark in here, Joey.

JOEY: Get him out, you witch! Get him outa me!

LEON: (*Over PA.*) How can you stand it?

JOEY: (*To Leon.*) I can't, you idiot! Why do you think I want to die?!

LEON: (*Over PA.*) Well, let's let some light in.

JOEY: (*To Leon.*) I'll let some light in, all right!

(*Joey goes for gun. He points it at his own head. As Leon talks Joey stares at Gina strangely.*)

LEON: (*Over PA.*) A little light, Joey. Right there in front of you. Lookit how her eyes are so open-brown and deep. You could disappear inside them, couldn't you? Just fall forever slow like flight.

GINA: (*In response to Joey's stare.*) What?

LEON: (*Over PA.*) And how her voice gurgles in your chest like warm bath water.

JOEY: (*To Leon in his head.*) Shut up, Leon! Shut up or I'll pop you!

GINA: (*With a laugh.*) What's he saying?

LEON: (*Over PA.*) And how her laugh tingles the hair at the back of your neck.

(*Joey slowly lowers the gun.*)

LEON: And how her skin, Joey, if you just get a little closer, breathes warmth like fresh bread from the oven.

(*Joey approaches Gina. She smiles.*)

JOEY: Did anyone ever tell you your smile's a – (*To Leon inside.*) A what?

LEON: (*Coaching Joey.*) A candle-lit window on a lightless night.

JOEY: (*Overlaps as he repeats along with Leon.*) ... a candle-lit window on a lightless night?

GINA: Is that what you see?

LEON: (*Over PA.*) Little light makes a world of difference, didn't I say, Joey?

JOEY: It's what anybody'd see if he'd just close his eyes and ...

(*Joey and Gina close their eyes and kiss. Music. Leon is heard throughout the kiss and as lights fade to black.*)

LEON: (*Over PA.*) You know what you and Gina could do, Joe?

JOEY: (*In the midst of kiss.*) Shut up, Leon.

LEON: Tell the police an accident. Insurance money, Hawaii honeymoon.

GINA: (*In the midst of kiss.*) Shut up, Leon.

LEON: Hey, we could open that burrito stand we always wanted! (*Beat, in darkness.*) Joey ... ?

END OF PLAY

Who Made Robert DeNiro King of America?

A One-Act Play
by Jason Katims

BIOGRAPHY

Jason Katims' other plays include *Driving Lessons* (Samuel French), *Catch!*, and *The Man Who Couldn't Dance* (*More 10-Minute Plays from Actors Theatre of Louisville*). They have been performed in New York, Los Angeles, Paris and regionally throughout the United States. Katims is the cowriter and coproducer of *The Pallbearer* (Miramax Pictures 1996) and was also an executive story editor for ABC's critically acclaimed television series, *My So-Called Life*.

ORIGINAL PRODUCTION

Who Made Robert DeNiro King of America? was produced by Act One in association with Showtime Networks Inc., Paramount Network Television, Viacom Productions and Grammnet Productions for *Act One '95: A Festival of New One-Act Plays*, at The Met Theatre in Los Angeles, CA in May 1995. It was directed by Asaad Kelada with the following cast:

Red..Christopher Meloni
Maggie ....Susan Knight
Samantha ....Joanna Gleason

TIME

The present.

PLACE

The living room of an apartment in Manhattan. There is a small office area above which a framed poster of Maggie's novel, *A Conversation With Emily*, is displayed.

Who Made Robert DeNiro King of America?

SCENE 1

At rise: Maggie sits at her desk in the office area. She is motionless, staring at her computer monitor, dumb struck. She doesn't type a word. Red on the other hand leans forward on the couch persistently hunting and pecking away at a clunky old electric typewriter (IBM Series B) on the coffee table.

After a moment Maggie turns away from her computer, looks at him. Red doesn't look up until a sound of some sort is emitted from Maggie – something like clearing her throat. Red looks up. Maggie smiles. He smiles back absently, but turns immediately back and continues typing. Maggie looks back at her computer, types a few words then stops again, frustrated.

Maggie rises, crosses to Red, ostensibly to adjust the placement of a knick knack that Red has inadvertently moved from its correct position on the coffee table. Red, slightly distracted from his writing, looks up at her. She smiles at him.

MAGGIE: (*Whispering.*) Sorry …
RED: Mag, I'm doin' something here.
MAGGIE: Yeah, I have to get back to work myself.
RED: You do that.
MAGGIE: I just wanted to remind you that Sam will be here any minute.
RED: No problem.
MAGGIE: Good. I just hope it isn't any inconvenience.
RED: Actually, it's extremely convenient. I've been wanting to meet this Sam guy.

(*Beat. Maggie realizes Red has misinterpreted her point. Red, oblivious, goes back to typing.*)

MAGGIE: Well, actually? I mean, aren't you going to need a break?

RED: If only I had that luxury.

MAGGIE: Red, what I'm trying to get across here is, I'll baste your roast while you're out of the house.

RED: What are you saying, Mag?

MAGGIE: I'm just saying I will not neglect your roast.

RED: Mag, I'm at a critical moment in my movie here.

MAGGIE: (*As delicately as possible.*) Red, I don't want you to be here when Sam gets here. All right?

RED: I see.

MAGGIE: Yeah. It would be just a little … awkward.

RED: I understand. Unfortunately, I can't leave.

MAGGIE: What?

RED: You gave me six weeks before I have to go out and get work. I have two weeks left. You can't throw me out of the apartment. I'm trying to finish this thing off.

MAGGIE: Red, I'm not throwing you … Wait a second. "Finish it off?" What are you saying? Are you saying you intend to finish an entire screenplay in six weeks?

RED: No, I'm going to finish it in four weeks. In six weeks I'm going to have it sold.

MAGGIE: Red. Honey. No one writes and sells a screenplay in six weeks.

RED: Yeah, well, for your information they do.

MAGGIE: For my information?

RED: That's right. I'm on a system.

MAGGIE: What system?

RED: Forget it, Mag. You'll make fun of me. You'll pasteurize me.

MAGGIE: I'll pasteurize you?

RED: One way or the other you'll pasteurize me.

MAGGIE: "Patronize"?

RED: Whatever.

MAGGIE: Red, what "system" are you on? Is this costing us money?
(*Red slips his hand under one of the pillows of the couch and produces a book. He hands it to Maggie.*)

MAGGIE: (*Reading the title.*) "Arnold Boyle's Miracle System for Writing and Selling Your Screenplay in Six Weeks."

RED: I knew it. There's that superior tone.

(*Maggie flips through the book with an air of superiority.*)

MAGGIE: Red. Look. You had a traumatic experience at work. I understand that. It's not easy to deal with being fired.

RED: I wasn't fired, I was persecuted.

MAGGIE: Now, Red, you weren't persecuted. Your boss wanted you to do a job a certain way and you flew off the handle.

RED: Mario Sanzilli never laid a board of drywall in his life. He's gonna tell me how to do my work?! I don't think so, Mag.

MAGGIE: Red, it wouldn't kill you to compromise once in your life.

RED: Mag? I'm a sheetrocker, Mag. I do solid, lasting work. Mario Sanzilli on the other hand does shit. And I get fired? He should be the one that gets fired.

MAGGIE: Well, that's not the way it usually works, Red. The way it usually works is the employee gets fired and the boss hires someone else.

RED: I know how it usually works. Thank you.

MAGGIE: I'm just pointing out that you let your emotions take over and you're the one that ends up losing.

RED: Not yet, Mag. I haven't lost yet. I intend to expose Mario Sanzilli.

MAGGIE: Expose him? As what?!

RED: As a jerk. And at the same time bang out a crackerjack script that will sell big and entertain the masses.

MAGGIE: Red, writing a fully realized work doesn't happen in six weeks. It's a long, grueling, process. A hellish process, Red. One that can go on for several years. Or longer. And even after years of suffering can ultimately result in a terrible, terrible unthinkable failure.

RED: Look, Mag, I understand how this situation might be a little … difficult for you.

MAGGIE: (*Looks at him for a beat.*) What situation?

RED: You know, with me taking up writing and all.

MAGGIE: "Taking up writing." You don't "take up" writing. It's not a water sport.

RED: All right, let's just put this puppy out on the table. I've obviously been putting in some major writing days the past few weeks and that can't be easy for you. I mean, with what you're going through.

MAGGIE: (*Dangerous territory.*) What am I *going through*?

RED: I'm just saying it's been four years since *A Conversation With Emily.*

MAGGIE: I see. So you're saying … What are you saying? Are you trying to say that I'm …

RED: What …

MAGGIE: You know! That I'm …

RED: Blocked?

MAGGIE: (*She lets go.*) Don't ever use that word in the house again.

RED: Arnold Boyle does a whole chapter on unplugging your plugged up creativity.

MAGGIE: Would you stop evoking the name of that idiot hack?!

RED: Mag, seriously. You might want to take a look at Chapter Seven.

MAGGIE: I don't think so, Red. I don't think I want to read your little book. I am a professional writer. I believe Joyce Carol Oates wrote in her New York Times review, "Ms. Sorenson's work is drenched with the energy and fury comparable only to the first works of such writers as Fitzgerald and Hemingway. This reviewer awaits her next work with fervent anticipation."

RED: You've got them memorized now?

MAGGIE: The point is, *Red*. That I am not writing the sort of book you just "bang out." I am writing a sensitive, subtle, fragile work about the interiors of human beings. It's not some nonsense about a sheetrocker getting fired from his job which, believe me, no one really cares about.

RED: Is that right? It just so happens it's a perfect part for Pacino.

MAGGIE: Pacino? Al Pacino? Why are you bringing up Al Pacino?

RED: I'm just saying my Uncle Joey did give me his personal home phone number.

MAGGIE: You're not still living in the fantasy world that Al Pacino will even read your screenplay.

RED: He *is* family, Mag.

MAGGIE: He is not family.

RED: He might as well be. There's a deep bond.

MAGGIE: Red, your family sold pork to relatives of Al Pacino. That's not what I'd call family.

RED: This is an excellent point you make. I can't depend on him. Which is why I would really appreciate it if you could introduce me to Sam. I shake the guy's hand, plug my movie and that's all. You have your meeting.

MAGGIE: (*Dawning realization.*) Oh my God. You don't actually intend to push your little screenplay to my agent!?

RED: My screenplay is the opposite of "little." And *yes*, I fully intend to mention it.

MAGGIE: Red, that isn't going to happen. All right?

RED: Let me ask you something? Why can't I ever meet Sam? What are you ashamed of me or something?

MAGGIE: Ashamed of you? No! Look, I want you two to meet. I've tried to arrange something. But Sam's an extremely busy person.

RED: Look Mag, it's extremely important at this tender stage in my development as a writer to meet as many agents and industry people as possible.

MAGGIE: Is that Arnold Boyle's philosophy?

RED: Chapter four.

(*Doorbell rings. Maggie, suddenly serious, looks at Red.*)

MAGGIE: Say hello and leave.

(*Maggie opens the door to Samantha, an attractive woman dressed to accentuate her every curve. There's a silent, loaded moment as Red and Samantha regard each other.*)

RED: Hello?

SAMANTHA: Hi.

MAGGIE: Great! I'm so happy you two got a chance to meet. Bye, Red.

SAMANTHA: Don't tell me I'm actually meeting the mystery man.

MAGGIE: Actually, Red was just leaving so …

RED: *You're* Sam?

SAMANTHA: In the flesh.

RED: You're a woman.

SAMANTHA: Why thank you. It's a pleasure to finally meet you, Professor.

RED: Professor?

MAGGIE: You can call him Red.

RED: Maggie, what's … ?

MAGGIE: Hush-hush, *sweetheart.*

SAMANTHA: I've always been fascinated with the field of biology.

RED: What?

MAGGIE: She likes biology, Red. Is there something wrong with that?

RED: Of course not. I've personally always hated it.

SAMANTHA: *You've* always hated it?

RED: Couldn't pass it in high school.

SAMANTHA: Maggie, he's hysterical. (*To Red.*) I've been trying to get Maggie to bring you out for ages.

RED: (*To Maggie.*) Is that right? (*To Sam.*) Well, now that we've finally hooked up, why don't you stay for dinner?

MAGGIE: I'm sure Sam has dinner plans.

SAMANTHA: Actually, I do. But that does smell divine. What is it?

RED: That would be my world famous roast beef, ma'am. Served with homemade mashed potatoes buried in gravy. And an infinite supply of Pillsbury crescent rolls.

SAMANTHA: I love Pillsbury crescent rolls.

RED: And for dessert. Maggie's famous homemade apple pie.

MAGGIE: Red. That would be impossible.

RED: Anything is possible. Served with a ridiculous helping of whipped cream.

SAMANTHA: That's it. I'm staying.

RED: Excellent.

MAGGIE: Really, Samantha, you don't have to –

SAMANTHA: Forget it. It's settled. You couldn't throw me out of here if you tried.

RED: You won't regret this. Now I know you ladies have a lot of professional things to discuss in a professional manner and I don't want to interrupt. So you have your meeting and I'll be in the kitchen quietly working my magic.

(*Red exits to the kitchen. Samantha looks at Maggie.*)

SAMANTHA: Maggie, I absolutely love him.

MAGGIE: Thanks.

SAMANTHA: Doctor of science, charming, and he cooks! No wonder you keep him hidden away. And I've never pictured biologists quite so … muscular.

MAGGIE: Yeah, well, he does have to lift a lot of … test tubes and so forth.

SAMANTHA: And where did you two met?

MAGGIE: I hired him to fix my toilet and somehow he never left.

SAMANTHA: You hired a biologist to fix your plumbing? Is he a marine biologist?

MAGGIE: He used to do handywork, to put himself through, you know, biology school.

SAMANTHA: A scientist who's good with his hands. He's like a fantasy.

(*From the kitchen, Red begins to sing Italian opera.*)

SAMANTHA: He sings? Of course he sings.

(*Maggie walks over and shuts the kitchen door so we can't hear Red.*)

MAGGIE: Anyway!

SAMANTHA: Right. Maggie, I am so excited to finally read the next work in the Maggie Sorenson oeuvre.

MAGGIE: Sam, I think maybe we'd better talk.

SAMANTHA: Talk-schmalk. Let's have the pages, you tease.

MAGGIE: Well, actually ...

SAMANTHA: Maggie, I understand it's a rough draft.

MAGGIE: I just feel if we waited just a little bit longer ...

SAMANTHA: I want the book, Maggie. I *want* it.

MAGGIE: Look, Sam, the truth is ... There isn't actually any actual manuscript.

(*Long pause.*)

SAMANTHA: Sorry?

MAGGIE: I mean, to say that a manuscript actually existed at this exact moment would be a little bit overly optimistic at this, you know, point.

SAMANTHA: Oh.

MAGGIE: Now, I feel strongly that I am right on the cusp of a breakthrough. I mean, if things keep going the way they have been this book could potentially be ...

SAMANTHA: Finished?

MAGGIE: Well, yeah. I know that I'm a few months behind on my deadline ...

SAMANTHA: Fourteen.

MAGGIE: But I just truly feel that given three more ...

SAMANTHA: Weeks?

MAGGIE: Well, months.

SAMANTHA: Three months!

MAGGIE: I just really feel that given a little more time ... I mean, take for example, fine wines. Like the truly great wines, must be aged, for, well, God knows how long really, before they're actually ... you know *great*. And until they're great, the truth is – I mean, not that I'm the big expert on winemaking –

SAMANTHA: (*Cutting her off, at wit's end.*) Maggie, is this all leading to something?

MAGGIE: I don't know. I'm just afraid that I'm ...

SAMANTHA: Blocked?

MAGGIE: (*Blurting out.*) Don't ever use that word in this house again! (*Calming herself.*) Sorry, I don't know what got into me.

SAMANTHA: Maggie, You're a brilliant writer. *A Conversation With Emily* was a home run.

MAGGIE: Sam, you know how I hate all those baseball metaphors.

SAMANTHA: Sorry ...

MAGGIE: But since you started ...

SAMANTHA: Home run. Boom! Out of the park. You had two hundred thousand bored Americans in the stand and you woke them up. But it's time to step back up to the plate.

MAGGIE: But what if the next book isn't a home run?

SAMANTHA: What are you saying, Mag?

MAGGIE: I mean, right now I just feel like I'm, I don't know, losing yardage.

SAMANTHA: Well, give me a double off the wall and you're right on track to be the next Ann Tyler.

MAGGIE: Now you know how I hate to be compared to other writers.

SAMANTHA: I know. I'm sorry.

MAGGIE: Ann Tyler? Really?

SAMANTHA: Bigger. Now Maggie, I've got to fend off Peter while you finish. Can you give me a hundred pages?

MAGGIE: Well, can't we just wait until I finish the whole book?

SAMANTHA: Give me ninety pages.

MAGGIE: This is ridiculous. I'm not going to negotiate with you on how many pages I ...

SAMANTHA: Eighty.

MAGGIE: Fifty.

SAMANTHA: Seventy.

MAGGIE: Sixty.

SAMANTHA: Done. Let's have them.

(*Red enters.*)

RED: Okay, we're very close to having one of the greatest meals in history. Maggie, maybe you should get in there and work on that pie.

MAGGIE: Red, I am not going to make pie.

SAMANTHA: (*Devastated.*) Oh ... No pie? I love apple pie.

MAGGIE: It's just ... I don't even have a crust ...

RED: There's a crust in the freezer, hon.

(*Maggie smiles, defeated.*)

RED: Fear not, I'll keep Sam entertained.

(*As Maggie leaves she pulls Red into a sudden hug, so she could whisper to him without Sam hearing:*)

MAGGIE: If you bring up your screenplay, I will kill you. (*Maggie exits.*)

RED: (*Without missing a beat.*) So tell me, Sam. Any interest in a juicy screenplay?

SAMANTHA: Are you kidding, I butter my crescent rolls with screenplays.

RED: Sex scenes that make *Showgirls* look like an after school special, action that makes *Die Hard* seem like an afternoon nap, and more gags than The Three Stooges on speed.

SAMANTHA: Well … Do you know someone who –

RED: Take a seat, darling.

(*Red takes a handful of manuscript pages and hands them to Samantha.*)

SAMANTHA: Oh, *you* wrote this.

RED: Well, it isn't completely finished yet. I have about twenty pages left.

SAMANTHA: Well, maybe I should wait until you finish before I read it.

RED: That's okay. I'll finish it up right now.

SAMANTHA: What?

RED: I'll finish it up while you read.

SAMANTHA: You said you have twenty pages left.

RED: That's right.

SAMANTHA: It will take me a couple hours to read this. How are you going to write twenty pages of a screenplay in two hours.

RED: (*Indicating the typewriter.*) Oh you don't understand. This is an electric.

(*Blackout.*)

SCENE 2

Two hours later. In blackness we hear a big laugh from Samantha, then: Lights up! Samantha lays on the floor near the typewriter deeply engrossed in Red's script as she savors a slice of apple pie. Red maniacally types. Maggie paces, concerned. Red finishes a page and hands it to Samantha who eagerly grabs it from him and reads. She emotes as she reads:

SAMANTHA: Wooooo! Wooooo! (*Suddenly sad.*) Oh, no! No! (*Then disbelieving.*) I can't believe this! Is he going to do it!? I can't believe he's going to do it!

(*Sam finishes reading the page and immediately turns to Red who is typing at a clip:*)

SAMANTHA: More! *More!*

(*Red rips a page from his typewriter. Hands it to Samantha and literally collapses into the couch, exhausted.*)

RED: Finished.

MAGGIE: Finished!!?

(*Samantha reads the last page. She is suddenly overcome with emotion, and begins weeping. Then, she begins to smile through her tears, warmed and moved. She places the final page in place in the manuscript and holds the screenplay up dramatically.*)

RED: Well?

SAMANTHA: Well ... Let me formulate my thoughts. Red, I feel you have written a brilliantly sardonic yet sobering manifesto for the twentieth century working man.

RED: Oh well. I gave it my best shot.

MAGGIE: She liked it, Red.

RED: You liked it?

SAMANTHA: I've never thought I could feel so deeply for a hard hat.

RED: That's senior sheetrocker.

SAMANTHA: And I love the title – "Sheetrocker In Paradise."

MAGGIE: Jesus.

SAMANTHA: I'm gonna think twice the next time I pass a construction site. I had such feelings for Dirk.

MAGGIE: *Dirk?*

RED: He was kind of persecuted, wasn't he?

MAGGIE: Dirk?

SAMANTHA: Red, what can I say, you've knocked it out of the ballpark.

MAGGIE: What?

SAMANTHA: You've hit a home run, Red.

MAGGIE: (*To Sam.*) I can't believe you.

RED: Thank you, Sam.

SAMANTHA: Red, I'd like to show this to a few people, if that would be all right.

MAGGIE: People! What people?!

RED: Absolutely. Listen, if you happen to talk to Pacino's people you might want to mention my family owns Russo's Pork Palace in Brooklyn.

MAGGIE: (*Aside to Sam.*) This is how you let him down easy?

SAMANTHA: Maggie, he's really got something here. By the way, does Red have some kind of contact with construction workers or something? I'd like to know who this Dirk character really is. I could use a man like that in me.

MAGGIE: You could use him *in* you?

SAMANTHA: In my life. (*Moving to Red.*) Red, can you get me a copy of the screenplay first thing in the morning?

RED: You got it darling.

SAMANTHA: All I can say is – Wonderful roast; great screenplay. I'm truly impressed.

(*Sam is about to leave.*)

MAGGIE: Sam? Aren't you forgetting something?

SAMANTHA: Oh yeah, nice pie, Mag.

MAGGIE: My sixty pages.

SAMANTHA: Oh. Of course. (*She takes the manuscript.*) I'll get right to this. Chow fun, people!

(*Samantha exits. Maggie and Red exchange looks of utter disbelief.*)

MAGGIE: Dirk?

RED: Biology professor?

(*Blackout.*)

SCENE 3

A few days later. Applause is heard. Lights up on Red, responding to the applause with humbled appreciation. He moves downstage, and speaks toward the audience in a daydream.

RED: I want to thank the members of the Academy. And everyone that's supported me through this. My agent, Sam whatever her last name is.

(*Maggie enters unnoticed, watches.*)

RED: And well ... of course Mr. Al Pacino. I love you cuz. And last but hardly least my lovely wife and not a bad writer herself, Maggie Sorenson ... Thanks, Mag.

MAGGIE: Anytime.

(*Red swings around, startled.*)

RED: Jesus! How long have you … ?

MAGGIE: I came in when you were thanking Cousin Al.

RED: I can't believe three days go by and I don't hear from Sam.

MAGGIE: Red, don't tell me you're sitting around waiting for the phone to ring.

RED: Well, yeah.

MAGGIE: Red, look at me. I've just given sixty pages of my manuscript out. Sure in my fantasy world Sam's going to burst through that door any second saying she loved it. But I can't get caught up in that whole mindframe. I just have to keep going with my life.

RED: Maybe you're right.

MAGGIE: Of course I am.

(*The doorbell rings. Maggie and Red stare at each other for a moment then simultaneously rush for the door. Samantha enters speaking on a cell phone.*)

SAMANTHA: Nicky, you dog. You fucking dog. – No, you listen. *You* listen. As a decent human being I am trying to make this happen with you because you came to me first. You've got a tuna on the line, Nicky. We're talking about Bobby DeNiro for a Fall start date. That's a lock. That's real. Now I better hear some real numbers and I better hear them fast. – You want an exclusive? On the basis of what? One roll in the hay? Don't flatter yourself, dollface. Better come back to me quick. You have my numbers.

(*She hangs up and immediately collapses on the couch.*)

SAMANTHA: Water, water.

MAGGIE: What's going on?

SAMANTHA: Oh my God, I'm dehydrating. WATER!

(*Red flies back from the kitchen with water. Sam downs the whole thing.*)

SAMANTHA: This is the deal of a lifetime. What is that, tap!? Jesus.

RED: What's happening?

SAMANTHA: Bidding war. Sheetrocker.

MAGGIE: What?!

RED: What does that mean?

SAMANTHA: It basically means you've graded your last biology exam, my friend. I've got MGM bidding against Tri Star.

RED: Are they good?

MAGGIE: Red, MGM is the roaring lion, and Tri Star is the white winged horse.

RED: Oh my God. They're good!

SAMANTHA: Sign this, doll.

(*Samantha pulls out a thick set of stapled papers.*)

RED: What is this?

SAMANTHA: Agency papers. Standard. (*She hands the papers to Red.*) Oh my God. I got a call Saturday morning from Nicky Alvers. Guy I used to work with. You wouldn't believe the arrogance of this guy, Mag. He calls me and says he's just in New York for the morning, do I have any interest in thirty minutes of sex?

MAGGIE: What an idiot.

SAMANTHA: Ditto. So afterwards we're lying in bed and he asks me if —

MAGGIE: You slept with him?

SAMANTHA: He's an excellent contact, Mag. Anyway ...

MAGGIE: You slept with an idiot like that because he's a good contact?

SAMANTHA: Of course. Maggie, if I didn't let Peter Kipper give me a little thrill, *Conversation* would be gathering dust in your filing cabinet right now.

MAGGIE: Are you saying you slept with Peter?

SAMANTHA: Maggie. Child. Wake up.

MAGGIE: I can't believe that *Conversation* being published had anything to do with —

RED: Would you let her finish the goddamn story, Maggie. So what happened?

SAMANTHA: Nicky says he's desperate because they just lost this project that DeNiro was supposed to do this Fall. So they have DeNiro and no script, right? So I think of *Sheetrocker*. Boom! I make Nicky read it right there in bed. Boom! He loves it. Boom! It gets pouched to DeNiro in Fiji, or Bali, or Ibiza or wherever. Boom! I leak it to the studios. Boom! Bidding war.

RED: Oh Jesus. Maggie, are you hearing this?

MAGGIE: (*Not thrilled.*) Incredible.

RED: So are you saying DeNiro actually read it? He liked it?

SAMANTHA: He loves it. He has only one problem. The role of Dirk's wife, the frustrated novelist. She's just too depressing.

MAGGIE: I can't believe you.

RED: I'll liven her up.

MAGGIE: Sam, have you gotten a chance to look at those sixty pages.

SAMANTHA: Yeah, right. This is the deal of a lifetime, Mag. Red, sign

the papers. I'll close this deal, and you'll never drink tap water
again.

(*Red flips through the many pages of contract. Maggie comes up to
him.*)

MAGGIE: Red, just to give you some professional advice. Never sign
anything until a lawyer looks at it.

RED: Thanks, Mag. On this day of … blah, blah, blah, blah, blah.
Looks good.

(*He signs it. Maggie looks at him, askance. Sam's cell phone rings.
Everything stops. Sam lets the phone ring several times for effect. Red
can barely contain himself. Samantha does a few leg, arm and neck
stretches as if gearing up for an athletic event. Then she does a few
forced breathing exercises and calmly picks up the phone.*)

SAMANTHA: Speak to me. – Uh-huh, uh-huh, uh-huh. Well, you're
getting closer. Nice back end. Very nice. I admit that openly.

(*The other phone rings. Maggie picks it up.*)

MAGGIE: Hello? (*Her expression sours.*) Sure.

(*Maggie hands the phone to Samantha. Before Samantha takes the
phone, she produces a bottle of Champagne and hands it to Maggie.*)

SAMANTHA: Mag, we're getting pretty close to blast off here. Could you
prep this?

(*Maggie smiles, annoyed. She take the Champagne and stands there
holding it. Samantha takes the other phone in her other hand, speaks
into it.*)

SAMANTHA: Speak to me. Uh-huh, uh-huh, uh-huh. Okay. Okay. We're
very close. (*Samantha starts to rapidly change from one phone to the
other:*) Nicky? No more bullshit. Let's hear where you're willing to
go. Uh-huh. Uh-huh. (*Into other phone:*) Scott. Nicky's up to three
hundred. Uh-huh. Uh-huh. (*Into both phones:*) All right fellas. On
the count of three you both have one shot to be in bed with me
and DeNiro this Fall. Ready? – One … Two … (*Aside to Maggie.*)
Maggie! The Champagne!

(*Maggie exits to the kitchen with the Champagne.*)

SAMANTHA: … Three! (*Beat as she listens. A smile forms on her face.*)

SAMANTHA: Scott. Welcome, aboard. You've got sixty minutes to fax me
á deal memo. (*Into other phone:*) Nicky? Better luck next time. (*Into
both phones:*) It's been a pleasure, boys. Chow fun. (*She hangs up.
Looks at Red.*)

RED: So?

SAMANTHA: Red. Welcome to the wild side, my friend. Welcome to life.

RED: So ... You sold it?

SAMANTHA: No, I didn't "sell" it. I caressed it. I made love to it. I expertly sculpted it. I just lifted deal making to a level of high art.

RED: So ... I mean ... How much do I get?

SAMANTHA: Four hundred.

RED: Four hundred dollars? Well, I guess it's a start.

SAMANTHA: Red. Four hundred thousand.

RED: (*In shock.*) Oh. I see.

SAMANTHA: I thought that would be acceptable for your first effort. Plus, you have one of the most beautiful back ends in the business. Your back end is unprecedented.

(*Red could be in a coma. But suddenly, he snaps to, and just starts screaming.*)

RED: Ahhhhhhhhhhh! I can't believe it! I sold a fucking screenplay!

SAMANTHA: (*Also exploding.*) WOOOOOO!

(*Samantha holds out her arms. Red dives into them. They hug. Suddenly, they find themselves silent and locked in embrace, bodies pressed together. Obviously aroused.*)

SAMANTHA: Come here.

(*Samantha pulls Red into her. Red tries to pull away, but perhaps not as forcefully as he could. They fall into a passionate kiss. Maggie walks in with a tray full of champagne glasses. She stops short, dropping the tray. The glasses shatter. Red and Samantha break apart, caught.*)

SAMANTHA: (*Brightly.*) Well! I should push off. Red, fix the frustrated novelist. Mag, we'll talk real soon. Chow fun, people. (*Samantha exits.*)

RED: So. Did you hear? Four hundred thousand dollars. Plus Samantha says I have one of the best back ends in the business.

MAGGIE: I'm glad she likes it.

RED: Mag ... Look, I know Sam got a little excited ...

MAGGIE: Sam?

RED: Maggie, I was trying to pull myself away. That's a very forceful woman we're talking about. I mean, that is a woman who obviously works out.

MAGGIE: Red, get out of here, all right? Just get out of here.

RED: Look, it was a mistake.

MAGGIE: No kidding, Red.

RED: Mag, come on. Four hundred grand! We could buy a house in the country. We could –

MAGGIE: Red, leave.

(*There is a silence. Finally, Red takes his coat and exits through the front door.*)

(*Blackout.*)

SCENE 4

The next morning. Maggie sits alone on the couch intently reading Red's screenplay. She turns the last page over, finished. The doorbell rings. Maggie steels herself, then walks to the door.

MAGGIE: Red, where have you … ?

(*Maggie opens the door. It's Samantha. Maggie's completely stone faced.*)

SAMANTHA: Hi, doll.

MAGGIE: Red's not here, so …

SAMANTHA: I came to talk to you, Mag.

MAGGIE: Look, Sam, I've decided to seek other representation.

SAMANTHA: Maggie. What's going on? Did I do something?

MAGGIE: Did you *do* something?

SAMANTHA: Oh God, what did you hear? Did Nicky Alvers call here?

MAGGIE: Sam! It's not about Red's deal!

SAMANTHA: Maggie, I'm going to make this right, but I need to know what's on your mind. Confide in me, girlfriend.

MAGGIE: Well, *girlfriend*. It sort of has to do with you jamming your tongue down my husband's throat.

SAMANTHA: (*Relieved.*) Oh that.

MAGGIE: "Oh that?"

SAMANTHA: From that tone you take I thought this was something serious.

MAGGIE: I can't believe you!

SAMANTHA: Now Mag. Let's stay calm here.

MAGGIE: But I'm not calm!

SAMANTHA: Look, what if I sent flowers?

MAGGIE: Do you really think that sending flowers –

SAMANTHA: You're absolutely right. Make it a case of Crystal.

MAGGIE: Get out of here.

SAMANTHA: Now, Maggie-Waggie …

MAGGIE: Get out!

SAMANTHA: You don't mean that, Mag.

RED: Maggie …

(*Maggie turns to see Red in the doorway.*)

MAGGIE: Both of you. Just get out. Leave me alone.

RED: Mag, I'm sorry.

MAGGIE: Forget it, Red.

RED: I don't know what happened to me. I became swept up with the script. I forgot who I was.

MAGGIE: Well, let me remind you. You were married to *me* and you were kissing *her.*

SAMANTHA: Let me know when you folks are done with your little married people's thing so I can finish up here.

RED: Look, Sam. Maggie and I need to talk, so maybe you could skedaddle.

SAMANTHA: Fine. No problemo. Just wanted to talk to Maggie about her manuscript. But it could wait.

(*Samantha starts to leave. Maggie eyes her, burning with curiosity. Finally:*)

MAGGIE: Sam.

SAMANTHA: Yes, love?

MAGGIE: So … you read it?

SAMANTHA: I did peruse it, yes. Astonishing. Quite astonishing. But we'll talk later. Chow fun.

MAGGIE: Good …

(*Samantha exits. Maggie looks at the door, possessed.*)

RED: Mag, the thing I realize is? The most important thing is just us. You know? You and me.

(*Maggie suddenly makes a mad dash for the door:*)

MAGGIE: Sam!

(*Maggie opens the door. Samantha enters, already talking.*)

SAMANTHA: Mag, *Conversation* was an incredible first effort. But *The Choreography* establishes you as an important writer.

MAGGIE: Important?

SAMANTHA: I'm afraid so, Mag. You've hit a grand slam, here.

MAGGIE: Grand Slam?

SAMANTHA: We're talking top of best seller list.

MAGGIE: Wait, has Peter read it?

SAMANTHA: I haven't heard Peter Kipper so excited since the time he and I ... Well, the point is, he's literally bouncing off the walls. Peter is now legally insane.

MAGGIE: Really!?

SAMANTHA: He keeps babbling this nonsense about getting it in the stores for Christmas.

MAGGIE: Christmas! Isn't that impossible?

(Red tries to edge his way in:)

RED: Maggie, shouldn't we talk?

SAMANTHA: Oh Red, I should bring you up on *Sheetrocker.*

RED: Sam, my relationship with Maggie is more important than a screenplay, all right.

SAMANTHA: Okey-dokey.

RED: *(360-degree turnaround.)* Why, is there a problem or something?

SAMANTHA: Let me finish with Maggie first. Why don't you get your wife a drink?

RED: Mag ...

MAGGIE: Red wine, Red.

SAMANTHA: Make it two.

(Defeated, Red exits to kitchen.)

SAMANTHA: Anyway. They want a rough draft in three weeks –

MAGGIE: Three weeks!

SAMANTHA: Exactly my point. I yelled at Peter at the top of my lungs. I told him that Maggie Sorenson is an artist. Maggie Sorenson will finish when she finishes. Don't worry, Mag. I am here to protect you from that salivating money hungry insane person.

MAGGIE: Let's say I could finish in three weeks.

SAMANTHA: Maggie, the fact that getting it into stores for Christmas would triple the sales you did on *Conversation* should be the last thing on your mind.

MAGGIE: *(Like a soldier.)* I can do it.

SAMANTHA: Yes!

MAGGIE: Sam, the dancer. Did you find her to be a likable character?

SAMANTHA: She was more than likable. I wanted to *be* her.

MAGGIE: So she wasn't upstaged by the man?

SAMANTHA: Maggie, the man is just there to serve a function for the heroine. He's just a servant.

(Red returns with the wine.)

RED: Wine.

SAMANTHA: Thanks, Dirk. Maggie, dive into that computer and don't come up for air until you've typed "the end."

MAGGIE: Okay, okay. I'll try.

(*Maggie heads to the computer and just starts typing. Samantha breathes a sigh of relief. Then looks at Red.*)

SAMANTHA: Now, Red. How could I put this delicately? *Sheetrocker's* dead.

RED: What?!

SAMANTHA: Apparently, DeNiro wasn't as thrilled with it on the second read.

RED: Wait a second. What didn't he like? I could change it.

SAMANTHA: I'm afraid it's too late. He's onto another project.

RED: Another project!? I can't believe this. He can't just do this. He can't just pull out. Can he?

SAMANTHA: He's Robert DeNiro. He can do whatever the fuck he wants. MGM says no DeNiro, no dinero.

RED: The hell with MGM. Can't we go somewhere else? What about the white winged horse?!

SAMANTHA: The white winged horse has a full slate.

RED: Well, there are other places, aren't there? What about the one with the woman holding the torch?

SAMANTHA: *Sheetrocker's* yesterday's news, amigo.

RED: Jesus. How quickly do things happen in this business!?

SAMANTHA: Gotta keep your dancing shoes on, my friend. Look. We'll talk soon.

(*Samantha exits. Red looks at Maggie who is completely immersed, typing furiously.*)

RED: Mag ... Maggie?

MAGGIE: (*Writing.*) Not now.

RED: Mag, please. About what happened yesterday.

MAGGIE: Red, look ... (*Beat.*) Everything's going to be okay.

RED: Mag. It is so great to hear you say that.

MAGGIE: Grandpa will sell the farm!

RED: Mag ... Hello?

MAGGIE: And that's why the dancer leaves Oklahoma! It's perfect.

(*Maggie swings around and starts fervently typing. Red looks at Maggie, realizes saying anything would be futile. He paces the room, frustrated. Finally, he takes a crumpled piece of paper out of his pocket.*)

He looks at it for a long beat, considering. Resolved, he lifts the cordless phone and dials.)

RED: Hello. Al Pacino please.

(Maggie turns, looks at Red.)

MAGGIE: Red, what are you ... ?

RED: Mr. Pacino. This is Red Russo. Let me begin by saying your family has enjoyed my family's pork products for close to forty years. Now Al. I mean, can I call you Al? Mr. Pacino, right. No problem. So what I'm calling about is, see I wrote this screenplay – Mr. Pacino? Please don't yell, Mr. Pacino. Of course you don't have to change your number. – Mr. Pacino! Please don't hang up! Look, this is my life here. – Okay, okay. Sixty seconds. This is the role of a lifetime, Al. You're Dirk LaBella. Dirk the Beautiful. Got it? I guarantee an Oscar for this. – That's right. My personal guarantee. It's a story of hope, Al. The little guy triumphs. –

Right. Get to the story.

You're a senior sheetrocker, Al. You get fired for no good reason. True story. From here on in is where I took the truth and gently stretched it into what my agent described as a home run. – What's that, Al? Great, thirty seconds is all I need. You discover your boss is involved with the mob. You hook up with Sharon Stone, beat reporter by day, striptease artist by night. The two of you go undercover into the sleazy underworld of organized crime and corrupt unions where you meet up with every actor of Italian American descent alive. You get shot at by Joe Pesci, chased by John Travolta and double crossed by Palmenteri. It all leads to the final showdown on Marlon Brando's tropical island. Everyone's there. You, Brando, Travolta, Montegna, Aiello, DeVito, Pesci, Scorsese. In fact, about the only person who isn't there is DeNiro. They were going to *do* this, Al. And because *one guy*. Because *Mr. DeNiro* decided he had better things to do, the whole thing is dead. The point is, Al. *(Change of tone.)* The point is when I wrote this thing ... When I did this. It's like the best thing I've ever done in my life. It was like I was *alive*, you know? I mean, my people don't do this kind of thing. You know, we're in pork. Not to sneeze at the pork industry; there's more to it than meets the eye. But the idea that I could do this thing. That I could create something out of nothing. That was just really amazing, Al.

(Hearing this, Maggie rises. She walks toward Red.)

RED: Yes. I'm sure Robert DeNiro's a great guy. All I'm saying is …
Right, right. Regards to your family too. Thanks. (*Red hangs up.
Long pause.*)

RED: I'll make some calls tomorrow. Find some work.

MAGGIE: I read your screenplay.

(*Pause. Red looks at her.*)

MAGGIE: You're a writer, Red.

RED: No, I'm not, Mag. I'm an unemployed construction worker who
just wasted six weeks.

MAGGIE: No, you're a writer who just coincidentally – just through
circumstances – never wrote anything. Until now.

(*Red listens, silent.*)

MAGGIE: I can't tell you how much I hate to admit this, but you've got
to start a new script.

RED: So what're you saying? You'll give me six more weeks?

MAGGIE: Better make it a little longer. The second one tends to really be
a nuisance.

RED: Look, it's no good. I don't know how to write. I think I just
needed to get this thing out of my system. It's over.

MAGGIE: Well, if that's how you feel –

RED: Of course, I did have an idea.

(*Maggie smiles.*)

RED: It's like this period piece. Like hundreds of years ago in England
or whatever. So it's about this beautiful princess who falls in love
with just this guy – this pauper. I mean, she can have anyone in the
world, but for some reason she chooses *him*. I guess she kind of
gets a charge out of him or whatever. And for him – well, he just
really worships her, you know. Just knowing her changes his whole
life. But they have to hide their relationship from the king. So they
can only meet in this secret cave. But the thing is they get lost in
the cave. They can't find their way out.

MAGGIE: So the cave is a metaphor.

RED: Exactly … What's that?

MAGGIE: It's like the cave represents their relationship. Incredibly
intimate, but kind of hidden away from the world.

RED: Exactly. And it gets so they can't breathe in there.

MAGGIE: So it's about their journey out of the cave. Both literally and
figuratively.

RED: Right, whatever. And the thing that they learn, like when they finally get out of the cave? Like after all they've been through?

MAGGIE: Is that they're really not so different after all?

RED: No. There are aliens.

MAGGIE: Aliens?

RED: In the forest.

MAGGIE: (*Not pleased.*) Wait a second. You're saying this movie has aliens?

RED: Hundreds of them. Slimy little green creatures.

MAGGIE: Red …

RED: And the thing is these aliens are resilient little bastards. There's no killing them. And they multiply like rabbits.

MAGGIE: Red, think of what you're saying. You're watching this wonderful bittersweet love story and then all of a sudden there are these ridiculous aliens. What is that?

RED: *That* is a movie I love.

(*And as Red feeds a page into the typewriter we:*)
(*Blackout.*)

END OF PLAY.

Betrayed By Everyone
by Kenneth Lonergan

BIOGRAPHY
Kenneth Lonergan's work has been performed in New York at Naked Angels, Atlantic Theatre Company, Circle Rep., Playwrights Horizons, Manhattan Punchline and the HB Playwrights Foundation; in London, at The Royal Court Theatre and The Bridge Lane; and in Los Angeles at The Coast Playhouse. He is a member of Naked Angels. He is also a screenwriter.

ORIGINAL PRODUCTION
Betrayed by Everyone was produced by Act One in association with Showtime Networks Inc., Paramount Network Television, Viacom Productions and Grammnet Productions for *Act One '95: A Festival of New One-Act Plays*, at The Met Theatre in Los Angeles, CA in April 1995. It was directed by Frank Pugliese with the following cast:

Warren ....Mark Ruffalo
Jessica...Ria Pavia

CHARACTERS
WARREN, a young man, around nineteen or twenty
JESSICA, a young woman around the same age

SETTING
A small apartment on the Upper West Side of Manhattan.

Betrayed By Everyone

A small pillbox apartment on the Upper West Side of Manhattan, furnished scantily and arbitrarily. In one corner is a duffel bag and a cardboard box full of antique toys. It is after midnight on a Friday. Traffic noises can be heard out the window. Warren has just opened the door for Jessica. He is nineteen or twenty. He wears enormous pants, Hi-top sneakers and hair cut short very recently – probably for the first time in years. Jessica is the same age, wearing heavy but effective makeup, dressed in big shoes and a tight little dress. They are good-looking kids, but they would both look better if they eased up on their personal styles a little.

WARREN: How you doin', Jessica? You're looking very automated tonight.

JESSICA: What is that supposed to mean?

WARREN: Nothing. It's just a fashion concept.

JESSICA: What?

WARREN: Um – Nothing. Do you want to come in?

(*She takes a few steps into the room.*)

JESSICA: Hey. Where is everybody?

WARREN: They just went to get drugs. They'll be right back.

JESSICA: Well – what do you mean? How long are they gonna be gone?

WARREN: I don't know. Twenty minutes?

JESSICA: Well, how far did they have to go?

WARREN: The East 80s?

JESSICA: OK … I don't mean to be paranoid. I just don't want to be the victim of some teenage matchmaking scheme.

WARREN: Noted.

JESSICA: You know? If I'm gonna get set up, I'm gonna do it myself. I don't need anybody's help getting fucked.

WARREN: Well nobody's setting you up and nobody wants to fuck you, so calm down.

JESSICA: Oh you can't see why I would think that?

WARREN: I don't know or care what you fuckin' think, Jessica. I'm just staying here because my Dad threw me out of the house. But go home. It's fine with me.

JESSICA: OK ... Sorry. (*She comes in.*) You probably think I'm like a total bitch now, right?

WARREN: I don't think anything. I don't even know what you're talking about.

(*He shuts the door and locks it. She turns her head at the sound of the lock.*)

WARREN: And now ... you're *mine.*

JESSICA: No *way.*

WARREN: I'm kidding. Calm down,

JESSICA: (*Simultaneous with "calm."*) That's not funny at *all.*

WARREN: I'm just kidding.

JESSICA: It's not funny.

WARREN: Noted.

(*She sits down. He sits down across the room from her.*)

JESSICA: Well, is it OK if I smoke in here?

WARREN: Go ahead. It's not my house.

JESSICA: Is there any ashtray or something I can use?

WARREN: I'm sure there's one somewhere ...

(*He looks around for an ashtray and finds one around the same time she finds an empty soda can.*)

WARREN: Here you go.

JESSICA: No it's OK, I can use this. Thanks.

(*He puts down the ashtray and sits down across the room from her. She lights up. Silence. She smokes in silence. Warren watches her.*)

WARREN: So are you like a really big cigarette smoker?

JESSICA: I guess so.

WARREN: How many cigarettes would you say you smoke in the average day?

JESSICA: I don't know. Like a pack and a half a day, on a really heavy smoking day. Maybe like a half a pack a day if I'm like, in the country.

WARREN: Yeah ... I never really got into the whole cigarette scene, myself. But I hear great things about it.

JESSICA: Well, but if you smoke pot all the time it's much worse for your lungs than cigarettes.

WARREN: Well ... I guess my lungs are pretty severely damaged.

JESSICA: Well I'm not about to get hysterical about it. I'm nineteen years old, why should I give a shit what I do?

WARREN: That's pretty much how I feel. (*Pause.*)

JESSICA: So – Did those guys go to get, um, to get coke?

WARREN: That was the plan ... And we're getting some Dom Perignon to top it off, so it should be pretty good.

JESSICA: Sounds good ... (*Pause.*) So why did your Dad throw you out of the house? What did you do?

WARREN: Nothing. I got stoned and he came home and was like, "I want that smell out of this house." And then he was like, "No, actually, I want *you* out of this house," and then he threw a few hundred bucks on the floor and was like, "here's some cash, now pack up your shit and get out before I beat your fuckin' head in." And I was like, "Whatever." So I'm just gonna crash with Dennis for a few days till I figure out what I'm doing.

JESSICA: What *are* you gonna do?

WARREN: I don't know. I was thinking I might just buy a bus ticket and head out West. I have a buddy who lives in Seattle so I might just go see him ... I definitely wanna get out of *this – pit*. That's for sure.

JESSICA: You mean New York? You don't like living here?

WARREN: What's to like? You go outside and it *smells* bad. You know? And I live on Park Avenue.

JESSICA: Yeah ...

WARREN: I like the out*doors*.

JESSICA: I know, but –

WARREN: Like last winter I went to visit this buddy of mine who lives in Jackson Hole? In Wyoming? And we'd just *ski* every day, you know? And bus tables at night. And when you get up in the morning and open the front door, it's like, *silent*. You know? You go outside and it's like, the *mountains*. And *snow*. And nobody around for *miles*. And like the whole ... *sky* over your head. You know? So what the fuck am I doing languishing on *this* trash heap for? The intellectual stimulation? I'm not getting any. All I do is smoke pot. I can do that anywhere. I can just bring that *with* me, you know?

JESSICA: Yeah. I don't really take advantage of the city's facilities at all, and it just seems like such a total waste ...

WARREN: Yeah. I mean ... yeah. (*Pause.*)

JESSICA: Hey, is there anything to drink here? I've got this really bad taste in my mouth.

WARREN: (*Gets up.*) I think there's some water ...

JESSICA: (*Starts to get up.*) I'll get it ...

WARREN: That's all right. "Chivalry is not dead. It just smells funny."
(*She does not know how to respond to this attempt at humor. He exits. She checks her hair. He returns with a glass of water which he brings to her.*)

JESSICA: Thanks a lot. (*She drinks.*) God, I was so thirsty.
(*He sits down again, next to her, instead of across the room. But he doesn't look at her or say anything and it is making them both very nervous. She gets up, looks at the photographs on the wall.*)

JESSICA: So who are all these photos of? Are you on this wall?

WARREN: Yeah, I'm represented.

JESSICA: God, your friend Dennis is *so* handsome ...

WARREN: You think?

JESSICA: Oh my God, are you kidding? Is this Dennis as a baby? What a tough little guy with a little football helmet.

WARREN: I guess.

JESSICA: Hey, is that his Mom? She's beautiful ...

WARREN: It's an incredibly attractive family.

JESSICA: What does she do?

WARREN: Um ... She's like a big city social worker administrator of some kind ... She's always like, installing swimming pools for the poor or something.

JESSICA: What?

WARREN: Nothing. She runs these programs for the city government or something. She like designs social work programs for homeless kids and kids with AIDS and stuff like that. But she's a fuckin' psycho.

JESSICA: Why do you say that? Just because she's a social worker?

WARREN: No – because of her behavior.

JESSICA: Why? What does she do?

WARREN: I don't know. She's just really *strident*. She's like a bleeding heart dominatrix, with like a *hairdo*. She –
(*Overlapping dialogue.*)

JESSICA: "Bleeding heart?"

WARREN: – I don't know. Yeah!
(*End overlapping dialogue.*)

JESSICA: What are you like a big Republican or something?

WARREN: Not at all. I'm a total Democrat. I just –

JESSICA: So why do you *say* that about her?

WARREN: Because that's what she's *like*. I don't know. I don't really *care*. Maybe she's really nice. I don't really want to get into an *argument* about it.

JESSICA: No, it's just – my sister's a social worker, and I really –

WARREN: I didn't say anything *about* your sister.

JESSICA: I know you didn't.

I just –	WARREN: I didn't know you *had* a sister.
I *know* – but I just think it's like a really good thing to do with your life and I j– OK, I *know*. I just admire people who dedicate themselves like that, and I –	And I was not attempting to vilify the entire social worker community!

WARREN: So do *I*. What she *does* is fine. It's just how she *is*. I think it's totally brave to do that kind of work. Unless you're just …

JESSICA: Unless what?

WARREN: Unless you just have no *sense* of people. No – Like if your *mission* overrides your – actual moral *opinion*, but – forget it. It's not – It doesn't matter.

JESSICA: All right. I certainly didn't mean to offend you.

WARREN: I'm not offended.

(*Silence. She goes to the corner where Warren's stuff is piled up. She looks in the cardboard box.*)

JESSICA: Hey – what's this stuff?

WARREN: Those are just some of my belongings.

JESSICA: What are these?

WARREN: It's just some fuckin' shit.

JESSICA: What are these, like antique toys or something?

WARREN: Um, for the most part …

JESSICA: These are really cool.

WARREN: You think?

JESSICA: Yeah, they remind me of the stuff my brothers had when I was a little kid. I always wanted to play with their toys and they were like, "Go play with dolls, you little bitch." And I was like "Fuck *you.*" I *love* old toys.

WARREN: I have a fair amount of this kind of thing.

JESSICA: Do you know how many toys I had – I mean how much, of the stuff I had when I was little, I wish I had now? Like, I think of some of those toys and I just look back on them with this *longing* … You know?

WARREN: Definitely.

JESSICA: Who are these guys?

WARREN: That's my Major Matt Mason collection. You know Major Matt Mason?

(*She shakes her head.*)

WARREN: Come on. Major Matt Mason – when we were kids. He's a spaceman, and he has these helmets, aw he's the best. I have a complete set, all in prime condition.

JESSICA: Really cool.

WARREN: And this is my amazing toaster. "Toaster Amazing;" I call it. Come here and look at this. It's really something.

(*She looks.*)

WARREN: Yeah, G.E. made only like a few hundred of this model like in the '50s, and then they recalled them because they were like exploding in people's kitchens at breakfast and burning down their homes. So only a few hundred actually exist. I got one from this dealer I know in Seattle and he had *no* idea what he was selling me.

JESSICA: Huh.

WARREN: I have made toast with it and nothing bad has happened to me. But I don't really use it too much because it really depreciates in value. But it's great to know I have one of the only ones in existence.

JESSICA: So you're really into collecting, huh?

WARREN: Not really. Not much. Just stuff I like.

JESSICA: What's your favorite thing in this collection?

WARREN: Definitely my Wrigley Field Opening Day baseball cap my grandfather gave me. No contest.

JESSICA: What's that?

(*Warren takes out an ancient blue and white baseball cap.*)

WARREN: This is a real collectors' item, like an *amazing* collectors' item, actually. My Mom's Dad got it the first day at Wrigley Field when he was totally like a little kid, in 1914.

(*Jessica reads what's embroidered on the cap.*)

JESSICA: "Wrigley Field, Home of the Chicago Cubs, Opening Day." (*Reads off the other side.*) "True Value."

WARREN: True Value Hardware, all *right*.

(*She puts the hat on.*)

WARREN: Looks good, Jessica …

JESSICA: So…are your parents divorced?

WARREN: Yeah. They got divorced a while after my sister died. And then my Mom moved to San Diego.

JESSICA: God, so why don't you go stay with her? That's supposed to be pretty nice.

(*She takes the hat off and walks around the room.*)

WARREN: Well, I don't particularly want to live in California, for one thing.

JESSICA: Why not?

WARREN: Because of the people in it. Plus my Mom lives with her boyfriend … and anyway, she's kind of freaked out generally. So it's kind of tough to be around her for very long at one stretch.

JESSICA: Why? Because of your sister?

WARREN: I guess.

JESSICA: What did your sister die of?

WARREN: Um – she was murdered.

JESSICA: Oh my God, is that true?

WARREN: No, that's just a little joke we have about it in the family.

JESSICA: What?

WARREN: Yeah it's *true*.

JESSICA: I'm sorry: I didn't mean, "Is that true?" I just meant … You know, "Oh my God." How old were you?

WARREN: Ten.

JESSICA: Wow. How did it happen? Do you mind talking about it … ?

WARREN: Not really. Do you want any pot? (*He picks up half a joint.*)

JESSICA: No, no thanks. But you go ahead.

WARREN: Um – That's all right. (*He puts down the joint.*)

JESSICA: So what happened? That is so horrible.

WARREN: Um, nothing. She was going out with this guy named Julian. Who she was living with. And my parents were kind of freaked out that she was living with this guy because she was only nineteen, and he was much older. And my Dad was like, "I'll pay for you to live in your own apartment if you just *don't* live with Julian." So after a lot of fights and stuff she basically agreed. And then she went home, ostensibly to tell Julian, and as far as anybody knows, they had some tremendous argument, at which point it was revealed that he was actually like really out of his mind. So the next thing we knew, I was home with my Mom and the doorbell rang, and I got the door, and it was these two police detectives. And they asked to speak to my Mom, and I was invited to leave the room, and then they told my Mom that my sister had been murdered and they needed her to come identify the body.

JESSICA: Oh my God.

WARREN: So ...

JESSICA: All just because she was gonna move out?

WARREN: No, because the guy was *crazy*. I mean I'm sure that was the issue at *hand,* but nobody really knows, because –

JESSICA: But like ... Did he like ... I mean, do you think it was premeditated, or ...

WARREN: I really don't know.

JESSICA: Well I mean, did he go to jail? Or did he just –

WARREN: Um, no. He just vanished. They think he like, fled the country, but they don't really know. The police said it was definitely him that did it, but unfortunately they were too fuckin' stupid to ever find him. So as far as we know, he basically like, just, basically got away with it.

JESSICA: Wow ...

WARREN: Anyway, so not long after that my Mom just couldn't take it, I guess, you know, just being around the house, so she moved away, and then I guess they eventually got a divorce and ... that's pretty much it.

JESSICA: That is so horrible ... Nothing like that has ever happened to me.

WARREN: I would hope not.

JESSICA: I once saw a woman get her leg cut off by a bus ...

WARREN: Oh yeah?

JESSICA: Yeah. It was really horrible. I mean, it was really ...

WARREN: Was it somebody you knew?

JESSICA: No no.

WARREN: Did she die?

JESSICA: Um, yeah.

WARREN: Where were you? Were you right there?

JESSICA: Yeah. I was sort of holding her hand when she died.

WARREN: When was this?

JESSICA: Two years ago.

WARREN: So what happened? Was it the driver's fault, or was it just –

JESSICA: Well – Is this too morbid?

WARREN: Not at all.

JESSICA: Well, OK, see, that's the weird thing. Because the day this happened, I was out looking for a cowboy hat ...

WARREN: What?

JESSICA: I wanted to buy a cowboy hat, but I didn't know where to get one, so I was just walking down Broadway, looking in store windows ...

WARREN: Yeah?

JESSICA: And then this bus went by me, and I saw the bus driver was wearing this really nice cowboy hat. So I was looking at him, and he waved at me. And he was kind of cute, so I kind of waved back, and that's when he hit this woman.

WARREN: Whoa.

JESSICA: But when the cops came and they asked me if I saw what happened, the bus driver and I just sort of looked at each other, but I didn't say anything. I mean I just said I thought it was an accident.

WARREN: Huh.

JESSICA: But when I went home and told my family about it, you know, I didn't say anything about the guy waving at me. You know. Because I thought they would think it was my fault. Which it ... you know, which I think it was. But then I finally decided to tell my mother about it. And she was so nice about it – she was just like, "You didn't do it, it was an accident ... " But when I asked her if I should say something to the police, she was like, "Well, you should really think about that. Because you could really destroy the guy's whole life, and you should really think about whether you want to *do* that or not."

WARREN: What?

JESSICA: Well –

WARREN: But I mean – that guy should be *exterminated.*

JESSICA: That is *so* arrogant!

WARREN: How so?

JESSICA: What are you saying, you know *you* would have told the cops right away?

WARREN: Not at all! I'm sure you were in a very difficult position. But I do think if you're driving a fucking *bus,* you shouldn't be waving at chicks! I have no idea what course of action I would actually take, but regardless of that, the guy deserves to fry.

JESSICA: Well, anyway … I didn't know what to do. So finally I called the bus company and got the guy's phone number, and I called him – I actually called him at home. I'm not sure what I wanted to say, but I really felt like I had to talk to him, or ask him about it, or something. But when he picked up, I don't know, I couldn't say anything – like I just froze. So I just hung up. (*Pause.*) But I mean I think about that accident like *every* day. I mean it completely *haunts* me, and I'm sure my whole personality is different now because of it. Because why *shouldn't* I have told the police what happened? You know? *He's* the one who ran her over because he was looking at me. And I'm the only one who knows that. So why didn't anybody just, like, encourage me to just say what *happened?* You know?

WARREN: I don't know.

JESSICA: You know? So anyway, since then I've really realized you just gotta make your own decisions, and make it your own business to make sure you're covered. You know what I mean?

WARREN: Well, it's definitely an advantage. I mean … it's something you can always fall back on, no matter what the specific circumstances are.

JESSICA: Yeah … Anyway. Let's change the subject.

WARREN: All right.

(*Jessica looks out the window.*)

JESSICA: The Wild City. (*A moment.*) Hey, you want to put on some music?

WARREN: (*Getting up.*) Sure. These are my authentic first release '60s albums, all in perfect condition. Got the whole thing here: Early Mothers, Captain Beefheart, Herman's Hermits, everything. (*He puts on a slow ballad.*)

JESSICA: Oh. OK. Goes for the slow song. I get it.

WARREN: Of course. Care for a spin?

JESSICA: OK. I'm game.

(*He holds out his hands. She starts to take them.*)

JESSICA: Wait. (*She lets go.*) I've got a hair in my mouth.

(*She extracts the hair from her mouth, shakes it off her finger and puts her hands back up. They dance, not entirely gracelessly.*)

WARREN: I'm definitely into actual dancing.

JESSICA: Yeah I think our generation definitely missed out in the dancing department.

WARREN: Yeah … I guess like, whoever the genius was who decided you didn't need *steps* should have come up with something else instead.

JESSICA: Yeah, right?
(*He dips her.*)
JESSICA: Check him *out*. Mr. *Dip*.
WARREN: Um – Listen. I gotta say – I find you incredibly attractive.
JESSICA: Relax, will you?
WARREN: So listen: Would you be mortally offended if I kissed you for just a second?
JESSICA: Well, I mean, what's the rush?
WARREN: No rush. I'd just like to get rid of this knot in my stomach.
JESSICA: Oh, sure, I mean – whatever's expedient.
(*He kisses her. She kisses back. It gets very heavy very fast, until she breaks away.*)
JESSICA: They're gonna walk in and I'm gonna be really embarrassed.
WARREN: Yeah – me too.
(*She takes a few steps away.*)
JESSICA: So … do you like me, Warren, or what?
WARREN: Of course I do. Can't you tell?
JESSICA: I don't know. Maybe you just – I don't know, maybe you just want to mess around or something. (*Unconsciously she picks up the baseball cap and toys with it.*)
WARREN: Um, I do. *And* I like you. I completely enjoy talking to you …
JESSICA: Well, which would you prefer if you had to choose?
WARREN: That would depend on which one we'd already been doing more of.
JESSICA: All right. I'm sorry. Pay no attention. I'm just being weird. (*Pause.*) It's just – I'm just always getting drawn into these situations and then getting hurt really badly. So…
WARREN: Noted.
JESSICA: Can I have a present?
WARREN: Name it.
JESSICA: Um … Can I have the hat?
WARREN: Oh … No way. Sentimental value of enormous proportions.
JESSICA: Come on, I'll take good care of it. Look, it's filthy and everything. You're gonna ruin it.
WARREN: Um … I guess you don't want one of my surplus Major Matt Masons?
(*She shakes her head.*)
WARREN: Don't ask for that. (*Pause.*)
JESSICA: OK. Sorry. That was really stupid. Forget I said anything. (*She

gives him the hat.) I'm sorry. (*She goes to the window.*) Where do you think they *are?*

WARREN: Listen, I'm sorry ... uh ... I –

JESSICA: That's OK. Forget about it. That was a really stupid thing to ask for.

WARREN: Well ... I wanna give you something else.

JESSICA: You don't have to say that. I mean, you barely know me.

WARREN: Well – Are you angry? I mean, it seemed like we were getting along pretty well up to a minute ago –

JESSICA: I'm just embarrassed. I shouldn't have asked for it. Keep it for some – never mind.

WARREN: For some what? That's my special hat.

JESSICA: Yeah, I *get* it. But you can relax now, because I don't want it. I'm completely embarrassed that I asked for it and I'd really like to change the subject. OK?

(*Pause. Warren picks up the hat and offers it to her.*)

WARREN: Here. I want you to have it.

JESSICA: Don't if you don't want to.

WARREN: I really want to. (*Pause.*)

JESSICA: Well ... OK. (*She takes the hat and puts it on.*) I just *love* it. It's so *old.*

WARREN: Looks great on you ...

(*She starts dancing again.*)

JESSICA: Uh huh, uh huh, come on, don't you want to?

WARREN: Yeah.

(*He starts dancing too, but he is clearly in distress. She takes the hat off and throws it at him.*)

JESSICA: Why did you give it to me if you don't want me to have it?! Just keep it!

WARREN: But I really want you to have it!

JESSICA: But you obviously *don't!*

WARREN: No! God *damn!* What do I have to like *beg* you to take it from me? (*A moment.*)

JESSICA: OK. I'm sorry.

(*She picks up the hat, hesitates, then guiltily puts it on her head. Warren watches.*)*

WARREN: Thank you.

(*Fade out.*)

END OF PLAY

Broken Bones
A One-Act Play
by Drew McWeeny and Scott Swan

BIOGRAPHIES

Drew McWeeny was born in New York, but has lived all over the country in his first twentysomething years. His interest in film was initially sparked by *Star Wars*, and he spent most of his teen years watching any and every film he could get his hands on. He credits his imaginative skills to a mostly thrill-free childhood.

Scott Swan was born in Pittsburgh and raised in Washington, Pennsylvania. As an only child, he turned to his imagination early in life, writing stories and drawing their "storyboards" to entertain himself. At the age of ten, he utilized his talents writing, directing and playing the lead role in his class play. An average student, Scott spent much of his time writing plays and studying on his own, educating himself in a way the school system could not. Inspired by the films of George Lucas and Steven Spielberg, Scott focused on screenwriting in his early teens.

Drew and Scott met while attending Armwood High School in Tampa, Florida, where they were the top Television Production students. Their work on a closed circuit morning show that was broadcast live to thousands of students each day (and garnered them several awards during the two years they worked on it) led them to collaborate on a screenplay together. Since moving to Los Angeles in 1990 they have written twenty-two feature length screenplays, two full length plays, and four one-act plays. Their first produced work was *Sticks and Stones*, which snagged industry attention, leading them to a feature version of that play. The duo are currently at work developing two original features with Avalon Films and directing their own no-budget feature, *Walter Did It ...*

AUTHORS' NOTE

It's been almost six months since *Broken Bones* closed on stage as we sit down to write this. It's been a busy six months for us, and the entire *Bones* process seems so far away now. This play was not, by any means, an easy birth. Everyone who was involved with it had an opinion as to how it should open, why they should be fighting, how it should end ... honestly, this was the most arduous development process we've been through yet. And through it all, the characters of Jamie and Steven stayed remarkably consistent. No matter how much people tried to bend the characters to fit their own agendas, the characters demanded that they be written a certain way. To our minds, the hero of this piece is Don McManus, a friend and a great guy in general. He believed in the material from day one, and fought to do it the right way. Our cast, Willie Garson and Michelle Joyner, were wonderful in demanding, unpleasant roles, and they brought such grounded reality to the piece that we will owe them forever. Debra Jo Rupp, the last in a long series of almost-Megs, ended up being the one that we were looking for all along. In the time since we started work on the piece, the OJ Simpson trial focused a national spotlight on the issue of domestic violence, and we've heard about it almost ad infinitum. Still, for our money, there is no comment more effective than actually being there and seeing how it happens, hearing what leads up to it, and witnessing the way it can ruin lives, just like that. Watching this play on the stage was a shattering experience on the best nights. We saw people leave in tears. We saw other people leave angry. Most of all, though, we saw that we had affected them in some deep and meaningful way, and that is the greatest reward we could have had.

ORIGINAL PRODUCTION

Broken Bones was produced by Act One in association with Showtime Networks Inc., Paramount Network Television, Viacom Productions and Grammnet Productions for *Act One '95: A Festival of New One-Act Plays*, at The Met Theatre in Los Angeles, CA in April 1995. It was directed by Don R. McManus with the following cast:

Steven .... Willie Garson
Jamie .... Michelle Joyner
Meg .... Debra Jo Rupp

Broken Bones

It's late, after midnight, and we are in the living room of a good-sized apartment in Seattle. Outside, there's a light rain falling. The room is set up so the back of the TV faces the audience. A hallway leads to the bedroom and the bathroom, and a counter separates this room from the kitchen.

A computer workstation has been set up, with the system taking up one corner of the room. The computer is on, and there is a screen saver running. This provides the only light in the room.

There are also several boxes full of what looks like trash around the room, as well as a mannequin spattered in red and black paint, and what looks like a welded collage of auto parts.

Music plays softly from hidden speakers, more driving beat than anything. We hear someone moving around offstage, in the bedroom. Steven Todd enters from the back hallway, flipping through a notebook. He's dressed in jeans, socks, an oversized T-shirt. At thirty, he's still got a boyish quality to him, something perpetually rumpled in his manner.

Steven takes a seat in front of the computer, paging through the notebook, completely wrapped up in what he's doing.

He starts to type something on his keyboard, working rapidly without looking at the screen. His concentration is broken from the sound of someone approaching in the hallway outside the apartment. The person, a woman, is muttering to herself, low, obviously agitated. She stops outside the door, tries it, realizes it's locked.

WOMAN: (*Offstage.*) ... shit ... (*She starts to pound on the door, the sound echoing loudly in the hallway.*) Come on, Steven ... I know you're here. I saw the car downstairs. (*Pause.*) I don't have my keys ...

(*Steven rises and crosses to the door. He unlocks it, but doesn't open it.*)

WOMAN: (*Offstage.*) Dammit, I can *hear* you in there ...

(*Steven's not quite to his desk when the woman tries the door again, this time opening it easily. Jamie Todd enters, soaking wet, dressed for a formal occasion. Under the best of circumstances, Jamie has an open, friendly charm. Right now, she just exudes quiet rage.*)

JAMIE: You are a fucking son of a bitch ... you know that?

(*She slams the front door, walks slowly into the room. Steven sits down, facing the screen, not giving Jamie an audience, not looking at her.*)

STEVEN: I'm glad you got back okay.

JAMIE: I'll bet. (*She shrugs off her coat and tosses it onto the couch with a wet thud. She drops her purse by the couch on the floor, then heads for the bedroom, kicking off her shoes in transit.*) Why didn't you answer the phone?

STEVEN: I did. You already hung up ...

JAMIE: (*Offstage.*) ... it rang *forever* ...

STEVEN: I was doing something. It happens ...

JAMIE: (*Offstage.*) I didn't even know you left. You could have told me ...

STEVEN: You were busy. Now, I'm busy ...

(*Jamie peeks back around the corner as she worms her way out of her dress.*)

JAMIE: You can take a break for a minute ...

STEVEN: ... have to finish this ...

JAMIE: ... I wanna know what's going on. (*Jamie picks the discarded dress up, vanishes back into the bedroom again. Offstage.*) Come in here while I wash my face ...

(*Steven hears her turn the water in the bathroom on, looks over at her coat on the couch. He gets up, goes over, picks the coat up, shakes some of the water out of it. He looks around for a place to put it, ends up draping it over the mannequin's shoulders. He picks up her purse and her shoes and heads for the bedroom.*)

JAMIE: (*Offstage.*) You left before I could tell you ... I sold one of the big pieces ...

(*Upon hearing this, he changes his mind, tosses her things back onto the floor, goes back to the computer, sits. The water continues running for a long moment, then we can hear Jamie moving around in the bedroom.*)

JAMIE: (*Offstage.*) Steven ... ? (*Pause; low.*) ... goddammit ... (*Finally, she emerges, dressed in a dry T-shirt and shorts, still towel drying her hair.*) Steven, are you listening to me?

(*She walks over to the stereo, turns the music down to the point of being practically inaudible. Steven finally glares over at her. When he speaks, it's in low, even tones, like you would talk to a child.*)

STEVEN: I'm working, okay?

JAMIE: No. It's not okay. *You left me.*

STEVEN: I had things I needed to do. I have a job, too, remember?

JAMIE: I mean, one minute, you're there, we're talking ...

STEVEN: We were *not* talking ...

JAMIE: ... then I turn around a few minutes later, you're just gone ...

STEVEN: I tried to talk to you, but you were busy. I figured you'd be able to catch a ride ...

JAMIE: I didn't know I needed to. I thought you were still there and just, you know, giving me some room ... by the time I realized, everyone had already left. I had to call a fucking cab ... almost twenty dollars, Steven ...

(*Steven reaches over, turns the music back up, then kind of half shrugs as he goes back to what he was doing.*)

STEVEN: Yeah, well ... sorry 'bout that.

(*Jamie just stands there, looking at him for a moment, waiting for something more.*)

JAMIE: You don't even care, do you? You don't care that I had to stand outside the gallery for thirty minutes waiting for the cab to show up? (*When nothing is forthcoming, she twists the towel tightly. A smile creeps onto her face, nothing playful about it.*) You'd better turn around and talk to me ... (*She practices popping the towel at him once, missing by a good foot.*)

STEVEN: Don't play like that ...

JAMIE: Are you going to turn around? (*Pause.*) Last chance, dear ...

(*Thwack! She pops the towel again, this time catching him square between the shoulder blades. Steven is up on his feet immediately, but stock still, in too much pain to turn around.*)

STEVEN: (*Finally.*) Are you out of your mind?

JAMIE: (*Shrugs; smiles.*) Yeah, well ... sorry 'bout that.

STEVEN: How many times have I said it since you got home? Huh? I have work that I have to fucking do ...

JAMIE: I'm asking for ten minutes of your time ...

STEVEN: I can't. Not right now.

(*He sits down again, back to her, and the conversation is over, just like that. She stands there for a moment, miserable, wanting desperately to talk to him. Finally, she turns and walks out, back to the bedroom. It takes him a long moment to relax again, start working. Jamie walks back out, walks over to the stereo. She checks the CD case, reads it, inspects the cover, her obvious distaste for the music written all over her face. She turns it down, just a touch, when she's sure Steven isn't looking. She ends up wandering over to the sofa where she dropped her jacket. She realizes it's not there now, looks around.)*

JAMIE: Steven ... did you ... ? (*She spots the jacket on the mannequin.*) Oh, fuck. (*She darts over and, carefully, peels the jacket off of the mannequin. She checks the inside of the jacket, and groans loudly when she sees the red paint that stains the lining of the jacket.*) Steven, you fucking ... you ruined my jacket!

STEVEN: I just hung it up for you ...

JAMIE: Look! Look! (*She marches over, waves the jacket in Steven's face.*) That's paint from the fucking dummy. You didn't even look at what you were doing ...

STEVEN: You came in and tossed your wet coat on the couch ...

JAMIE: It's only wet because of you ...

STEVEN: ... should know better than that ...

JAMIE: ... can put it anywhere I want to ...

STEVEN: ... ruin the couch ... is that what you want to do?

JAMIE: Don't talk to me about ruining things, Steven! It's a good thing I sold a piece tonight ... a good goddamn thing ... (*She walks over and slams the jacket into the trash can.*) It adds up, your little tantrum ... I think you've made your point, whatever that may be. You win. Okay? I don't want to fight with you.

STEVEN: Then don't. Fine with me.

(*He goes back to his work, and Jamie walks back over to the mannequin, begins to check it out.*)

JAMIE: ... no respect for my things ...

(*She finishes looking the mannequin over, then walks back to the bedroom for a moment. The CD that is playing ends, and there is just the sound of Steven typing for a moment. He finishes his thought, sits back for a moment. He notices that the music has ended, reaches over and turns it back on. Jamie finally comes back into the room, looks at the stereo.*)

JAMIE: Are you going to listen to this?

STEVEN: It's on ... why?

JAMIE: I wanna watch some TV. (*Pause.*) ... if you're done.

STEVEN: You can turn it off if you want.

JAMIE: Are you sure?

STEVEN: Yeah. It's fine.

JAMIE: If you're still listening to it …

STEVEN: I'm done. Watch TV.

(*Jamie goes to the stereo and takes out the CD, shuts the system down. She sits down on the couch, picks up a remote and turns the TV on. She begins to flip through the channels, past all sorts of late night dreck, talk shows, sports, three different Spanish channels. She stops on The Weather Channel, stares blankly at the screen. The only sound for a long moment is the cheesy elevator music.*)

STEVEN: (*Finally.*) Would you at least find something you can watch?

JAMIE: I'm watching this.

STEVEN: Something real …

JAMIE: C'mon, Steven … in Pittsburgh, it's 47 degrees right now. I mean, that's real.

STEVEN: You know what I mean …

JAMIE: In Miami, they had a record high of 73 degrees today. I need to know this. You never know when something like that could come in handy …

(*When she realizes he's ignoring her, she flips past an infomercial which she stops on for a moment, then continues to flip until she locates a boxing match. She stops, sets the remote down. We can see the tension building in Steven's neck, his posture, the way he fidgets with the keyboard, unable to continue typing.*)

STEVEN: (*Explodes.*) For chrissakes, would you turn that thing off?!

JAMIE: All right, fine! (*Pause.*) I was kidding with you, Steven. I didn't realize that you were determined to be an asshole all night.

STEVEN: … trying to piss me off and you're doing a pretty fucking good job of it …

(*Jamie looks at him for a moment, trying to decide how to play this. Finally, she turns the TV down quite a bit.*)

JAMIE: Steven … I wanna talk to you … and it doesn't have to be about anything. It can be good news … just positive only, y'know? Like … like we could talk about what you want to do with all the money we made tonight.

STEVEN: We didn't make anything tonight. It was your show.

JAMIE: Come on … your half is four thousand dollars, partner. What do you do first?

STEVEN: I don't know …

JAMIE: Any impulse at all … just tell me the first thing you think of …

STEVEN: I'm no good at this kind of …

JAMIE: Try.

STEVEN: Um … I'd get an office. With a door.

JAMIE: (*Not amused.*) You're not trying very hard.

STEVEN: Yes, I am. I'm trying very hard to solve a format compatibility problem. If you can help me with that, then I'm very interested in what you have to say. If not …

JAMIE: I want to help however I can.

STEVEN: … you can let me do this in peace … that would be a big fucking help …

JAMIE: Do you want me to go away?

STEVEN: I didn't say that …

JAMIE: Do you?

STEVEN: Well, it's a little difficult trying to work with you out here, dicking around with the TV. It's the middle of the night. You never watch TV right now … I know that. I know you want to talk, or share, or some fucking thing, but this is my time right now, and you're cutting in on it. I don't come home in the middle of the day and fuck up your space when you're trying to, uh … to create or whatever. Give me this, huh?

JAMIE: All right. Fine. That's … that's fair. But promise me something …

STEVEN: What?

JAMIE: That you'll tell me what's wrong. It doesn't have to be tonight … but I want to know.

STEVEN: It's nothing.

(*Jamie studies Steven for a long moment.*)

JAMIE: It's something.

STEVEN: I don't want to get into this.

JAMIE: So we'll talk about it later.

STEVEN: Maybe I don't want to talk about it later. I don't think I'm required to discuss every fucking thought that crosses my mind with you …

JAMIE: I don't want to know every thought that crosses your mind … just the ones that directly impact me.

STEVEN: I never said it had a goddamn thing to do with you! Why are you so fucking convinced that it's you?!

JAMIE: I can read you like a book …

STEVEN: The hell you can.

JAMIE: I know you're mad at me.

STEVEN: Okay! You're right ... congratulations. You're a fucking genius.

JAMIE: I know it's got something to do with my show.

STEVEN: No, it doesn't.

JAMIE: Well, that's where it happened.

STEVEN: Nothing happened, goddammit. I just felt like leaving. You were busy with other people, and me being there was just a waste of time ...

JAMIE: It was my first real show, Steven ... I was in charge. I got to do things the way I wanted. It was important to me that you be there ... you know that ...

STEVEN: How many times did you even talk to me tonight?

JAMIE: That's not the point ...

STEVEN: Once.

JAMIE: Having you there is the important part. Knowing that you care about what I do ...

STEVEN: Like you care about what I do?

JAMIE: Exactly.

STEVEN: Do you?

JAMIE: Do I ... what, care? Of course ...

STEVEN: Of course. You're always there for me ...

JAMIE: I think you're talented, and, uh ...

STEVEN: You're a real inspiration ... supportive ...

JAMIE: Stop it! Why are you being so sarcastic?

STEVEN: You don't know?

JAMIE: No ...

STEVEN: Then it's no big deal. Leave it alone.

JAMIE: I'd be happy to, but if I do, you're just going to sit out here all night and brood.

STEVEN: Talking isn't going to make me feel better, Jamie ... I need to deal with it ... my way, 'cause it's my problem.

JAMIE: If it's about me ...

STEVEN: ... then it's still none of your fucking business.

(*Steven starts to shut his computer down. Jamie watches him, wanting to say something. In the end, she opts to cross to stand behind Steven. As he shuts down various Windows screens, backs out of the system, she reaches up and begins to knead his shoulders. Steven pulls away from her, but not dramatically. She just takes a moment, then goes back to it, trying to massage his shoulders, loosen them up.*)

STEVEN: Jamie …

JAMIE: Shhh … we'll talk about it later …

(*She bends so she can kiss his neck. She runs her hands over his chest, down his front. Steven closes his eyes, is silent for a moment. He looks like he is torn, both relieved and repulsed by her touch. Finally, he jerks away from her. She reluctantly stops, backs away. He finishes up, shuts the computer off so that light spills in from the bedroom, and from the TV, which is turned almost all the way down. He doesn't stand for a moment.*)

STEVEN: I'm going to bed.

(*He rises, pushes past her, heads for the bedroom. She hesitates a moment, then follows.*)

STEVEN: (*Offstage.*) Jamie …

(*Steven walks back out, Jamie still behind him.*)

JAMIE: Now I can't go to bed?

STEVEN: Look … I need to do some thinking …

JAMIE: … what, you can't sleep with me all of the sudden?

STEVEN: I want some time to myself, okay?

JAMIE: Don't be ridiculous, Steven …

STEVEN: No … I'll take the couch.

(*Steven walks back into the bedroom as Jamie tries to understand all this.*)

JAMIE: Okay, Steven, stop it now …

STEVEN: (*Offstage.*) I'm taking one of the pillows.

JAMIE: Stop it. Tell me what I can do …

(*Steven walks in, pillow and blanket in his arms.*)

JAMIE: I'm sorry … whatever it is …

STEVEN: No, you're not.

JAMIE: I am.

(*Steven drops the blanket and the pillow on the couch, then sits down.*)

STEVEN: Fine. You are. Good night.

(*She starts to sit down on the end of the couch.*)

STEVEN: Don't …

JAMIE: I'm really trying to remember, Steven … did I say something wrong to you? We spoke the one time …

(*He tries to lay down, ignore her. He pushes her with his feet.*)

STEVEN: Get up.

JAMIE: … you seemed fine. You had a drink, you were smiling …

(*He pushes her, hard, knocking her onto the floor.*)

STEVEN: Leave me alone!

(*Jamie begins to pace a little, watching Steven stretch out on the couch and cover his face with the pillow.*)

JAMIE: I hate this, Steven. I hate feeling like the bad guy ... I mean, I'm at least making the effort ... y'know?

STEVEN: (*Muffled.*) I'm trying to go to sleep.

JAMIE: You're shutting down. You think I don't notice, or that I don't know what it means ...

STEVEN: Jamie, it's 1:15 in the goddamn morning. I have to go to work tomorrow ... *today* ...

JAMIE: Don't use that as an excuse. You don't want to talk to me.

STEVEN: God, what do you ... you're right. I don't. Anything I say to you is going to give you fucking ammo ...

JAMIE: Give me ammo? You're the one who took the car, locked me out ... and you won't even tell me why. I mean ... should I be worried here?

STEVEN: ... please, can't we do this in the ... ?

JAMIE: No. Now.

STEVEN: What's the big fucking deal?! You didn't give a rat's ass about how I felt earlier tonight ... why do you care now?

JAMIE: Don't be stupid. That's stupid. I always care.

STEVEN: You're right. You're a wonderful wife. The problem is me. You should do yourself a favor, just tell me to go fuck myself, then go to bed. You had a busy night ...

JAMIE: Take the pillow off your face, Steven. Sit up.

STEVEN: I'm tired ...

(*She snatches the pillow from him.*)

JAMIE: So am I. You know, you've spent the last, what is it, four months now pulling this shit ... ? I'm tired of it.

STEVEN: I'm sorry I'm not more like you ...

JAMIE: Don't apologize. I don't care if you're like me ... I just want you to act like yourself. You are in this fucking mood, and I have no idea what you want from me. You dance around things, Steven. You take it out on me in all your little ways, but you never tell me what I did ... you never tell me so that maybe, y'know, I can do something, or change something ...

STEVEN: You can't change it ... it's done.

JAMIE: Then, next time ...

STEVEN: What next time?! Huh?! People don't get fucking next times, Jamie ...

JAMIE: What are you talking about?

STEVEN: It's nothing you have anything to do with, okay? It's work ...
(*With that, Steven erupts off the sofa. Jamie draws back, startled, as he heads into the kitchen.*)

JAMIE: This is about work?
(*Without turning the lights on, Steven crosses to the cupboards, gets a glass. He opens the fridge as Jamie walks in. She turns the overhead light on, suddenly flooding the room with harsh florescent light. He winces.*)

STEVEN: Give me a fucking break with the light, huh?

JAMIE: I don't understand ...
(*Steven walks over, without a word, and turns the lights back off. He crosses to the refrigerator again, gets the water out.*)

JAMIE: Steven ... ? You've been beating me up all night over your work?

STEVEN: Do you ever listen to me when I talk about what I'm doing?

JAMIE: Of course ...

STEVEN: I don't mean, do you stand silently and listen to the sounds I make? I wanna know if you really hear me.

JAMIE: Yes, goddammit. I listen ...

STEVEN: Then tell me who Alex Corder is.
(*He finishes pouring his water as Jamie thinks about it. She's drawing a big blank on this one, though. He puts the bottle back and turns to her, taking a long sip.*)

STEVEN: Give up?

JAMIE: It sounds familiar ... I know the name ...

STEVEN: I'll give you a hint ... now, this might make it too easy, but ... Omnitech Software.

JAMIE: He's in the software business.

STEVEN: Very good ... but, specifically ...

JAMIE: You talk about a lot of different companies ...

STEVEN: You don't know.

JAMIE: Did you work for him?

STEVEN: Just admit it. You don't know.

JAMIE: (*Finally.*) You don't have to be a bastard about this. I have nothing to do with your work. You don't remember any of the people I have to ...

STEVEN: He's the president of Omnitech ... the company that has an option on my Wildfire program ...

JAMIE: Oh, right ...

STEVEN: Stop it!

(Steven is practically shaking from anger, on the verge of really losing control. Jamie begins to realize just how angry he is.)

STEVEN: You don't get to act like you knew that ... because you didn't. You had no idea ... because you don't care.

JAMIE: But I know now ... it's the company you're having the problems with ...

STEVEN: Shut up. You don't get a second chance ...

JAMIE: But ...

STEVEN: You blew it. If you paid even the slightest bit of attention, you'd have known that name tonight when you heard it ...

(He heads back into the living room, past her. She is torn between wanting to let him have it and wanting to make it better, and it's written on her face.)

STEVEN: ... four months of me getting my balls busted every fucking day, and the one guy who can make it all better is right there, right in front of me tonight, and my wife ... *(Pause.)* ... my partner ... doesn't say a fucking word.

JAMIE: He was there tonight?

STEVEN: Yep ... you talked to him.

JAMIE: I don't remember ...

STEVEN: He walked up to you, started talking, and as soon as I saw you, I started to walk over, because I knew that you would hear his name and recognize it. You would know exactly what to do. I knew that you were talking him up for me ... telling him how hard I've been working to fix this thing ... and I knew that I'd be able to sell him tonight on my changes ... all I needed was that intro. For months, all I can get out of his secretary is he's out of the office or in a meeting or on a business trip, and now, out of the fucking blue, here he is, talking to my wife. *(Pause.)* And when I walk up, and I slide my arm around you, I hear you laugh, and I hear him say how much he's enjoyed the show, and just as I start to think that, indeed, there is a God, he turns ... and he walks away. And I realize that you weren't talking about me. The name hadn't triggered a single fucking thought in your head. It was just the successful artist, chatting it up with the rich, handsome executive. You hadn't even registered ... you just let him slip away ... and take my last fucking shot with him.

JAMIE: I didn't know … I mean, I don't think he even said his name … and you didn't …

STEVEN: You didn't give me a chance … I mean, I come all the way across the room, it's obvious I'm trying to get an introduction.

JAMIE: You could have said …

STEVEN: I nudged you …

JAMIE: And I'm supposed to know what that means?! I thought you had too much to drink, you were having trouble standing …

STEVEN: It was a nudge … a signal. You know what a nudge is … all you had to say was, "This is my husband, Steven Todd." That would have been enough.

JAMIE: But you didn't nudge me.

STEVEN: Yes, I did. I put my arm around you, I nudged you, and all you did is turn, give me a little Hollywood kiss on the cheek, then go right back into the conversation, like I wasn't even there.

JAMIE: I didn't know that you were signaling me …

STEVEN: How could you not know?!

JAMIE: Because I didn't! I just didn't! If it was that important to you, you should have broken in, said something …

STEVEN: How? You were talking …

JAMIE: You could have interrupted.

STEVEN: That would look so desperate …

JAMIE: Listen to you! You are desperate, Steven. Only someone who's desperate would put me … or himself … through this …

STEVEN: You don't know enough about me to call me desperate. You have no idea …

JAMIE: I know you …

STEVEN: No. Just save yourself the fucking embarrassment and go to bed. You've talked this fucking thing to death …

JAMIE: So, that's it, then? You get to go to bed, you get to say, "No more … we're done"?

STEVEN: That's right. (*He drops onto the couch again.*)

JAMIE: I think that's bullshit. I have tried to be civil about this since I got home because I know what a fucking baby you can be, but I really don't care now … your feelings are hurt? Good. I'm glad. I'm glad you know what it feels like. When I realized you had walked out on me … (*Pause.*) Steven, what do you think the last five years has been about? I care, goddammit. That's why I came home tonight … that's why I stay here … that's why I try to talk to you. I know how you are, shutting down, keeping me out … but I keep trying, because I know what you have in you … I know what kind of person you can be … and sometimes, you can be the most wonderful person I've ever met … and sometimes, you're just a selfish fuck.

STEVEN: Selfish?! Ten fucking seconds is selfish? I have put months and months of my own work into this, into this whole goddamn back and forth with goddamn Omnitech, and it could have been over and done with and fucking resolved … if you'd just taken a second to think, "Wait … Steven is trying to do business with this man, with his company, and I know he's having problems. Here's an opportunity … "

JAMIE: How dare you … ?! It was my opportunity! It was my night!

(There is nothing for a long moment, and Steven finally nods.)

STEVEN: Well … thanks for being honest. *(He stands, weary, tired of all of this.)* Let me go to sleep now, okay? You can have the bedroom, or you can sleep out here …

JAMIE: I don't care.

STEVEN: Then enjoy the couch.

(He heads for the bedroom, closing the door with a solid sound. For a long moment, she doesn't know how to react. Finally, she takes a seat on the sofa. The TV is the only light in the room, and we watch as she seems to slowly crumble from within, breaking down in silent, angry tears. After a moment, she manages to gain some control of her emotions, and she shuts the TV off. She throws the remote at the bedroom wall, hard.)

JAMIE: … asshole … *(As she wipes away the last of her tears, she stands and heads for the bedroom.)*

[Note to Director: In the following sequence, any violence takes place offstage, with only sound to indicate what is happening.]

(Jamie begins to knock on the door, tentatively at first, but gaining passion the longer she knocks.)

JAMIE: *(Offstage.)* Steven … open the door. *(Pause.)* You can't just throw me out of my bedroom. This is my home, too … *(Pause.)* I can't say I'm sorry any other way, can I? I'm sorry … now open up. *(Pause.)* Goddammit, Steven … I mean it …

(She ends up practically pounding at the door, until Steven jerks the door open suddenly.)

STEVEN: *(Offstage.)* What the fuck is wrong with you?!

JAMIE: (*Offstage.*) You can't …
STEVEN: (*Offstage.*) All I want to do is be alone!
JAMIE: (*Offstage.*) It's my bedroom, too! I can do anything I …
STEVEN: (*Offstage.*) Fuck! Fuck this shit!
(*There is the sound of something being kicked, bashed around. Suddenly, Steven comes into view, just for a moment, dragging Jamie, who begins to shriek.*)
STEVEN: I fucking asked you!
JAMIE: Get your hands … !
(*She pulls free of him and lunges back into the bedroom, with him in hot pursuit. There is another sound, unmistakable, someone getting punched. There is the sound of a struggle, swearing, a few traded slaps. Steven begins to bellow, unintelligible, more like a primal sound than actual words. There are several more loud punches, and then the sound of furniture or something being kicked and smashed. Finally, after no more than ten or twenty total seconds, there is just silence. Several seconds go by before we hear the very soft sound of Jamie, crying.*)
STEVEN: (*Offstage.*) … oh my fucking God … look at this … look …
(*Steven walks back out into the living room, visibly shaken. His knuckles and his forehead are both bloody. He paces in small circles for a moment. He notices the remote on the floor, picks it up, and at the same time, notices the blood on his hand. He stands, looking at the blood for a moment, listening to Jamie, still crying in the other room, then sets the remote on the TV. The only light now comes from the bedroom, and from outside.*)
(*Steven goes into the kitchen, washes his hands in the sink, not turning any lights on. While he is at the sink, there is a knock on the front door. Steven just ignores it as he finishes washing his hands. There is another knock, this one more insistent. Steven gets a drink of water, carries it with him as he walks back into the living room. The knocking continues, and, very slowly, obviously annoyed, Steven crosses to the door. He opens it, his face a blank, to see Meg, a woman in her thirties in jeans and a sweatshirt. She looks like she has been sleeping and just woke up. She sees the blood on Steven's forehead and bites back a gasp.*)
STEVEN: What do you want?
MEG: I'm really sorry to disturb you … (*Pause.*) Um … I, I was … um … this would be easier, I think, if I could talk to, to your wife …
STEVEN: It's one in the morning.
MEG: … just want to see her for a minute …

STEVEN: She's asleep. I'll tell her you stopped by.

MEG: Listen ... I, uh ... (*Pause.*) ... jeez, I really don't know how to ... (*Pause.*) I heard you two just now ...

STEVEN: Yeah, well, we'll try to keep it down ...

MEG: I mean, I wouldn't bother you, but ... it's just that my, uh, bedroom is on the other side of the wall from yours, y'know ...

STEVEN: I'm sorry if we woke you. Good night. (*Steven goes to close the door.*)

MEG: No, no ... wait a minute, okay? I need to know if you're hurt ...

STEVEN: What ... ?

MEG: Your forehead. It's bleeding.

(*Steven reaches up, touches his forehead, sees blood on his fingers. He stops, surprised.*)

STEVEN: ... she, uh ... she threw some stuff at me. I guess I got hit, didn't even know it. I feel fine, though.

MEG: I don't mean to embarrass you, coming over here and all ...

STEVEN: I'm not embarrassed.

MEG: That's, uh ... that's not your blood, is it?

(*This really throws Steven. Sensing this, Meg takes advantage of the moment to step in.*)

MEG: I, I called, um ... 911 ...

(*Steven looks like he's been punched in the gut, like he can't breathe.*)

MEG: ... and I wasn't going to come over ... I didn't want to make it worse ... it's just, they asked me if anyone needed an ambulance ... and I told them I didn't know ... (*Pause.*) The 911 lady didn't want me to come over and ask, but I figured ...

STEVEN: You ... called the cops on me?

MEG: No ... I mean, I called them, yes, but not on you. I was worried ...

(*Steven processes this, then visibly changes modes, trying now to sound reasonable, trying to turn on whatever little charm he can muster.*)

STEVEN: Listen ... what was your name again?

MEG: Meg.

STEVEN: Listen, Meg ... was there some reason you couldn't come over and ask me what was going on first?

MEG: It was pretty obvious.

STEVEN: We had an argument, and she slapped me, then threw some stuff at me. I beat the shit out of the dresser ... that was all the noise.

MEG: I heard what happened ...

STEVEN: I know we were yelling, and I told you ... I'm sorry ...

MEG: No ... I heard you ... I heard you hit her ...

(*Steven stops moving, and his smile fades.*)

STEVEN: Watch it. You don't know what you heard …

MEG: These walls are paper thin … I mean, I can hear what you're watching on TV sometimes …

STEVEN: It's pretty easy to make a mistake …

MEG: I'm sorry if I assumed something, but I just couldn't sit there and listen to …

STEVEN: You weren't listening to anything. I mean, it was an argument, sure, but …

MEG: … I mean, I want to be fair. I don't want to presume something …

STEVEN: … it's not a big deal. It's over. We both had this shit all built up from today, and it just fucking boiled over, but that's it … finished …

MEG: Then let me see her.

STEVEN: The thing is … (*Pause.*) Tonight was a big night for her. You know how it is … she had a lot to drink. When she drinks, she gets louder … and when she starts yelling, I'll admit it … sometimes I yell back. (*Steven speaks in reassuring, measured tones, moving closer to Meg as he does, a subtle smile locked in place.*) I'm sorry we disturbed you. Really … but we've got it all under control now …

MEG: Two minutes … that's all …

STEVEN: … and, besides … it's none of your business, is it?

MEG: … one minute …

STEVEN: If it'll make you feel better, I'll have her stop by tomorrow morning, okay? Once she's had a chance to sleep it off …

MEG: She's gonna have to wake up when the police get here anyway …

STEVEN: I want to give her as long as I can. (*Pointed.*) After all, she didn't call the cops. She just wanted to get some sleep. It's fine, though … I'll talk to them, we'll get this fucking thing squared away. You, though … you should go home.

(*He practically backs her into the door, and she stops, hand on it. Steven stands in front of her, arms crossed, daring her to do anything but leave.*)

STEVEN: Really … everything's okay.

(*Jamie appears in the doorway from the bedroom, behind Steven. She is a truly shocking sight, her face stained with blood, her white T-shirt soaked in places, her lip already swollen, one eye closed. She moves like she's a little disoriented, like she's in slow-motion. Meg spots her at once, and her mouth drops open in shock, her eyes welling with angry tears. Her first instinct is to run, and she grabs the doorknob.*)

MEG: Oh, my … God …
> (*Steven turns and sees Jamie, and panic washes over him.*)

STEVEN: Jamie … honey …

MEG: … motherfucker …
> (*Steven turns on her, angry now.*)

STEVEN: Shut up! What do you know about anything?!
> (*Meg flinches away, struggling to stand her ground, as Steven turns back to Jamie.*)

STEVEN: You should go back in and lay down, Jamie …

MEG: No …
> (*Meg starts to move towards Jamie, but Steven gets in her way.*)

MEG: You're not okay … you need to have someone look at you …

STEVEN: (*To Meg.*) I'm not fucking around with you anymore. Back off.
> (*Meg tries to look past Steven, talk directly to Jamie, who is totally unresponsive.*)

MEG: I came over 'cause I heard you guys … (*Pause.*) Listen, the police are on their way, and they're gonna wanna take a look at you. Is that enough, or … ?

JAMIE: Who called the police?

MEG: I did.

JAMIE: It's not that bad …

MEG: You haven't looked in a mirror yet, have you? It's bad.

STEVEN: Are you satisfied? You've seen her, and she says she's fine. Will you please leave now?
> (*Steven slowly moves closer to Jamie, trying to put himself between Meg and Jamie.*)

MEG: Do yourself a favor. Put some distance between you and him right now … so you can take care of yourself …

STEVEN: I'll take care of her.

MEG: … it's not like you're walking out for good. Just for right now …

STEVEN: Man, you are some kinda fucking pushy. I've told you to leave, and it's obvious she doesn't want anything from you, either. Now, I want you outa here before …

MEG: Before what? What are you going to do? (*Pause; to Jamie.*) He'll do it again …
> (*Steven isn't putting up with this. He practically leaps across the room, and Meg cries out, just a bit, as she ducks back.*)

STEVEN: Get out of here!

MEG: Don't touch me!

STEVEN: You come into my house, you start telling me how things are going to be ... why the fuck shouldn't I knock you on your ass?

MEG: The police are on the way ...

STEVEN: Yeah, I know. I got that. Don't worry about it ... I wouldn't touch you. I'm not that kind of guy. Despite what you think, you don't know me.

MEG: No ... but I know your type.

STEVEN: Oh, yeah? What's my type?

MEG: I don't want to debate this with you ...

STEVEN: I invited you to leave, but you didn't want to go. So, tell me ... what's my type?

MEG: Look at your wife's face! That's your type.

(*Steven tries to look at Jamie, and can't.*)

MEG: That's your wife. You're supposed to keep shit like this from happening to her. Cherish and honor and all that ...

STEVEN: (*Low.*) You don't know us. You don't know me. My wife, she can tell you ... you've got the wrong idea ...

(*Outside we hear sirens, in the distance at first, then getting closer. Red and blue light begins to play over one of the walls from the street below.*)

MEG: I'm gonna go down and, uh ... let them in ... (*Opens the door.*) We'll be right back ...

(*Meg lets herself out and pulls the door closed. It's the sound of the door closing that finally brings Steven back. He notices the lights coming in from outside.*)

STEVEN: Jamie ... baby ... I'd like to take a look at you ... clean you up a little ...

(*Jamie watches him go into the kitchen, wet a rag. She doesn't move, doesn't show any reaction at all. Steven mumbles to himself as he stands at the sink, then comes back into the room. He moves to wipe her face off, and she flinches away, backing up as far as she can, ending up against a wall.*)

STEVEN: Jamie ... please ...

(*He tries again, but she won't let him touch her. She smacks his hands away, her motions panicked, almost disconnected. Steven backs off, terribly upset now, and leans against the armrest of the couch.*)

STEVEN: I swear to God, Jamie ... I didn't mean for this to happen. I know what you must be thinking right now, but I want to put this right ... and I need you to help me if that's gonna happen ...

(*She can't even look at him. This seems to bother Steven more than anything else.*)

STEVEN: Whatever this is ... we can take care of it. We can deal with it

... it's just one of those things. If I went too far, if you went too ... who's to say who's right and who's wrong? I love you. Don't throw that away over ten fucking minutes of mistakes, okay? (*Pause.*) Jamie? Honey?

JAMIE: (*Low.*) ... you hurt me.

STEVEN: I lost my temper ... it's never happened before, right? It's just this one thing ... I don't know, it got to be too much and I ... I went crazy. That doesn't mean that we can't work this out. I mean, we've been together for a hell of a long time ... (*Pause.*) We're committed, you and me ... (*Tries a smile.*) We should be committed ... acting like this. I don't know what the fuck I was thinking. It's only because it's you ... you're my fucking everything. We're stuck with each other, y'know ... (*Pause.*) I mean ... we made a promise. That means good and bad, and I'm sorry that it got this fucking bad, baby, but that's just this one time. I mean, this'll never ... I'm so fucking scared here ... this'll never happen again. I swear to God, Jamie. For better or for worse ... right, Jamie? (*Pause.*) Please?

(*Someone begins to knock on the door, and we hear the squawk of a walkie-talkie outside. Steven looks over at the door, naked fear on his face. He looks like he's about to be sick.*)

STEVEN: Jamie ... I have to get that ... I have to let them in ...

(*The knocking continues, more insistent now.*)

STEVEN: I just want you to know ... whatever happens here ... I'm sorry. Oh, God ... I want to do this all over again ... (*Pause.*) I mean, you know me. I'm not like that. I'm not a, a, a whatever you wanna call it ... this was just a mistake. That's all. I'm not like that. This is me ... this is Steven. (*Starts to cry softly.*) I'm not like that.

(*He waits for an answer for a moment. When none is forthcoming, he stands and heads for the door, every step an effort.*) I'm not like that ...

(*Just as he reaches the door, Jamie speaks in a voice so low he almost doesn't hear.*)

JAMIE: I know.

(*He looks back at her for a second, then goes to open the door. As he does, we hold for a moment, in silence, as Steven begins to talk to the officer at the door. Finally, Lights Down.*)

END OF PLAY

Dearborn Heights
by Cassandra Medley

*This play is dedicated to
all of the Ladies of Anabelle Street in Southwest Detroit.*

BIOGRAPHY

Plays include *Ms. Mae,* one of several individual sketches which comprise the Off-Broadway musical, *A...My Name is Alice,* which received the 1984 Outer Drama Critics Circle Award and is still currently touring regional theatres and Europe. Other plays include *Ma Rose, Waking Women, By The Still Waters,* and *Terrain,* all presented and produced throughout the U.S. For her screenplay *Ma Rose,* Cassandra was awarded the Walt Disney Screenwriting Fellowship in 1990. She is also the recipient of the 1986 New York Foundation for the Arts Grant and a New York State Council on the Arts Grant for 1987, was a 1989 finalist for the Susan Smith Blackburn Award in Playwriting, won the 1990 National Endowment for the Arts Grant in Playwriting, the 1995 New Professional Theatre Award and the 1995 Marilyn Simpson Award. She teaches playwriting at Sarah Lawrence College and Columbia University and has also served as guest artist at the University of Iowa Playwrights Workshop.

AUTHOR'S NOTE

Dearborn Heights is one in a planned series of short plays I am writing that concern the legacy of self-hatred within the African-American cultural context, the result of the long and enduring history of racial oppression in America. Americans of all ethnic backgrounds tend to want to either dismiss history or to invent a nostalgic, mythic, idealized past that never was. We love our heroes larger-than-life and without ambivalent weaknesses or flaws.

The two characters in *Dearborn Heights* represent what I believe are the complexities involved in "heroic" survival and endurance; complexities found within any group of people faced with contempt, bias, exclusion. The heart of the play occurred in a "burst of inspiration." A writer should only be so lucky at least once in her or his career.

ORIGINAL PRODUCTION

Dearborn Heights was produced by Act One in association with Showtime Networks Inc., Paramount Network Television, Viacom Productions and Grammnet Productions for Act One '95: A Festival of New One-Act Plays, at The Met Theatre in Los Angeles, CA in May 1995. It was directed by Kate Baggot with the following cast:

Grace ....Michole White
Clare ....Tina Lifford

Dearborn Heights was first produced at The Ensemble Studio Theatre One-Act Play Marathon 1995 One-Act Festival. It was directed by Irving Vincent (stage manager, Gwen Arment) with the following cast:

Grace ....Linda Powell
Clare..Cecelia Antoinette

CHARACTERS

GRACE: A very light-skinned African-American woman in her late 20s. She is thin and rather, "slight". She carries a studied "air" of self-conscious "refinement" and speaks with a soft, lilting Tennessee accent.

CLARE: Dark-skinned African-American woman, mid-30s. Rather hefty with a deliberate "commanding" bravado that disguises her vulnerability underneath.

TIME

A mid-summer day, 1951.

SETTING

A "homestyle" diner in Dearborn Heights, Michigan.

Dearborn Heights

Grace is a very light-skinned Black Woman, late 20s, early 30s. She is dressed in the "dress up" style of the early 50s: A close-fitting hat banded around the top of her head, perhaps with a bit of a small veil attached. She wears summer net gloves, stockings with the seams down the back, 50s style high heels, a "smart summer suit" of the mass-produced variety based on "high fashion." Her pocketbook, which usually dangles from her wrist, is resting in her lap.

She is seated at a restaurant table. The table draped in checkered cloth, napkin dispenser, a tiny vase with a single plastic flower stem. It should give the feeling of a "homestyle" restaurant-diner. Several shopping bags and packages surround Grace underneath the table. She takes out a large, folded newspaper article from her purse, admires it.

The Andrews Sisters: "I'll Be Seeing You in Apple Blossom Time" plays in background, coming from an unseen juke box. Grace is clearly waiting for someone, she sips the lemon coke in front of her. A basket of fresh bread has been already placed before her. There is a second table setting with a second lemon coke placed across from Grace. She should appear to be glancing out of an imaginary window.

A few more beats and then suddenly her face lights up and she "waves" to someone unseen. She quickly folds her newspaper, returns it to her purse and waits.

Sound of a door chime jingling.

Enter Clare, dark-skinned Black woman, same age as Grace and dressed in the same style. Clare faces the audience. Grace waves as though through a window and gestures. Clare turns, crosses to the table with her shopping bags in tow.

CLARE: *(Fanning her perspiration.)* Whew! If it ain't hot as all-get out, out there!
(Smiling, Grace helps Clare with the packages which they tuck underneath their seats.)
GRACE: Oh you should feel "Knoxville" you think this is aggravating! I thought moving to Michigan was my release from "the fiery furnace", I see I was mistaken...truth is I done pulled off my shoes ha...I'm *(Whispering.)* "in my stocking feet."
CLARE: Ha. Well I'm 'bout to pull mine off right behind you girl...got a bunion that's "sounding off" like a bugle at the V-E Day parade!
GRACE: *(Gazing around.)* Ain't this a sweet place?
CLARE: *(Glancing around.)* Well...yeah...I guess...I mean why is it...well...empty?
GRACE: Chile, I come here everytime I come to Dearborn shopping...
CLARE: Oh?
GRACE: Copied their way of doing "tuna salad"...
CLARE: Where's the waitress hiding out? *(Looking around for a beat, she then smiles and gives a brief friendly nod to an unseen waitress in the distance.)* Oh...good...
GRACE: *(Indicating the drinks on the table.)* See? Got us our lemon cokes
CLARE: *(Still staring out, puzzled.)* Y'see that?
GRACE: I been here couple times, trust me. I promise she won't be as slow as that salesgirl in the "Lingerie Department."
CLARE: *(Distracted.)* Ummm? Don't mind me girl I just...well when a place is empty makes me "jittery"...*(She "cackles" with a wave of her hand.)*...Starts me to wonder "what am I gonna be spending my money on"? Funny food or something...?
(Sound of a door chime jingling.)
GRACE: Ha...your turn to be the "stranger" and have me show "you" a new place!...See? here come a couple of people...
CLARE: Oh! wonderful! *(Settling into her seat, relaxing, buttering her bread.)* I am ready to "chow"—my stomach is about to "mutiny"...
GRACE: *(Pause.)* Well what happened? What did I miss?
CLARE: Humph! The "so and so" of ah Floor Manager finally decided to put in a appearance...
GRACE: *(Glancing at her watch.)* Girl, I was wondering if I should have the waitress hold the table. I started to go back 'cross the street to check on you...wondered how long they'd keep you waiting.
(Clare stops and reaches down into her packages. She pulls out a box and reveals a pair of long white evening gloves. She salutes Grace "army" style.)
CLARE: "Mission accomplished" under enemy fire.

GRACE: *(Impressed.)* Well!

CLARE: I tole you if I waited there long enough and held out for that store manager...

GRACE: *(Overlapping.)* And they finally let you exchange them for the right fit.

CLARE: That's right! Boils me how they try and treat "us" when we shop in these suburbs...

GRACE: Well I'm impressed...

CLARE: They up there trying to tell me they "can't exchange my gloves cause they was purchased in the De-troit Montgomery Wards and not this here Dearborn Heights branch of Montgomery..."

GRACE: *(Overlapping.)* ...Wards.

CLARE: Yeah you heard they "crap"! That's all it was! "Crap."

GRACE: *(Glancing at the menu)* ...You gonna have fries or...you still on your diet...?

CLARE: *(Putting on one of the formal gloves as she speaks.)* I just explained to them with a smile on my face *(She illustrates "smile".)* that fine "I wil! make sure to write 'The Chronicle', Michigan's largest Negro newspaper and to tell all my church members to make sure not to shop at Montgomery Wards" period.

GRACE: That did it huh?

CLARE: And I tole him I say, "You know Wards got no business putting better quality merchandise in the Dearborn stores then they got in the Detroit stores *anyway*"...like we "enjoy" driving out all this way into the suburbs just to get us decent...

GRACE: Well it's so "pretty" out this way...but no you right...you right...

CLARE: *(Pauses, shrugs.)* I guess they just figured, "Let's just get this colored B.I.T.C.H. out the way, what the hell."

GRACE: Nunno! No! What you did was...y'know...I admire...I mean... anything large or small that we do for the "Race"...
(Clare carefully packing the gloves back in their box, she then takes up her menu.)

CLARE: Dearborn is a very long way to come to shop if you don't drive...

GRACE: Is it? *(Pause.)* ...Driving out here with you was nice but I like the bus...I don't mind...*(Stiffly smiling.)*
(The door chime sounds again as other unseen customers enter.)

CLARE: *(Smiling.)* Ha. *(Pause.)* That is one "sharp" hat you got...been meaning to tell you all morning...

GRACE: *(Touching her hat, smiling.)* Oh I collect hats, I love hats...thank you...you so sweet...didn't know if I should wear it just for shopping.

CLARE: It's gorgeous on you girl! If you "got" it why not "flaunt it."

GRACE: People…well…don't want folks to think one is you know *(She makes a silent gesture to indicate "stuck on oneself".)*…people can think things you know…

CLARE: *(Placing her hand on top of Grace's hand.)* Girl…when that Moving Van pulled up and you and your husband got out…and next thing I know there you are out there putting in rosebushes along ya driveway, and I thought to myself, "thank you Jesus"… cause see we on our street are "vigilant"…the last thing we want is a bunch of "sorry", shiftless Colored Folk "ruining" what we all trying to build!

GRACE: Didn't mean for two months to go by 'fore I came over.

CLARE: You're a little on the "shy side" ain't ya?

GRACE: *(Smiles.)* My husband teases me…I thought you maybe thought…took it for granted I was…you know…*(She makes a gesture to indicate "stuck up".)*

CLARE: *(Smiling, waving off suggestion.)* Child pal-lease! Okay now the question is do I have the "BLT" dripping in mayo or…oh and "by the by"…they delivering me and O.Z's new television set tomorrow…Well ah right!

GRACE: *(Pauses rather uncertain)* Well yeah…I think I'm gonna "miss" the radio…

CLARE: Now you can keep up with that crazy "Lucy" every week…

GRACE: Something well I dunno something "cultivated" bout the radio.

CLARE: Child, last night, "Lucy" dyed her hair jet black, would you believe, and "Ricky" got hisself on this "quiz show" he had no business fooling with…oh they had me "in stitches" so I nearly choked to death!…"cultivated"…*(Pause.)* You got such a…"sweet" way with words I been admiring all morning how you…

GRACE: Some Negros get excellent educations down South contrary to what you might hear 'bout us!

CLARE: Course you gotta be "word-fancy" if you gonna qualify as "telephone operator." *(Graciously.)* Oh we must order something extra special, you're my first new girlfriend to celebrate!
(Grace offers a toast with her coke.)

CLARE: I'm living right next door to "one of the first five Negro women to be hired by the phone company", I tole my Momma 'bout it.

GRACE: Ah ain't you sweet! Ain't you the sweetest thing!

CLARE: Well the whole entire street is proud! My goodness! *(Pause.)* You make sure you preserve that pic-ture they had of you in the "Chronicle" for your children! *(Pause, staring at her)* 'Bout time some Negro women got hired to do something more worthwhile then that ole "mop and pail" stuff I be doing up at the Hospital!

(They toast with their lemon cokes. Pause.) I tell you, here I am living right next door to a Negro Pioneer!

GRACE: Truth be told, when I went for the interview my hands were shaking so…I could barely hear my voice…

CLARE: Who cares? For the very first time in De-troit, whenever we call "Information" it could be one of five new Negro operators…Could be you…Don't worry…if I recognize your voice I won't "chat"…I know how to act as opposed to "some" of our people…

GRACE: *(Graciously).* Well now you got something to be proud of yourself now…standing up for yourself like that!…Whew that's what I luv bout being up North! Back down in Knoxville you wouldn't dare…They don't even allow us to try the clothes on, just have to take our chances…and you don't dare return it if it don't fit…

CLARE: Well I am proud to say I've never been "South" of Dayton, Ohio where I'm from.

GRACE: *(Glancing over the menu.)* This being our first shopping trip together and a day of celebration…I say we "sin" and have hot fudge sundaes…

(The door chime sounds again as other unseen customers enter.)

CLARE: Let's see the pic-ture.

GRACE: Well…I dunno…I mean…

CLARE: Naw-naw…don't you carry it 'round with ya? I would, you couldn't stop me from showing it 'round if it was "me"…

GRACE: We don't want folks accusing me of the "sin of pride" now do we?

CLARE: So how's your hubby like driving for the Bus Company? Course my Clyde's got "lifetime" job security at Chryslers…

(Grace takes out a folded newsprint photo from her purse and hands it over to Clare. Clare reads from the paper)

CLARE: "July 23, 1952"…Course I have my "own" copy back at the house…

GRACE: Ain't you the sweetest thing! *(Pause.)*

CLARE: Some Colored folks might think I was causing too much of a "rucus" over a pair of gloves…

GRACE: Girl you don't know me! *(Laughing.)*…Wait till you get to know me better…I admire "spunk", "grit" as we call it back down home.

CLARE: Well like you say…our very first "girls day out"…didn't wanna embarrass you.

GRACE: The first of many! *(They toast.)*

CLARE: Folks keep staring at us Grace…don't look…

(Grace on reflex reaches her hand to her hat to make sure it's on right.

Door chime sounds. Clare slowly gazes around. The door chime jingles as more "unseen" patrons enter. There is the soft sound of murmuring.)

CLARE: Act like nothing's wrong...

GRACE: What is wrong?

CLARE: Oh gawd...

GRACE: What?

CLARE: Oh mercy...

GRACE: What is it?

CLARE: Oh Jesus, my Jesus...don't stare! Sorry but...don't let 'em know we know...

GRACE: What? What do we know?

CLARE: Girl you made a mistake in coming to this place...

GRACE: You don't mean...

CLARE: That's right, that's the ticket all right...

GRACE: But...

CLARE: Everybody else is being served over there, over there...over there...

GRACE: But they served me! They always serve...

(Embarrassed pause between the two women.)

CLARE: Well! *(Pause.)* I guess they realize now that they "took a few things for granted" didn't they?

GRACE: Oh God...

CLARE: You had them "fooled."

GRACE: Gawd...

CLARE: Now they realize you...

GRACE: Don't "say" it...

CLARE: Ain't the shade they "assumed" you was...

GRACE: Jesus in Heaven...

CLARE: We better call on somebody...

GRACE: *(Mortified.)* Clare...I'm so...I'm so...

CLARE: Nunno...don't get up...Don't let 'em think "we know"...

GRACE: 'Least down South they got...we got "signs" up...

CLARE: Well I never been down South, couldn't drag me down South.

GRACE: I'm still not used to dealing with up "here"...the signals to go by...That waitress has always been so nice to me...How could I be so stupid...

CLARE: *Keep your seat*...Keep your face in the menu for the time being...*(Pause.)*...We came here to have "lunch" and by-golly have lunch is what we gonna "have"!! They'll have to serve us or throw us out! *(Pause.)* Now then...*(Clare reaches into her bag and pulls out a ribboned broach the size of a small badge. She hands it to Grace.)*... "The Southwest Detroit Ladies Cavaliers" wants to welcome you as a new member!

(Grace distractedly waves off "broach".)
GRACE: Shouldn't we just get up and go…
CLARE: *(Reaching down.)* Don't look around…pretend nothing's wrong
(Smiling self-consciously.)…now uh the "grapevine" tells me you
being uh…shall we say "approached" by the "Metropolitan Ladies
of Triumph"…
GRACE: Well…they have you know…uh…
CLARE: Oh I know they "after ya" right? They always scrounging 'round
for "new blood" like "gnats at a picnic"…not that I'm bragging but
they ain't the Ladies Club for a Colored Woman of "quality"…
believe me…
GRACE: Look why cause a whole lotta fuss? Let's just…
CLARE: Keep smiling so they don't know we're upset…hate it when
Colored People don't know how to keep their dignity in public?…
GRACE: I am so so embarrassed! *(Pause.)* How do you tell up North
where "we" can go and can't go?
CLARE: Grace you gotta learn the difference 'tween De-troit and the
suburbs—Detroit and Dearborn, Dearborn and Detroit…me
being President of Cavaliers means I can you know, "guide" you
more easily then they can in "Ladies of Triumph"…*(Pause.)*
relax…lean back, let 'em know we ain't to be "budged" and we ain't
to be "bothered"! Now then. *(Pause.)* Every year we "Cavaliers"
happen to raise more than "Ladies of Triumph" do for the
NAACP…why "they" was so "low-class" they held they "Annual
Fashion Show" at the "Y"! "We" at least rent the Elks Lodge over
on Livernois and 9 Mile…
GRACE: "Up North" was supposed to be so "easy"…come to find out it's
even more complicated…
CLARE: You just gotta fine-tune your sense of place! Look for other
Negroes and if you don't sense 'em there then they don't want us
there! Feel out the air around you!…We sponsor this "Gospel
Jubilee" in the Spring that'll send you to Heaven and back…
GRACE: Down South it is clearly marked…please please pardon me…
CLARE: It is very unusual for any "newcomer" to get a "unanimous" vote
from our membership.
GRACE: I shoulda sensed something…No wonder everybody's sitting so
spread out away from this table…Lord the "cook" is peering out at
us from the kitchen…!
CLARE: Let him…see when "we" shop in these here suburbs we gotta be
armour plated inside girl…Don't let "them" push us around…!
That's the spirit of a Lady in "Cavaliers"! *(Pause.)* Plus, as an added
bonus…I'll teach you how to drive…guarantee you'll pass "the

road test"...and don't you dare ask me to accept no fee! *(She guffaws softly.)*

GRACE: My man's the, you know, the basic "ole-fashioned" Southern type...he prefers to do the driving in our...

CLARE: Chile you up North now!! We the "new Negro" women up here!...*(Leaning in on her and softly poking her.)* I can tell ya want to...tell the truth...ain't you tempted by just a itty-bitty bit of independence?

GRACE: Thing of it is they know me here!...the waitress is "Mattie" over there...told me all 'bout her "bunions"...even promised me the recipe for "chicken-a-la-king"...

CLARE: "Mattie" huh? Ooough if I just had it "in" me to "lay her out" to her face!

GRACE: Clare please...

CLARE: I'm not blaming you—don't think that, you made a honest mistake...but see now this is the very reason why you need to join us "Cavaliers."

GRACE: *(Graciously smiling.)*...To tell the truth, very soon I'm gonna be in need of the "restroom facilities"...oh otherwise I'd be all for sitting this out...*(Pause.)* 'Sides *(Smiling.)* I seriously doubt if I'm gonna be able to you know, "receive" the proper "impression" of Cavaliers—I don't think your Club Members want me to be famished in the process...

CLARE: ...*(Pause.)* Ha. *(Pause.)* Sweetness. *(Pause.)* Let us leave this minute! Please—please pardon me!

GRACE: Nunno I'm the one got us into this...

CLARE: Nunno..."last" thing I want is for you to be put through...you know...stress and strain and and "devil-made" conniptions cause of "yours truly"...please...

GRACE: Nunno...it's "my" fault...but we'll just take our stomachs and our business to where we can get respect *and* so we can concentrate...ha...

CLARE: Fine...All we need to do is just "maneuver" out of this here with some lil bit of "dignity"...

GRACE: Just follow me to the door...

CLARE: Don't panic...worst thing is to panic...compose your face 'fore you get up...

GRACE: Everybody's eyeing us...Oh gawd...The longer we sit here it's just more awful!

CLARE: I will not give them the "satisfaction" of seeing me panic...Think they gonna "run me out" oh naw! Get up when I'm good and ready, "my time, not they time"...Grace control yourself!

GRACE: All their eyes trained on us!

CLARE: My dear just gimme one second...Don't come unstuck...You are not "down South" now just keep a steady hand till I get my shoes on...

GRACE: Fine...fine long as we don't get into no more monkey-business foolishness, let's go.

CLARE: What kinda "business" excuse me?

GRACE: Clare...please...

CLARE: Please "explain" that last remark...Calmly compose your face and then we will rise and get out of here.

GRACE: *(Pause.)* There is no need for you to "order" me around in such fashion...

CLARE: *(Taking a long gulp from her glass.)* Sons-of-bitches! *(To Grace.)* Excuse me, pardon me.

GRACE: Nunno under the circumstances I'd say the same 'cept I got too much of the "church woman" in me...
(They pat each other's hands in mutual comfort.)

CLARE: I'll sit here as long as I can stand it—ain't gonna run me off like no "whipped mongrel"!

GRACE: Thing of it is they don't...they don't snarl at us or...or yell at us or attack in the same way they do down home...

CLARE: No. I will not just "fold my tent" and like a lamb, "bleet" all the way home...Oh it gauls me...but they ain't gonna break me...!

GRACE: Pardon me but there is no need to make the situation any worse...

CLARE: I'm the "dark" one that's gotta get past their stares, walk through to that door over there!

GRACE: Now hold up Clare Henderson...just cause I'm light, don't mean I'm not feeling the same as you're feeling!

CLARE: *(Overlapping.)* Take it easy...Nobody's saying nothing 'bout your...

GRACE: Well what are you saying?

CLARE: Well who you calling a "monkey"?

GRACE: Now wait a minute here! We are not gonna lower ourselves to such a "level" now are we?

CLARE: Look if the "boot" fits then march in it!

GRACE: *(Pauses, then.)* Well! Trouble is "your kind" gets so...

CLARE: So?

GRACE: "Wound up."

CLARE: *(Folding her arms.)* Here we go! I knew you'd get to it sooner or later...the "darker" we come, the more we embarrass you huh?

GRACE: Look I'm the one they treated so nice "before"...

CLARE: Before me...

GRACE: Before!

CLARE: You wouldn't be treated like a leper "now" if I wasn't sitting up here, would ya!?

GRACE: You think it's easy? D'you think it's easy being taken for granted as "one thing" then facing the "flip" look when…

CLARE: Then you knew they was "taking it for granted" yet you lead me "in here!"

GRACE: *(Putting on her gloves, grabbing her packages to leave.)* I made an honest mistake. I'm "new" in this here city if you have the "decency" to recall.

CLARE: I got the "decency to recall" that soon as you and your high yella Clark Gable "wannabe" husband moved on the block, you've had your noses tipped in clouds, so high and mighty! *(Pause.)* Oh yeah anything to Lord yaselfs over the whole entire Street! The Block votes to get all new "look alike" Lamp Lighter Front Porch Lamps in front of each and every house…like in the white suburbs, but naw—naw! You and your husband gotta do something "fancier", something more "high tones"—just a tad one step above the rest.

GRACE: Humph!…Why don't you get yourself a "telescope" out of one of them Sears catalogues so you can keep your "busy-body" nose better in everybody's business? A neighbor can't "sneeze" and you report it to everyone!

CLARE: *(Pauses…studies Grace with contempt.)* And to think you had me "groveling"…at your feet to *(She snatches up the club brooch.)*…Oh all them "begged" me to take you out, show you shopping…lunch you as "our treat"…but I tole 'em I said, "I wonder if she's not too siddity, too 'high-toned' and stuck up for us."

GRACE: You are so damn "pushy" who would want to "join?" *(Grace reaches for her bags under the table.)*

CLARE: Damn you red-bone, "high yella", "lemon meringues." Always the first to be hired to the best jobs…always flaunting ya color, and every other Negro fawning over ya!

GRACE: That's right! "Vanilla" still beats out "chocolate" any day!

CLARE: Every night probably get down on ya damn knees and pray, "Thank you Jesus for making me light, bright and almost white." *(A pause, then,)*

GRACE: Is that what you would do in my place? *(Clare is stunned a little but struggles to hide it.)*

CLARE: I tole the Cavaliers you had no intentions of joining us anyway…*(She starts putting on her gloves.)*…Or do you think it entirely "escapes" me that Ladies of Triumph all happen to be just about as "pale" as they can find 'em?

(Grace remains stock still.)

GRACE: Nobody's telling me I ain't a dedicated Negro woman same as you!

CLARE: Ha…"dedicated"!? *(Mocking Grace.)* "Lez Go, lez go 'fore we cause mo' trouble"…You can't wait to go "shuffling" out of here with your tail between you legs…*(Pause.)* So your lil "diner" friends have "let you down"…well "ta-ta"…*(Clare gestures dismissively to Grace.)*

GRACE: Hell with you, I'll sit as long as I want to!

CLARE: Fact is the rest of "us"…don't want y'all "high tone types" …don't need ya…

GRACE: Oh you want us, you "crave" us…don't blame us if you faun all over us…

CLARE: Y'all don't have no real idea what real "color" feels like…

GRACE: And you do?…You and the way you just had to "throw your weight around" in that store 'bout those "gloves"…not the principle of the thing I minded but you had to be so loud, so "pronounced" about it…

CLARE: I? I was "standing up" for something? *(Gesturing with her gloved hand.)* But of course you got treated way more "courteous" by the salesgal…guess you thought I didn't notice?

GRACE: I noticed that the other Colored shoppers were "cringing" but of course you thought you were "displaying" your courage in front of each and every damn body…

(Clare cooly lights a cigarette and studies Grace.)

CLARE: What's it like being "accepted" everywhere you go?

GRACE: And what the hell is that supposed to mean?

CLARE: Taken for "granted" as just a…you know…"normal" everyday "pretty woman"…what's it feel like?

GRACE: Don't you dare start "toying with me"…

CLARE: Since I'm so "bossy" and "nosey" I'm gonna be sure and tell the "whole block"…*(Clare pauses smiling with a sardonic expression on her face. Grace rises to leave.)*

GRACE: *(Mocking expression.)* You are such a "small-minded" woman.

CLARE: Why sure not as "sharp as you" girl. After all, as you say yourself, "They know you here" right? What's it been like? Lemme guess…here you ain't been in De-troit two months and ya already staked out a "nice" friendly "homestyle diner" in Dearborn Heights where you "treat" yourself to cool, restful, summer lunches… *(Pause.)* Tell me what's it been like Grace, so I can tell the whole street!

GRACE: No hold up…! It…has never been my intention that I was…

CLARE: What's that? Sorry I'm too "simple-minded"…

(Grace's face contorts in sudden shock and pain. She drops her head in silence. A long beat. Suddenly a tight smile crosses Grace's face.)

GRACE: Don't try and pull that outlandish crap on me.

CLARE: So she does her passing on a "shopping spree" to the suburbs, now don't that beat all!

GRACE: You the one who would want to wouldn't ya?...not me.

CLARE: How many afternoons do ya treat yaself to "make believing" you a white "heifer"?

GRACE: Wouldn't you just like to know...Wouldn't you just like to be able to "dress yaself" in my dreams?!

CLARE: Thank God I was born with some real "paint" on my bones and not no poor "in-between"! Lease way's when folks "see" me they know what side of the fence I'm looking back from!

GRACE: "Fence"!? Oh and don't you just wish you could "open the gate!" Don't try and tell me you don't just—just *wish* you could scrub even just a "layer" of that "dirt color" down the drain...

CLARE: *(She is visibly trembling but softly taunting Grace.)* And we all know how ya got that "shade" of grey. Generations of "opening ya legs" for the wh—

GRACE: *(She is trembling.)* Don't care how much "face cream" and lipstick and "rouge" and...eye-shadow, and "Nu-nile" gloss on the nappy, hot-combed head, you still AIN'T gonna be *close* to being...

CLARE: *(Hurt but taunting.)* The real "true" woman you get to be everytime you "escape" ...right? Right? And you thank God you can "escape" ...don't cha! Don't cha!

GRACE: *(Nodding.)* Absolutely...Abso...*(Realizing what she's saying, she cringes, drops her head.)*
(Suddenly there is a ground swell of sound. The unseen white patrons begin banging tableware against glassware to protest Grace and Clare's presence. They both look up startled.)

CLARE: *(Softly, grabbing Grace's hand.)* Don't turn around Grace...Don't let 'em see your fear...

GRACE: But what if they...if they grab us...if they punch us...

CLARE: They too "gen-teel" for that...we're just "women" and it's just two of us...They won't go too far...*(Clare lifts her glass and shouts outloud, facing the audience)* Well I got a lemon coke out of it, nothing you can do about that can ya!! Smash the glass but you can't take the coke back!!

UNSEEN VOICE: Get on back to De-troit where you niggers belong!
(Grace takes a long sweeping look at the audience, she stares at Clare as they gather their packages.)

GRACE: Oh it "gauls me"...oh it "gauls me."

CLARE: *(Softly smiling.)* Welcome to the "Motor Capital of the World."

(They rise together. They stare out at the audience as they clutch each other's arms and hold their heads high. They take slow steps toward the audience. Soft "cackling" from an unseen "crowd" can be heard in background. They take slow "dignified" steps towards audience. They "cross" a lighted boundary, the door chime "sounds", traffic noise, they are standing face front to the audience with the impression that they are now outside the Diner. They still clutch each other for a few moments, then pull away.)

CLARE: *(Panting.)* Feels like I'm a icicle all over.

GRACE: My heart's racing…racing…

CLARE: Lemme just stop shaking…ha…

GRACE: My heart's pounding…

(Suddenly Clare checks her packages.)

CLARE: Did we get everything Grace?…*(Quickly counting her packages, pause, frantically.)* Whew!…we made it…ha…One day we'll tell our kids how we stood up to the crackers one summer day in Dearborn Heights!

(It is obvious they are too embarrassed to look each other in the face.)

GRACE: *(Pause, then:)* To think all that ugly could come out of my mouth…

CLARE: All that trash I was talking…please…don't see how you could ever "pardon" me…

(Grace tries to answer, cannot. Softly.)

CLARE: Did I have all the Colored cringing back at Montgomery Wards?

GRACE: *(Turning to her.)* Nunno…you stood up for…

CLARE: *(Overlapping.)*…No you were right…I embarrassed everybody…

GRACE: Colored Rights!

CLARE: I was so…so loud and bodacious…tell me true now…

GRACE: What could I say to you that you could possibly believe after today? *(Staring out in a daze.)* They…they…got to see the…"base" side of us that's what gets to me.

CLARE: *(Pause.)* You left me standing there at the counter, I must have been behaving pretty awful.

GRACE: *(Pause.)* Clare, *(Pause.)* understand something…I may have "crossed" the Mason-Dixon line but it's still in me…Even when I take the long ride out here on the bus just to go past all the lovely homes and gardens? Still can't bring myself to take a seat sit "up front" even though I know we're "allowed" to up North here…and I can't even tell my husband that.

(They both smile to each other a moment.)

CLARE: Know what we need? *(Pause.)* We need ta "shop" all this out our system…calm our nerves…ha ha…Okay Hudson's here we come… gonna get me some new patent-leather heels right now! Where'd I park m'car? I'm so frazzled.

(Clare begins to move off, Grace stops her with her voice.)

GRACE: First time I went there I really didn't "think" of it as "passing"... *(Pause.)* but then again, didn't I? And then the next time...and then the next...

CLARE: Don't start "unraveling" nothing!...Leave where it lays, forget it took place, come on...

GRACE: But...truth be told...when I really deep down think about it.

CLARE: *(Smiling.)* Oh to hell with the "truth"...thinking too much frays the nerves, don't you know that...

GRACE: Clare...! *(Pause.)* Everytime we meet up "today" is gonna be "behind" our eyes, our...smiles...our "hellos." *(Grace grabs Clare's hand for a moment as they still look away. Embarrassed, Clare pats Grace's hand, gently pulls off and "brightens".)*

CLARE: Now we gonna get the car, get back cross the line to De-troit and get us some food in us 'fore we faint from this heat...

GRACE: Will I tell O.Z. about today I wonder? Will you tell Clyde?

CLARE: I always say it's a wise woman who charts a clear course 'tween women's business and men's.

GRACE: Now if I join up with Cavaliers you'll probably think...

CLARE: No I will not...

GRACE: I'm feeling obliged in some way...

CLARE: No you mistake...*I don't intend to "think" about it ever...(Pause.)* I guess I "push against" folks...so I don't Break me...*(Pause, studies Grace, then.)*...I say we "toss" this whole day in the pile marked, "never happened" and stop feeding on it, period...

GRACE: It's not just gonna dissolve away...

CLARE: Don't fool yaself...pieces fall away bit by bit till finally it's just a haze of a recollection way, way back...then presto, it never happened.

GRACE: *(Pause.)* Wonder if one day we might end up "real buddies"...

CLARE: *(Pause. Smiling.)* Could be dangerous to your home life. *(Pause, smiles.)*...For one thing, you just might end up learning how to drive.

GRACE: *(Giggling.)* Ha. *(Then she suddenly turns somber.)*... "Toss it back and forget it ever happened..."?
(Pause. They stare off in different directions. Grace removes her sunglasses from her purse, puts them on. Clare takes out her compact, checks her face.)

CLARE: *(Her face is a smiling "mask".)* I already have...

GRACE: *(Pause, then.)* "Dearborn Heights." *(Fade out.)*

END OF PLAY

The Talk
by Frank Pugliese

BIOGRAPHY

Frank Pugliese's play *Aven'U Boys* won an Obie in 1993. Last year, he won the WGA award for his work on the television series *Homicide*. His plays also include *The Summer Winds* and *Dem Bums*. His screenplays include *Dion, Buddy Boys* and *Mob Girl*. He most recently directed *Hesh* at the Malaparte Theatre Co. and *The Question and The Passion Play* at Naked Angels. He is currently working on a film version of *Aven'U Boys*, which he will also direct. He will be directing *Hesh* again Off Broadway in the Fall. Frank is a member of Naked Angels.

ORIGINAL PRODUCTION

The Talk was produced by Act One in association with Showtime Networks Inc., Paramount Network Television, Viacom Productions and Grammnet Productions for *Act One '95: A Festival of New One-Act Plays*, at The Met Theatre in Los Angeles, CA in April 1995. It was directed by Fisher Stevens with the following cast:

Ricky ....Bruce MacVittie
Charlie ....David Eigenberg
Sammy ....Titus Welliver
Freddy..Saverio Guerra

The Talk

CHARLIE: I'll make the … coffee …

FREDDY: Shit.

RICKY: Stop, already … She is not here … to stop the fightin'.

SAMMY: It's-It's-It's—

FREDDY: Shit, mud and dirt and little pieces of paper, shit.

SAMMY:—Good, really good—

FREDDY: You got gas? Gas over there? And plugs? For electric things?

CHARLIE: Yeah, and food, and clothes, and friends, and relationships—
that work.

SAMMY: Man. You can really cook.

RICKY: … whatta ya sayin'?

SAMMY:—just—

FREDDY: You gotta see this dump. A door almost fell on me. This
fuckin' ape caught it.

CHARLIE: Are you tryin' to be racist.

FREDDY: Ape, albino ape, an ape is an ape …

RICKY: … whatta … whatta …

SAMMY: Nothin'.

CHARLIE: That ape's my roommate.

FREDDY: Roommate. Oh!

RICKY: No, whatta ya sayin'?—when you say—

SAMMY: Jesus …

CHARLIE: That ape saved your empty head … "OH?!"—No, wait.
WHY?

RICKY: Stop, the fighting. No more … she …

FREDDY: Nothin', shit, I'm not … Nothin', okay. Man, only, you don't
got doors but you got "relationships."

RICKY: WELL?!

SAMMY: You cook like mom—

RICKY:—Well, when mom—

SAMMY:—Yeah, like mom.

FREDDY: Only nothin', but, if mom—

CHARLIE: If mom what!?

SAMMY: Will you two shut the fuck up—

RICKY: Dad couldn't cook for himself—He was shakin' so bad.

CHARLIE: Like a bell ... Remember ... The cup in his hand, against the saucer, like a bell.

RICKY: Yeah!? How the hell—?

SAMMY:—He's here now.

RICKY: I don't need him now.

CHARLIE: Nobody called me!

FREDDY: You don't have a fuckin' phone!

CHARLIE: No ... I have a life. (*He rubs his eyes.*)

RICKY: I called that God Damn pay phone.

SAMMY: You okay?

CHARLIE: I miss her too, all right.

RICKY: Maybe, maybe a call now and then, is all.

CHARLIE: To hear you read to me about somebody who got shot on my street.

FREDDY: ... Hey!

SAMMY: ... to hear her ... to hear her voice ...

CHARLIE: You don't know ...

FREDDY: Shit! Mom woulda hated that dump.

CHARLIE:—Thank you for the ride. ALL RIGHT!

RICKY: She's not here to stop the fights, anymore.

SAMMY:—Did he, does he eat it?

RICKY: A little then, now, nothin'.

FREDDY: You had a grant.

CHARLIE: Don't start. I told you in the car. Tell him not to start.

SAMMY: Don't start.

FREDDY:—For paint and brushes and—

CHARLIE: I paint!

FREDDY: Not the walls of a burned out tenement–

CHARLIE:—squat—

FREDDY: —but in frames for bullshit soho galleries, or museums and shit.

CHARLIE: Please ...

SAMMY: But you had a grant!?

CHARLIE: I bought windows for the building.

FREDDY: You never could, you always. You never finished anything.

CHARLIE: Not like mom.

FREDDY: You fuckin-

RICKY: Stop—

SAMMY: You hit him … I'll kill you.

RICKY: We're not kids, and she's … Not! Here!

SAMMY: We used to have some brawls.

FREDDY: Wake up the dead.

SAMMY: Oh that's good.

FREDDY: … Sorry. Sorry.

RICKY: The house would scream. Scream.

CHARLIE:—I live there!

FREDDY: Nobody lives there. You're like a homeless person. Brains! It breaks your heart. It musta broken her heart—

SAMMY: Leave him alone.

FREDDY: Bad enough—

SAMMY:—We did this at the funeral.—

FREDDY:—you into that faggot painting shit to begin with, but not to—

CHARLIE:—fuck you.

RICKY: And how's your wife?

FREDDY: What!?

CHARLIE: Yeah, maybe I should go live at the Watering Hole Bar and Grill in Huntington fuckin' end of the world Long Island, and piss every night away too …

SAMMY: Did you tell him what you told me … ?

FREDDY: That's between you and me.

CHARLIE: He's never gonna leave …

FREDDY: Who told you!

CHARLIE: You did! In the car.

FREDDY: I am. I am. No … I am …

CHARLIE: He's too scared to sleep alone.

RICKY: … Alotta bald guys get laid.

FREDDY: I'm not bald.

SAMMY: Your follicles are numbered.

RICKY: A weave …

CHARLIE: Tattoos. A swirl or somethin'.

SAMMY: You're, you're, you're …

RICKY: He's not the president, he's the client …

SAMMY: You're, you're, you're ...

FREDDY: Your wife didn't even come to the wake. Not a mass card. Damn, a message on the machine. That's bullshit.

SAMMY: She's working.

FREDDY: Work. You people got no fuckin' idea.

SAMMY: Sorry. I don't make tools.

FREDDY: You make somethin' you can put in your hand. That's work.

SAMMY: I work!

FREDDY: You oughta do some work in your fuckin' bedroom.

SAMMY: I'm separated. Which means—

FREDDY: It's over.

SAMMY: She's experimenting ... We were too young.

FREDDY: She's thirty-five years old. For a woman, that's, that's like, like she's a designated hitter. She can't really play the field no more.

CHARLIE: It is probably over.

SAMMY: It's this business. Everything is a fantasy. Everything seems possible. You believe your own lies. You play house on location. You move from one place to the other so fast, you don't have to stand still and look at anything.

RICKY: Experimenting? She was screwing somebody outside her hotel room ...

FREDDY:—On the ice machine.

SAMMY: She didn't know I was in the room. I showed up to surprise her.

CHARLIE: Surprise.

FREDDY AND RICKY: Surprise ...

RICKY: All I'm sayin' is Mom didn't buy her a Christmas present.

SAMMY: Christmas!? Christmas presents. It's March.

RICKY: She bought everybody presents before ... for next year.

FREDDY: And ... and my wife?

RICKY: Your wife calls, called.

FREDDY: Mom buy my wife a Christmas present?

RICKY: She calls all the time ... His wife, waited till she died before she called.

SAMMY: Your wife calls everybody.

FREDDY: What!? She calls you?

SAMMY: She's not, you know, what's that word ... "happy."

FREDDY: You're talking' to my wife. She calls you!?

SAMMY: I called her first.

FREDDY: Oh, I see, you called her first.

SAMMY: Is this about what's her name, in tenth grade. 'Cause, Jesus Christ, I still got that scar over my eye. You know, she said, I told you back then, she said you smelled like bar-b-que potato chips all the time.

FREDDY: Wait, wait, wait. Forget about the tenth grade. You call my wife!

SAMMY: You said she was crazy. You said she fell asleep in the garage, with the, the, the thing running …

CHARLIE: Don't even start with the subject.

SAMMY:—The Car!

FREDDY: The door!—the garage door was open.

SAMMY: You don't wanna sleep with her, she can tell.

FREDDY: How!?

SAMMY: You sleep all over the house. Forget the couch. You sleep under the dining room table.

CHARLIE: You and your wife sleep alot.

SAMMY: That's not right.

RICKY: Anybody want, decaf? (*To Sammy.*) Coffee, sleepy?

SAMMY: Grumpy.

RICKY: Dopey.

CHARLIE: No, no, lemme—Pop, loves my coffee. When I burn it.

RICKY: You ain't made him coffee since you were ten.

FREDDY: She said that?!

CHARLIE: Maybe it'll wake him up … burnt …

RICKY: He's not sleepin'.

CHARLIE: Yeah, but, you know … It's worse than sleepin'. He's frozen.

FREDDY: She said that to you, "she's not happy." That's a private thing to say.

SAMMY: You called her a "cunt."

CHARLIE: I wanna make the coffee—when we were kids.

RICKY: Mom always made the—We're not! Kids!

SAMMY: Let him … What, you wanna get back in the kitchen so bad?

RICKY: What the fuck is that supposed to mean?!

FREDDY: Who the hell's gonna cook for him anyways.

CHARLIE: Him?

FREDDY: Him! (*Pointing to Ricky.*)

RICKY: I work nights. But I can cook in the day—

FREDDY: Yeah, work, right.

RICKY: … Yeah? Retail, is, what it's not, not, not …

CHARLIE: It's a mall.

RICKY: I got a time card.

SAMMY: That was Spencer gifts, now it's like what?

RICKY: Tracy's gifts.

SAMMY: Gifts, means, like what, crap, right?

RICKY: Posters and ...

CHARLIE: Yeah, posters and ...

SAMMY: Posters and, hard to find things.

FREDDY: I didn't mean, she was a "cunt."

SAMMY: Mom buy the "Christmas" presents at Tracy's gifts—

RICKY: NO!

FREDDY: Fuck that, she never shuts up. This bitch is a cunt.

CHARLIE: Will you stop sayin' that!

SAMMY: You gonna stay ...

RICKY: For now, I mean, I mean, where am I ...

CHARLIE: You should. Get your own place. I mean Mom would—

RICKY: He, he, he doesn't eat. He doesn't talk. He lays on that bed like he forgot how to get up. And I'm gonna leave. "Go get a place."

CHARLIE: There's always someone to take care of. But you, yourself ...

RICKY: I can't just ...

CHARLIE: No, I mean, you're still livin' in the basement like a Brady kid or ...

RICKY: I had a band.

CHARLIE: That was twenty years ago ...

SAMMY: You're forty-two years old.

CHARLIE: You're like an article in Time or Newsweek.

FREDDY: When's the last time you got—... the basement is still sound proof. You get yourself a screamer, a broad that screams. And give it to her.

RICKY: Pop, doesn't wanna live anymore. We should worry about him. I'm fine.

CHARLIE: We'll get him somebody. People.

RICKY: People? We are people.

FREDDY: When's the last time you got laid?

RICKY: Probably the last time you did.

SAMMY: Please. He's confused.

RICKY: Hey, you got somethin' to say, say it.

CHARLIE: Mom wanted you get out—

RICKY:—YOU DON'T KNOW WHAT MOM—

FREDDY: FUCK!

RICKY: I found her. I don't know where the fuck you were.

FREDDY: SHIT. FUCK. (*Tears burst out of his eyes.*)

SAMMY: What ... Yeah, I know ...

FREDDY: Why? I mean what? Did we ... Was it ...

CHARLIE: It was her choice.

RICKY: I called that fuckin' pay phone. I went to the fuckin' Four Seasons. And she ordered room service. That's why I don't think she wanted to die. She ordered a coffee with cream, and the paper. You see, what if she changed her mind. That, kills me, it keeps me up at night. Because, if she changed her mind—

CHARLIE: She took over a hundred sleeping pills. Two o'clock in the afternoon. She was wearing a new nightgown. She bought a nightgown.

SAMMY: She drank eight cups of coffee a day. With her insomnia. The shakes.—Orderin' coffee ... It's like reflex.

RICKY: But she ordered room service.

CHARLIE: Maybe it was late ... The room service ...

RICKY: Yeah, it was late ...

FREDDY: I can't think about anything else but why. I can't talk to no one. Woman, especially.

SAMMY: I know, I keep lookin' up to the sky, I don't even know why I'm doin'. I'm gonna get hit by a car or somethin'.

FREDDY: I'm so, damn, pissed off.

RICKY: How do you know she bought a nightgown?

CHARLIE: What!?

RICKY: That it was bought.

CHARLIE: I don't think, that's not important. Pop is ...

SAMMY: I'm so scared. That I'm never ...

FREDDY: It's true. I hate to be alone, to sleep alone. Even if she's in the other room. I don't wanna die alone.

SAMMY: No, I'm like, I'm never gonna be able to have a thing with a woman. And after this ...

CHARLIE: The thing now is Pop. What to do with Pop.

SAMMY: I call and I hang up when I hear her voice. I drive by and sit in my car until her lights are off. No, not like a creep. Just to make sure she's okay.

CHARLIE: You're separated. Separate.

SAMMY: I still love her ... Even if I can't be with her ...

CHARLIE: Don't make it about yourself, don't ...

SAMMY: I'm not!

FREDDY: Oh Mom, I don't remember the last conversation I had with her. I would come over. I would fix things. Fix things.

SAMMY: Did you talk to her. You lived here.

RICKY: No. I don't know, every day talk. Weather and …

SAMMY: And Pop?

RICKY: Really, I just would sit in the kitchen, with the TV, while she cooked, I watched her cook.

SAMMY: Pop talk to her.

CHARLIE: Not enough.

SAMMY: Don't blame him.

RICKY: Some people, they don't—

FREDDY: In the old days you didn't have to talk so much.

CHARLIE: He never asked her what was wrong. I mean, come on. Who we kiddin'. We all stopped talkin'. We're all so grand to think, we couldn't talk anymore. We couldn't help anymore … He avoided her. And now, he can't stop to the point of bein' silent.

FREDDY: Like you're a big expert on women. What, you and your roommate talk about marriage.

CHARLIE: Excuse me.

SAMMY: With my wife and the psycho-drama. With my wife, the parties, the clubs, the drinks. I never … and that's what hurts. I don't remember talkin' to her, Mom, anymore. I would come over here … and then go.

CHARLIE: Excuse me. What!? Sometimes, you really sound like Pop.

FREDDY: And you sound like Mom, okay.

RICKY: When's the last time you talked to her.

CHARLIE: Mom, had alot to say. But, you know what she's like. She doesn't volunteer. She needed someone to ask. And someone did?

RICKY: You?

CHARLIE: We have to talk to Pop. We have to wake him up and start talkin'. If you don't believe in that anymore. What else do we have?

FREDDY: Like you know about Pop. A workin' man. Eighteen hours a day. A man's man. You don't know nothin about bein' a man.

CHARLIE: Well Mom was in love with someone else.

FREDDY: Get the fuck—

CHARLIE: I saw Mom that day.

RICKY: Jesus Christ—

CHARLIE: We went shopping in the East Village.

RICKY: You tell us this now!

CHARLIE: She loved the little shops with crazy one of a kind things.

SAMMY: Mom? Yonkers, PTA, Library volunteer Mom. East village?

CHARLIE: God, she was so complicated. She needed somebody to talk to. Sometimes, she would just show up. With curtains, for the place. Always curtains. Nothin' hide, me, right. Wrong, she knew. I think she knew we were sellin' them for food and supplies. I actually used one of the curtains for a canvas. I paint! I paint the junkies. It's weird, the East Village. Your ideas get so limited in the face of all that freedom. But then, a place like this, with all the fences, people get so free. We went for a walk, shopping, Christmas in March. She was in love with someone else. And Dad knew it. But he never said anything. He didn't wanna talk about it.

FREDDY: Who!

CHARLIE: I don't think that's important.

FREDDY: Sometimes talkin' is not enough. So you better tell me fuckin' who?!

CHARLIE: She didn't do anything about it. It was a feeling she needed to talk about. She's stubborn. She's committed to Dad.

FREDDY: Who! Who! WHO!

CHARLIE: Sara. Over at the coffee shop, near the station. Coffee, paper and a little talk.

FREDDY: The waitress ... You're full of shit ...

SAMMY: I'm gonna need Analysis.

CHARLIE: Shut up!

RICKY: No, he's ...

CHARLIE: She couldn't tell us. No trust. That's not love. That's not taking care of someone you love.

FREDDY: You're so full of shit.

RICKY: No, she went to the coffee shop every morning. For coffee and a newspaper ...

CHARLIE: My, my, my friend and her bought the nightgown ... Mom was so happy to meet ...

FREDDY: Gay people, think everybody is gay.

CHARLIE: I'm gettin' married! But with the funeral and ...

FREDDY: Gettin' married to an ape. Where, at the zoo? Don't offend me. When two guys get married it's not a wedding, it's a drag show.

CHARLIE: That's my roommate.

FREDDY: RIGHT!

CHARLIE: I'm not gay! I'm gettin' married to my girlfriend.

SAMMY: You fuckin' idiot.

CHARLIE: Mom got to meet her, my wife, but she's, we're pregnant and ...

SAMMY: He's not. He's (*He points to Ricky.*)

RICKY: Go …

SAMMY: … you fuckin' idiot.

RICKY: … go ahead …

FREDDY: You're not gay?

CHARLIE: Jesus fuck. I'm not gay! And so what if I was?

RICKY: No, go ahead. Say it.

SAMMY: What?

RICKY: You been hintin' at it all night.

CHARLIE: Whatever it takes, we have to wake, Dad, we have to believe he wants to talk about it all. We can't just stop …

SAMMY: Whatta you talkin' about?

RICKY: Confused, huh, confused, what's that mean?

FREDDY: Confused my ass. Holy shit, no wonder, I can't have a healthy relationship with a woman. I come from a family of faggots.

SAMMY: Hey!

FREDDY: Call my wife, go ahead. Go hang out at the beauty parlor.

RICKY: Asshole.

FREDDY: Say it, just say it, I'm a faggot …

CHARLIE: She was tryin' to tell us something, God damn it. She wanted us to listen.

FREDDY: I don't give a shit if you're gettin' married, if you got a girlfriend, if you're pregnant, you probably still a fag.

(*Ricky punches Freddy. Freddy hits Ricky back. Charlie jumps on Freddy. Sammy tries to hold Ricky back. They all start rolling around on the floor. Then they suddenly stop. They turn to the audience.*)

SAMMY: Pop, we're just messin' around.

RICKY: You're up … Yeah.

FREDDY: Dad, I didn't start it.

(*Pause as they listen.*)

CHARLIE: Cream and sugar.

RICKY: Yeah, we would …

SAMMY: I'd like to …

FREDDY: Yeah …

CHARLIE: Lemme make the coffee first … No, you're right, let's start talkin, now.

END OF PLAY

Why the Beach Boys Are Like Opera
A One-Act Play
by Carole Real

BIOGRAPHY

Carole Real's play, *Why the Beach Boys Are Like Opera* was developed at Ensemble Studio Theatre's summer conference, and subsequently produced in New York at EST's Octoberfest, and in Los Angeles as part of the EST LA Project Summer Shorts festival of one-acts, as well as in the Act One Festival. Her one-act plays *Pray to Mary*, and *The Battle of Bull Run Always Makes Me Cry*, were included in EST's Octoberfest of 1994 and 1995. Carole is developing a full length play which recently was given a staged reading at Manhattan Class Company. A graduate of Yale University, Carole lives in Connecticut and is a member of the Aural Stages writers group in Manhattan.

AUTHOR'S NOTES:

Why the Beach Boys Are Like Opera was first staged at Ensemble Studio Theatre's summer conference in the summer of 1993 and later given workshop productions at Ensemble Studio Theatre and at Playwright's Horizons Theatre School Summerfest in New York. I'd like to thank the directors of those productions, Sara Chazen and David Friedlander, and both casts, for their insight and inspiration. I'd also like to thank John McCormack, Stuart Spencer and Neal Bell for their kind guidance and support.

ORIGINAL PRODUCTION

Why the Beach Boys Are Like Opera was produced by Act One in association with Showtime Networks Inc., Paramount Network Television, Viacom Productions and Grammnet Productions for *Act One '95: A Festival of New One-Act Plays*, at The Met Theatre in Los Angeles, CA in April 1995. It was directed by Ken Frankel with the following cast:

Karen	Anne DeSalvo
Janet	Debra Stricklin
Beth	Janet Zarish
Shane	Andy Lauer
Alec	Richard Steinmetz
Charles	Michael Kaufman
Harry	Don R. McManus

CHARACTERS

KAREN: In her mid-thirties, bright funny, angry, with a tendency to over-intellectualize, Karen has had little lasting happiness with men.

JANET: Karen's friend, also in her mid-thirties. Janet is attractive, physical, with a self-reliance that keeps people from getting too close.

SHANE: Mid-twenties, attractive, a construction worker with a high school education. Though not very communicative, Shane is astute about people.

HARRY: Shane's pal and coworker. In his late thirties, Harry has an active mind and is funny, lonely, and a little bitter.

BETH: Karen's friend from college. Smart and adept at most things, Beth's life is now defined by her house, her husband and her toddler, Christopher.

CHARLES: Beth's husband, Charles is nice to the point of having no edge at all.

ALEC: Beth's tenant, an attractive, self-absorbed artist.

Why the Beach Boys Are Like Opera

SCENE 1

Karen's living room at dawn. Shane enters from Karen's bedroom wearing jeans and no shirt. He finds his tee shirt on the floor and puts it on. He stands studying the wall down left. Karen enters from her bedroom wearing a short nightgown and robe.

SHANE: I could build you some really great shelves.

KAREN: (*Hugs him.*) You are different from every other boyfriend I've had. (*They kiss.*)

KAREN: What are you doing today?

SHANE: I'm supposed to knock down some walls.

KAREN: Oooo*oooooooo*. Would you like me to make you dinner?

SHANE: Dinner?

KAREN: Big thick steak … rare … baked potatoes … two if you want … salad … spaghetti on the side.

SHANE: Yeah. Sure.

KAREN: Okay.
(*They kiss.*)

KAREN: Bye.
(*They continue to kiss until Karen's buzzer rings.*)

KAREN: Who could that be?

SHANE: (*Mock jealous.*) Must be the other guy.

KAREN: There's no other guy.

SHANE: Better not be some other guy.
(*He grabs her and they kiss. There's a knock at the door. Karen opens it to reveal Janet, frazzled, carrying a gym bag, a blow dryer and a garment bag.*)

JANET: Hi. I'm sorry. Can I use your shower? I can't believe the boiler is broken at my place *and* my gym is closed *and* I have a big presentation to do. (*Janet sees Shane.*)

SHANE: Hi.

JANET: Oh, hi.

KAREN: This is Shane. Shane, this is Janet.
(*They shake hands.*)

SHANE: (*To Karen.*) I gotta go.
(*Shane and Karen kiss.*)

SHANE: (*To Janet.*) Hope you get your shower.

JANET: Thanks.

SHANE: All right.

KAREN: Bye!
(*Shane exits.*)

JANET: "Shane?"

KAREN: "Shane." As in "come back, Shane."

JANET: He is really cute. And young.

KAREN: (*Happy.*) Yes! He's too young for me! He's a carpenter. He's going to build me shelves.

JANET: Whoa!

KAREN: Janet, there's not a neurotic bone in his body. Tonight I'm going to cook for him all carbohydrates and protein. And he doesn't whine or ruminate or complain or gas on.

JANET: What do you guys talk about?

KAREN: (*Happily.*) We don't! We don't talk. I cook dinner and bring it to the table. He eats it. Then I do the dishes and he grabs me from behind and we start to make out. Then he carries me into the bedroom. I haven't been this happy in years.

JANET: It sounds like this relationship is entirely physical.

KAREN: Oh, it's entirely physical. He is entirely physical. I mean, Janet … This guy is as physical as you would want … and then some.

JANET: Yeah? Wow. Now I'm depressed. Now I have no hot water and no hot guy.

KAREN: Oh, Janet, he has tons of friends. All these guys who tear down walls, for a living.

JANET: I don't see me with a wall-tearer.

KAREN: They're really nice and upper bodies like you wouldn't believe. From tearing down the walls. (*Seeing something on one of her walls.*) Janet, Janet, look. (*She turns a switch and the lights gradually dim.*)

Dimmer switches! He must have put them in while I was asleep. Wasn't that sweet?

JANET: I'm sorry. I'm going to gag.

KAREN: All I can say is, when I hand him a beer, I feel like a woman. I know, Shane and Harry are going to tear out one of Beth's walls this weekend.

JANET: Who's Harry?

KAREN: One of Shane's wall-tearing buddies.

JANET: Oh, great.

KAREN: No, I've seen him. You've done worse, believe me. We can all go down and visit, and there's also that guy, in the cottage.

JANET: I am not traipsing out to the country to scrounge for men.

KAREN: Two available guys, one unattached woman – you.

JANET: It's humiliating. I won't do it.

KAREN: Janet, come on.

JANET: No!

KAREN: It'll be fun! I promise.

JANET: No, no, no! Absolutely, positively *no!*

SCENE 2

That weekend. Beth's cozy country kitchen. Karen and Janet enter.

JANET: I can't believe you got me to do this.

KAREN: What do you think of Harry?

JANET: He's weird. He kept talking about his sister-in-law getting stabbed.

KAREN: Yeah.

JANET: I mean, that was a murder!

KAREN: I know.

JANET: I just think that's a weird thing to talk about in a car with someone you've just met.

KAREN: He's usually very gentle. I don't know why he decided to talk about that.

JANET: Well, I'm sorry, but that's weird.

KAREN: Give him a chance.

JANET: He's weird! You fixed me up with a weird guy, I thank you very much.

KAREN: You don't even know him.

JANET: And what's with that shirt?

KAREN: What about his shirt?

JANET: His shirt! His shirt is awful. It's like a workshirt, but it's not really a workshirt. And that joke he told.

KAREN: Which joke?

JANET: "Be alert. America needs more lerts." And then he laughed really hard, like it was funny.

KAREN: Janet, you know, you can be pretty picky.

JANET: Picky?

KAREN: Yeah.

JANET: I'm picky because I want the guy to be normal?

KAREN: What's normal?

JANET: Not weird. Not weird is normal.

BETH: (*Entering.*) Hi.

KAREN: Did the guys get started?

BETH: Yeah, they said it'd be a piece of cake.

KAREN: What do you think of Shane?

BETH: He's too young for you, he's not your intellectual peer and he's very hot.

KAREN: I know. Janet thinks Harry is weird.

BETH: Oh?

JANET: He talked about his sister-in-law's murder in the car.

BETH: Maybe that was just his way of saying hi.

JANET: That's a weird way of saying hi.

BETH: Have you seen Alec, my tenant?

KAREN: No. Where is he, anyway?

BETH: He always works in the garden at noon. I always manage to be in the kitchen around noon.

JANET: Really?

BETH: Yeah, it's ...

(*She goes to the window. Janet and Karen follow.*)

BETH: ... here he comes ... worth it.

JANET: (*Sees the tenant.*) Yeah.

KAREN: Yeah. That's a "worth it" situation.

BETH: Wait a minute. Best part. Shirt off.

JANET: Yeah, that's worth it.

KAREN: Oh, yeah.

BETH: Oh, yeah.

(*They watch a minute in silence.*)

KAREN: He is really attractive.

BETH: Mmmmm.

JANET: Yeah.

(*Alec looks up as he's working and catches Beth's eye. He waves. She waves.*)

BETH: (*Waving and smiling.*) Act natural, not completely stunned.

(*Janet and Karen manage to smile and wave.*)

BETH: He's coming in.

ALEC: (*Entering.*) Hi.

BETH: Hi.

ALEC: (*To Karen and Janet.*) Hi. I'm Alec.

BETH: These are my friends Janet and Karen. They're visiting for the day from the city.

JANET: Hi.

KAREN: Hi.

BETH: Alec is a photographer. He's here preparing for a show.

KAREN: Oh, really?

ALEC: Yes. Beth, can I borrow your lawn mower?

BETH: Oh, sure. Whatever you want. Really. Mi casa, su casa, Alec.

ALEC: Thanks. Do you two live in the city?

JANET: Yeah.

ALEC: Me too, but I'm staying here for the spring. It's great being out here.

KAREN: It's nice, isn't it?

ALEC: Very relaxing.

JANET: Yeah, it's really peaceful.

ALEC: Yeah, peaceful, that's it. That describes it.

JANET: I'm thinking about moving. I mean, you can't live in the city forever.

ALEC: No, I was saying that the other day. I really can't picture myself living in the city twenty years from now. And what's the point living somewhere where you can't picture yourself growing old?

JANET: Yeah. It must be great to be able to leave for three months. What kind of stuff do you photograph?

ALEC: I do still life. But to make money I photograph structures.

JANET: Oh. I live in a structure.

ALEC: Do you?

BETH: You should see Alec's photos. He's a fabulous photographer.

KAREN: I think I'll take Shane some lemonade. Beth, why don't you help me take Shane some lemonade. (*She goes to the fridge and pours two glasses of lemonade.*)

BETH: Oh, you go ahead.

KAREN: I don't remember the way to the study.

BETH: It's right down the …

KAREN: Show me.

BETH: Oh. Okay.

   (*They exit.*)

ALEC: What kind of a structure do you live in?

JANET: A fifth floor, walk-up, hole-in-the-wall structure. Nah, it's okay. What kind of structure do you live in?

ALEC: A ground floor studio structure. Do you live alone in your structure?

JANET: Yes. And you? Do you live alone?

ALEC: Until February I lived with my girlfriend. But now I live alone.

JANET: Really? Did you always want to be a photographer?

ALEC: I went back to school for art. I'd been a psych major, but I didn't really know what I wanted to do.

JANET: I was a psych major.

ALEC: Really?

JANET: Yeah. So you were a psych major too. Huh. That's a coincidence.

ALEC: I enjoyed it but I didn't want to go into the field.

JANET: Yeah, me too.

ALEC: So I discovered the photography. And now I show once a year, and do industrial photography to support myself.

JANET: Oh. What's your work like?

ALEC: It's hard to describe. You should come see it. How long are you going to be here?

JANET: I think we're staying for dinner.

ALEC: Come over after dinner. Please. I'd like to show you my work.

JANET: Really? Okay. I'd like to see it.

ALEC: Great. Well, I'll get back to work. I'll see you later. (*He impulsively reaches out and gives a lock of her hair a little tug and then is embarrassed.*) 'Bye.

JANET: 'Bye.

   (*Alec exits. Karen and Beth reenter, almost as if they've been listening at the door.*)

KAREN: So?

JANET: He asked me over tonight, after dinner. To see his work.

KAREN: To see his "work."

JANET: He pulled my hair.

KAREN: He pulled your hair?

JANET: Yeah, he just reached out and yanked my hair.

KAREN: Huh. Like in fifth grade.

JANET: Yeah.

KAREN: Huh.

JANET: We were both psych majors. He seems really nice.

BETH: He is really nice.

KAREN: Are you glad we came out now?

JANET: Yeah.

BETH: Well, I better go check on Charles.

KAREN: Okay.

BETH: You guys make yourself at home. We can go to the mall in a bit. (*Beth exits.*)

KAREN: Then, dinner, then you can have your rendezvous ... see those etchings. And then ... full details.

JANET: I don't think there'll be details.

KAREN: No? I think he really liked you.

JANET: Well, we'll see. He really is cute.

KAREN: Yeah.

JANET: And smart. And sensitive. He's an artist.

KAREN: Um hmmm.

JANET: That's the kind of guy I see myself with. Not some weirdo.

KAREN: All right.

JANET: Someone with some class.

KAREN: Smart, classy guys can be real schmucks too, you know.

JANET: Thanks for being negative.

KAREN: Well, it's true. And its even worse then because even as they're being schmucky you lust after their smart classiness.

JANET: What are you talking about?

KAREN: Remember that guy I chased for years?

JANET: Howell?

KAREN: Yeah, Howell. I thought I was in love with him, but turns out I was really in love with his clothes.

JANET: Really?

KAREN: Yeah. Sometimes, when I was alone in his apartment, I'd get into his closet and just press up against his suits.

JANET: No! Do you do that with Shane? With his clothes?

KAREN: No. I touch his tools sometimes, but that's about it. Which is okay, because that suit stuff, that's all illusion. Dimmer switches, that's reality.

JANET: You know, I think you really care about Shane.

KAREN: Shane's a doll.

JANET: I think maybe you really ...

KAREN: Shane's a puppy. I love him like you love a puppy.

JANET: I think you really ...

KAREN: Shane's a doll, he's a bod, he's a puppy ...

JANET: ... might love Shane.

KAREN: Knock it off.

JANET: Why? What's the matter with that?

KAREN: Because that always ends so badly.

JANET: Not always.

KAREN: Oh, come on.

JANET: Well, but you can't let it get you down. You can't become negative. That's the key.

KAREN: That's the key?

JANET: That's the key. Just don't think about it. Keep moving.

KAREN: Keep moving? That's the key to happiness?

JANET: Don't think and keep moving.

KAREN: That's your philosophy of life? That's like what an aerobics teacher says.

JANET: Well, that's where I got it, from aerobics. But it works. And Karen, I honestly do think that two people can have a good relationship and really love one another and be really happy. I do.

SCENE 3

Charles and Beth in Charles' study.

BETH: (*Handing him a list she's just written.*) Here's your "to do" list.

CHARLES: (*Reading.*) "Mow lawn, buy groceries, quality time with Christopher ... " I'm playing racquetball ...

BETH: Racquetball!

CHARLES: ... with Henry at three.

BETH: I don't think so!

CHARLES: What?

BETH: You promised to pick up the groceries this afternoon.

CHARLES: Henry and I are working on a case.

BETH: Then why did you tell me you'd do the grocery shopping?

CHARLES: I forgot that I'd promised you. I'll do it after racquetball.

BETH: All the good vegetables will be gone.

CHARLES: All right! I'll call Henry and cancel.

BETH: Honestly ...

CHARLES: I said all right. Beth, I'm doing what you want. What do you want?

BETH: It's fine.

CHARLES: Beth …

BETH: It's fine. Never mind. I'll get the groceries. You go play racquetball.

CHARLES: I'll get the groceries.

BETH: No, I don't want you to. I'll do it.

CHARLES: Okay. (*He starts to exit.*)

BETH: Charles …

CHARLES: What?

BETH: The fence. You're using the wrong paint. You should use oil base.

CHARLES: What?

BETH: I saw you out there with the latex. What you need is oil base.

CHARLES: I …

BETH: Latex is bullshit.

CHARLES: (*Pause.*) Okay.

BETH: What do you mean "okay"?

CHARLES: I mean, okay, latex is bullshit.

BETH: How could you say that?

CHARLES: I didn't say it. You said it.

BETH: But you agreed with it. How could you agree with that?

CHARLES: I always agree with you.

BETH: Why? Why do you do that?

CHARLES: It's just … easier.

BETH: Easier than what?

CHARLES: Than trying to explain to you why I don't agree. I'd spend half my day doing that.

BETH: You should fight with me sometimes.

CHARLES: All right. I should fight with you.

BETH: I mean it.

CHARLES: I know. I agree.

BETH: You're like jello.

CHARLES: (*Laughs.*)

BETH: You're like a big thing of jello!

CHARLES: (*Laughs.*)

BETH: What are you laughing at?

CHARLES: You like jello. Jello is your favorite dessert. (*Tries to kiss her.*)

BETH: Don't.

CHARLES: Okay. (*He exits.*)

SCENE 4

*Beth's dining room. Harry, Shane, Charles, Beth, Janet and Karen
have just finished eating dinner.*

HARRY: Remember when we were tearing down that wall and we found
that poodle?

BETH: Oh, there was a poodle?

HARRY: Yeah. In the wall. Mummified. Looked like this. (*Imitates
mummified poodle.*) We had to tell the lady who owned the place.

SHANE: (*Laughs.*) Yeah.

HARRY: Fortunately she wasn't a dog lover.

SHANE: Nah.

HARRY: So we just carted it.

BETH: How on earth did a poodle get walled into an apartment
building?

HARRY: Guess some guy lived there and his dog died and he just
couldn't let go.

BETH: Oh, that's sad.

JANET: Could we not talk about death?

KAREN: Harry, tell us about being a Big Brother. (*To all.*) Harry is a Big
Brother for kids without dads.

HARRY: Yeah, I play basketball once a week with this little kid.

BETH: That must be gratifying.

HARRY: Oh, yeah. I usually win. (*Laughs.*)

JANET: You mean you play to win?

HARRY: Sure.

JANET: You get off on beating this poor little kid who doesn't have a dad?

HARRY: Hey, you don't want to baby them.

JANET: (*Little explosive noise of disgust.*)

HARRY: The world's a tough place.

JANET: Apparently.

(*We hear the sound of thunder.*)

BETH: Wow. It's really raining. I don't think you guys should drive back
in this.

KAREN: (*To Shane.*) I'm afraid of thunder.

(*Shane laughs and pats her thigh.*)

BETH: (*To Shane.*) Karen and I went to Princeton together. She double
majored in Poli Sci and English Literature.

SHANE: That sounds like a lot.

KAREN: It was a lot. Wasn't it, Beth? I think that pretty well describes it.

SHANE: My mom tried to get me to go to college. But it wasn't for me. I can't stand to be cooped up. That's why I like knocking down walls. And there's good money in it.

KAREN: Oh, and there's always plenty of walls to be knocked down.

SHANE: Yeah. It's like all these people have these great houses, but they're never satisfied with where the walls are. So I knock them down. Then, five years later, someone else owns the place and wants the walls someplace else, so I knock them down again. (*Laughs at the folly of man.*)

KAREN: I think that's a profound indictment of our inability to ever be satisfied with what we have. To always want more or something different.

SHANE: I think it's a waste of money. But hey, if they want to pay me to do it, I'll do it.

BETH: Shane, I might want some work done in our cottage, at the end of the summer, when our tenant leaves.

SHANE: Oh?

BETH: Do you think you might be able to do it?

SHANE: End of summer. I might not be around.

KAREN: What?

SHANE: I might be going with Phil on his boat.

KAREN: You're going with Phil?

SHANE: I might. (*To Beth.*) My buddy Phil has a sailboat and he asked me if I'd like to come sail it to Florida and Barbados, then through the Panama Canal and up the Mexican coast to California.

BETH: Oh, my. That sounds exciting.

HARRY: Phil is going to sail to L.A.?

SHANE: Yeah.

KAREN: How long does that take, anyway?

SHANE: He's going to do it in six months. Take it slow. Hang out.

KAREN: Six months! Why doesn't he just fly?

SHANE: That's not the point of sailing.

KAREN: What is the point of sailing?

SHANE: To hang, but be going someplace at the same time.

KAREN: Oh. Well.

SHANE: So, yeah, if I'm here, I'm available, but if I go with Phil I'll be, you know, on the high seas.

KAREN: So you might not go with Phil?

SHANE: I probably will.

KAREN: So, are you going or not?

SHANE: I'll probably go.
(*We hear thunder and the lights flicker.*)
CHARLES: Oh oh.
(*Thunder and the lights go out.*)
BETH: Shit.
CHARLES: It's ... I'll get the candles.
BETH: They're in the kitchen, by the ...
CHARLES: I know. (*He exits to kitchen.*)
BETH: The last time this happened we were without electricity for three days.
JANET: You're kidding.
BETH: No. This is a really terrible storm. You guys shouldn't leave tonight.
(*Charles reappears with candles and begins lighting and distributing them to everyone.*)
CHARLES: Okay everyone! Candles ...
(*Everyone ad libs as they get their candles.*)
CHARLES: I'm going to go down to the basement.
BETH: Be careful.
SHANE: I'll go down with you.
BETH: I'm going to go check on Christopher. (*She exits upstairs.*)
KAREN: (*Following her out.*) I'll go with you.
(*Left alone together in the living room, Harry and Janet are quiet for a moment and then look at one another.*)
HARRY: Want to slow dance?
JANET: No, I do not want to slow dance.
HARRY: You know, you're pretty stuck up but you have great legs.
JANET: Look, Harry, here's the deal. I don't like you.
(*He starts to laugh this off.*)
JANET: We're stuck here and I don't like you and your stories about dead dogs and I don't give a fuck about what you think of my legs.
HARRY: Well, all right.
JANET: So back off.
HARRY: All right.
(*They're quiet a moment.*)
HARRY: It's okay, you know, you don't have to pretend.
JANET: What?
HARRY: You don't have to pretend around me.
JANET: What are you talking about?
HARRY: You don't have to pretend that you have it all together.
JANET: What?

HARRY: That you have it all together and that you're not lonely.

JANET: I'm not lonely.

HARRY: It's not a crime. (*Pause.*) You know, when you're not insulting me you're very attractive. I could forget how stuck up you are.

JANET: (*She gets up and looks for an umbrella.*)

HARRY: Where are you going?

JANET: I'm going to the cottage.

HARRY: The cottage? Oh, the guy.

JANET: I'm going for a visit. Not that it's any of your business.

HARRY: The guy in the cottage. The photographer.

JANET: That's right.

HARRY: Going to see his photographs.

JANET: Yes, as a matter of fact.

HARRY: I took a look at them through the window. Lots of grainy, black and white photos of turnips. About fifty of them. I don't think you want to go.

JANET: Bullshit.

HARRY: See for yourself.

(*Janet exits with an umbrella.*)

HARRY: 'Bye beautiful.

(*Harry looks around a moment and heads down to the basement to help Charles and Shane.*)

SCENE 5

Karen and Beth on the landing outside Christopher's room.

BETH: At least the baby's asleep.

KAREN: (*Excited.*) I haven't been in a blackout since I was in high school.

BETH: Well, it's a pain in the butt when you have a house and a kid.

KAREN: Jesus. Beth, everything is a pain in the butt when you have a house and a kid.

BETH: Karen!

KAREN: You have all this stuff and you're always finding some way to complain.

BETH: What are you talking about?

KAREN: You're always complaining about really small things. Like when you called me up to tell me about Charles raking the lawn wrong.

BETH: Well, of course, you'd think that was a small thing because you don't have a yard, so you don't know.

KAREN: Or when you were really upset because he used the wrong stuff on the floor.

BETH: Just what is your point?

KAREN: I just think you kind of have it made and you could lighten up a bit and enjoy it.

BETH: Do you think this cozy country thing is easy? It's brutally hard work. I've been kicking this house uphill for three years. And Charles too. He was eating Spaghettios straight out of the can in a one room apartment when I met him. Now he makes more in a year than he did the four years we were dating. And his home is a showplace. It's worth twice what we paid for it because of the work I've done or had done.

KAREN: It's very nice.

BETH: So if I occasionally flirt with my tenant or some guy down at Home Depot, well I deserve a little fun sometimes.

KAREN: Okay.

BETH: If I didn't leave Charles a detailed list of things to do, he'd probably just stay in his study reading patent law journals. He didn't even know what a house was until I met him. So don't tell me he's "whipped."

KAREN: I never said Charles was "whipped."

BETH: But you think it.

KAREN: No, I don't think of him as "whipped."

BETH: Because this has been hard work and nothing but.

KAREN: No, I think of Charles more like ... more like ...

BETH: What?

KAREN: More like Gumby.

BETH: What?

KAREN: Like Gumby. Like you live with Gumby.

BETH: (*Offended.*) What?

KAREN: Well, you can pretty much bend him however you want. And he's got that rubbery look. (*Sees Beth's look.*) Oh now, don't get really pissed. I was kidding. He's not Gumby. He's full grown. He has a law degree. Beth ... Beth, I was joking!

BETH: You may think of him as Gumby. But at least I won't be growing old alone. (*Beth exits.*)

KAREN: No. You'll be growing old with Gumby.

(*Karen exits. Beth re-enters the living room when the doorbell rings. She answers the door to reveal Alec, in a wet rain poncho.*)

BETH: Alec!

ALEC: Hi. I'm sorry to disturb you, but I don't have any candles ...

BETH: Oh. Of course.

(*They cross into the kitchen.*)

BETH: We have lots. You can have some.

(*She hands him several candles from a box in the kitchen.*)

ALEC: When do you think the lights will come back?

BETH: Oh, I don't know. But you know, Alec, I really don't mind being in the dark with you.

ALEC: (*Embarrassed.*) Oh, well ...

BETH: Forget it. Just forget it.

ALEC: (*Notices she's crying.*) Are you okay?

BETH: I'm fine. It's just ... nothing is ever quite how I want it to be. Sometimes I just want to run away from everything and start over with a new name. Do you feel like that ever?

ALEC: Well, no.

(*She starts to sob.*)

ALEC: Oh, I'm sorry.

(*He wipes her tear away with his thumb. Beth looks at him and on impulse takes his face in her hands and kisses him passionately as Charles enters.*)

CHARLES: Beth, I ... (*Sees that she's kissing Alec.*)

CHARLES: Beth!

(*Beth and Alec break away.*)

BETH: Charles!

(*Charles turns and exits to the dining room, Beth follows him. Alec slinks out the kitchen door.*)

BETH: Charles! Listen ...

CHARLES: No!

BETH: I'm sorry. Listen ... nothing happened.

CHARLES: You're sorry? What does that mean? What's going on between you and that guy.

BETH: Nothing. Nothing is going on.

CHARLES: Tell me what's going on.

BETH: I am telling you. Nothing is going on.

CHARLES: Have you been fucking that guy?

BETH: No! No.

CHARLES: How could you do that in our home!

BETH: I'm sorry.

CHARLES: Beth, what do you want? What could you possibly want? I bend over backwards to be here for you. I don't have a fucking career because of the time I take for you and the baby. I'm a joke at the office and I come home and cook and do scut work so that you can stencil the dining room and renovate the pantry and whatever else you think of, because I want you to be happy. And this is how you pay me back? Thank you for fucking me in the head.

(*During Charles' monologue, Shane and Harry have come up the stairs from the basement and are quietly watching. Karen has come down the stairs from the bedrooms and is also quietly watching.*)

BETH: Charles …

CHARLES: You tell your photographer friend that tomorrow he packs his bags and he is out of here.

BETH: Charles, it wasn't his fault.

CHARLES: Or I'll fucking kill him. (*Charles turns and exits upstairs.*)

KAREN: Wow.

BETH: Charles … (*She follows him up.*)

KAREN: (*To Harry and Shane.*) Wow. I've never even heard him raise his voice.

HARRY: What happened?

SHANE: I think she smooched the turnip guy.

HARRY: Oooh.

BETH: (*Off.*) If you'd just let me explain.

CHARLES: (*Off.*) How could anything you say possibly, possibly explain?

KAREN: They're really fighting.

BETH: (*Off.*) Charles I just …

CHARLES: (*Off.*) No! I don't want to hear it!

SHANE: They'll work it out.

BETH: (*Off.*) Charles, I …

CHARLES: (*Off.*) No no no!

BETH: (*Off.*) But Charles, I …

CHARLES: (*Off.*) Not *one more word!*

(*Karen, Shane and Harry pause a moment to see if Beth will speak.*)

SHANE: (*To Karen.*) I hope I never see you with some turnip guy.

KAREN: I hope I never see you with some flight attendant.

SHANE: Or some … guy from TV.

KAREN: Or some … cocktail waitress.

SHANE: Or some … delivery boy.

(*They kiss passionately.*)

SCENE 6
Janet in Alec's cottage. Alec enters, shaken.

JANET: Did you get a flashlight?

ALEC: No.

JANET: No?

ALEC: But I have candles.
(Lights one and gives it to Janet.)
Here.

JANET: Candles! Candlelight is so special.

ALEC: *(Looking out the window at the house.)* Oh, yeah, it's okay I guess.

JANET: You're shaking. Did you get a chill?

ALEC: I'm okay. Do you see Charles out there?

JANET: Charles? No, I don't think so.
(Alec continues to look out the window.)

JANET: So, tell me all about your photos.

ALEC: Yes, my art. I work entirely with still life.

JANET: That must be fascinating.

ALEC: For the past four years, I've worked with one subject, so I could really hone.

JANET: ... hone ...

ALEC: *(Taking Janet's hand.)* Do you want to see my work?

JANET: Yes, I do.
(Alec shows Janet several large photos of turnips.)

JANET: These are ...

ALEC: Turnips.

JANET: You photograph ...

ALEC: Turnips. Just turnips.

JANET: Wow. Boy. They're really ...

ALEC: What do they say to you?

JANET: They ... well ... it's funny ...

ALEC: What?

JANET: It's funny ... I feel kind of sad for them.

ALEC: Excuse me?

JANET: They seem sort of lonely. The turnips.

ALEC: Lonely?

JANET: Yeah.

ALEC: They're vegetables.

JANET: I know.

ALEC: Vegetables don't have feelings.

JANET: No, I know. But when you look at them, they seem a little lonely in that big bowl.

ALEC: They're not lonely. They don't have lonely feelings. Still life is the perfect expression of the artist's ability with his craft because it's free of emotionalism. Here I was working with available light. Here with a flash. Here with available light and a flash fill. I think this one really works, don't you?

JANET: Oh, absolutely.

ALEC: Even upside down. See?

JANET: Yeah. Wow!

ALEC: Janet. You know what we could do?

JANET: What?

ALEC: We could photograph together! I could teach you.

JANET: Uh …

ALEC: Yeah! We could go out tomorrow morning at dawn and do some eggs. I started with eggs.

JANET: Oh!

ALEC: We can go into the swamp at dawn to get the morning light. Do you have some really high boots? Maybe I have some you can borrow. You can use my old Pentax. We can shoot five or six rolls of eggs at dawn. I can spend hours on eggs. I become the egg.

JANET: Yeah! Sure. But … what will we do until dawn?

ALEC: Well … (*He smiles to himself.*) I have lots to show you. All my photographs. The slides. The early work. Carrots. The line drawings I did from the photos … and the negatives, which are like works in themselves. Janet, I have over 400 photos. It will definitely take us until dawn.

JANET: Four hundred photos?

ALEC: Yeah! It's so great to talk to someone who can appreciate still life. Most people are bored by it.

JANET: Maybe I should get back and help Beth clean up, or …

ALEC: No, we have to get started right away. I want to be able to show you everything.

SCENE 7

Some time later. Harry is in the kitchen eating peanuts out of a jar with a couple of empty, crushed beer cans in front of him. Shane comes down the stairs shirtless and crosses to the kitchen as the electricity comes back on.

SHANE: Whoa! Electricity. (*To Harry.*) Hey.

HARRY: Hey.

SHANE: (*Shane looks into the fridge and drinks from a milk carton.*) What's up?

HARRY: Nada.

SHANE: Nada thing?

HARRY: Nada thing going on.

SHANE: Nada lotta. Where's Janet?

(*Harry indicates the cottage.*)

SHANE: Oh. I think she likes you.

HARRY: She hates me.

SHANE: Nah. She likes you. See, women are like walls.

HARRY: Oh, here we go.

SHANE: Each one is different. Some you can take right down, others, if you're not careful the whole ceiling can crack and then where are you. You have to know ...

HARRY: What?

SHANE: You have to know if the ceiling is going to crack.

HARRY: Right. What are you saying?

SHANE: With Janet, with women, you have to know what will make the ceiling crack.

HARRY: What the fuck are you talking about?

SHANE: With Karen. She's attractive, she's smart, she's fun, she's affectionate.

HARRY: Yeah, I noticed.

SHANE: She's very affectionate. But, if she thinks I'm serious about her, if she thinks I love her, the ceiling will crack.

HARRY: Oh?

SHANE: Yeah.

HARRY: Oh. Why is that?

SHANE: Don't ask me to figure it out. Her therapist, the guy she's making rich, he can't figure it out. If I let her know I love her, this will make her ceiling crack. Then we just have to put the wall back up again.

HARRY: Right.

SHANE: I'm so profound! So, with Janet, you just need to find out what will make her ceiling crack. And then avoid.

HARRY: Avoid. Right. Hey, what was that B.S. about you going sailing with Phil? The one time we went out on his boat you got sick.

SHANE: Yeah, I kacked.

HARRY: You puked repeatedly.

SHANE: I drove the porcelain bus.

HARRY: … on a long haul.

SHANE: I'm not sailing to L.A. with Phil. First, I puke when I sail, which would get old fast. Second, Phil is crazy! The other day I saw him reading a book about sailing, which I take as a bad sign, 'cause he should know how to sail if he's going to sail to Barbados, right? Then he starts talking about lashing yourself to the mast in case of a really bad storm and about this gadget that makes fresh water out of saltwater if you're stuck on a raft for a week. Man, if I ever, ever had any doubt about Phil being a crazy fuck, I no longer do, because, "A", you lash yourself to the mast you're never going to make it to the raft; "B", if you get to the raft there's no way that little gizmo's going to work. It'll be missing a part or something and you'll be fucked. You'd probably end up praying for a shark to eat you. Phil is a scary dude.

HARRY: He is.

SHANE: We'll be seeing him on TV one day.

HARRY: We will. So, what's with saying you're going with Phil?

SHANE: "Intermittent gratification."

HARRY: What does that mean?

SHANE: It means, if she thinks I'll always be around, Karen will decide I'm an asshole.

HARRY: Go to bed.

SHANE: I hate to see you unhappily downing Buds here.

HARRY: I was actually fairly content.

SHANE: I don't know. You look deeply lonely to me.

HARRY: Get out of here!

SHANE: Later.

HARRY: Right.

(*Shane exits.*)

SCENE 8

The middle of the night. Karen is in the guest room. She's awake, in her nightgown, upset. Shane enters.

SHANE: Hi.

KAREN: Where were you?

SHANE: I got hungry and went down to get something to eat. Got to talking to Harry.

KAREN: Oh. How is Harry?

SHANE: Harry's Harry.

KAREN: Oh.

SHANE: What's the matter?

KAREN: Nothing.

SHANE: Come on.

KAREN: Nothing's the matter.

SHANE: Come on.

KAREN: No, it's just. It's stupid.

SHANE: What?

KAREN: It's stupid.

SHANE: Tell me.

KAREN: I was scared that you were gone. It's dumb. I mean, where would you have gone?

SHANE: It's okay. (*He holds her.*) Karen, you know what?

KAREN: What?

SHANE: After I get done with your shelves, I'll put in a ceiling fan, right over your bed, would you like that?

KAREN: That'd be really nice.

SHANE: Then I'll replaster the walls so they'll be smooth. And sand the floors.

KAREN: Wow!

SHANE: And then ... one night, when you're asleep, I'll sneak into your bedroom with some putty and some glue and a little clamp and I will very, very carefully mend your heart. So you can't even see the cracks.

KAREN: (*Worried.*) Shane ... (*Stops herself.*)

SHANE: What?

KAREN: Nothing.

SHANE: Come on.

KAREN: I don't want you to sail to L.A. with Phil.

SHANE: No?

KAREN: No.

SHANE: Why not?

KAREN: Because you might get swept overboard.

SHANE: And ...

KAREN: And I'd miss you. If you drowned.

SHANE: What if I promise not to be swept overboard.

KAREN: I'd still miss you. Don't go.

SHANE: Don't go?

KAREN: No. Don't go. Please.

(*They kiss. Shane takes the medallion from around his neck and puts it around Karen's neck. They kiss again.*)

SCENE 9
The kitchen in half light. Charles and Beth are making out.

CHARLES: Bitch.

BETH: (*Pause.*) Say that again like that.

CHARLES: Vixen bitch.

BETH: (*Laughs.*) Charles!

CHARLES: Minxy vixen bitch.

(*Beth laughs again as she and Charles smooch, grope one another and tumble to the floor.*)

JANET: (*Entering from outside.*) Karen?

(*She turns on the light to reveal Beth and Charles on the floor, their clothing in disarray.*)

BETH: Oh, hi!

(*She and Charles untangle themselves as Harry enters the kitchen.*)

BETH: We were just ... running a load of dishes.

JANET: Oh.

(*Awkward pause all around.*)

JANET: The electricity is back.

BETH & CHARLES: (*Ad lib.*) Yes ... yeah.

BETH: Well, make yourself at home.

BETH, CHARLES, JANET & HARRY: (*Ad lib good nights as Beth and Charles exit.*)

HARRY: So, how was it?

JANET: What?

HARRY: Your visit?

JANET: He ... he ... (*She starts to laugh.*)

HARRY: What?

JANET: ... he actually showed me his photographs!

HARRY: Turnips.

JANET: He has well over 400 photographs. Well over. Then he gave me this. (*Shows Harry a postcard.*) It's an invitation to his show. (*Reading the card.*) Alec Lovegrove – Still Vegetables 1984-1995.

HARRY: I couldn't really picture you with the turnip guy.

JANET: No?

HARRY: No.

JANET: What kind of guy do you picture me with?

HARRY: A very lucky guy.

JANET: You're flirting.

HARRY: No, I mean it.

JANET: You're bullshitting me to get in my pants.

HARRY: That too.

(*They laugh. Janet sits at the end of the kitchen counter.*)

HARRY: So ... what happened to your boyfriend?

JANET: What, you mean Alec?

HARRY: No, I mean your boyfriend. The one you were really serious about.

JANET: You mean the guy from ... I haven't been serious about anyone since I was twenty-two.

HARRY: Yeah, that guy. What happened to him?

JANET: He ... Why do you want to know about him?

HARRY: I don't know.

JANET: He's somewhere in Maine. The party was never over for him.

HARRY: Oh?

JANET: He's a big drunk.

HARRY: Oh.

JANET: Yeah. After high school we lived in this house by the beach with a bunch of people and we were all always drinking and getting high and just working at bullshit jobs to pay the bills. And now, he's living in a big house with a bunch of people and drinking and working at bullshit jobs. Except he's thirty-seven.

HARRY: Oh.

JANET: And he doesn't look good.

HARRY: No.

JANET: So. That's what happened to my boyfriend. What happened to your girlfriend?

HARRY: She married some guy.

JANET: Oh.

HARRY: A dentist.

JANET: Oh.

HARRY: You know, I'm not really such a bad guy. That little kid I play basketball with? I usually let him win.

JANET: Really?

HARRY: Unless I've had a really bad week. Then I trip him.

JANET: Oh, there you go.

HARRY: What?

JANET: You can't go a minute without making some dumb joke or being gross.

HARRY: So? (*Pause.*) You know, I have a buddy, who works in the post office. He tells me that they're planning to start giving out awards to employees who work there 20 years without shooting a co-worker.

JANET: (*Smiles in spite of herself.*) That's dumb.

HARRY: You laughed. You did. Okay, no dumb jokes. (*Pause.*) A gorilla walks into a bar ...

JANET: (*Noise of disgust.*)

HARRY: And he sees a beautiful woman and he walks up to her ... (*He approaches Janet.*) ... and says "your eyes are so beautiful, when I look at them, I'm lost."

(*They look at one another a moment. We hear a Beach Boys tune coming from the radio.*)

JANET: The Beach Boys. I love them.

HARRY: Me too.

JANET: They're like opera.

HARRY: I've often said that.

JANET: Oh, you have not.

HARRY: No, I have. Ask Shane.

JANET: Oh yeah? So, why are the Beach Boys like opera?

HARRY: The Beach Boys are like opera because ... they express great yearning.

JANET: (*Laughs in recognition of the truth of this and then is serious.*) That is why they're like opera.

HARRY: Wanna dance?

(*They dance. Lights fade.*)

END OF PLAY

You Belong To Me
by Keith Reddin

BIOGRAPHY

Keith Reddin is a graduate of Northwestern University and the Yale Drama School. His plays include *Life and Limb, Rum and Coke, Highest Standard of Living, Big Time, Nebraska, Life During Wartime* and *The Innocent's Crusade*. Film credits including the Playwrights' Cinema - Turner Network Television Movie, *The Heart of Justice* and a film adaptation of his play *Big Time* for American Playhouse.

ORIGINAL PRODUCTION

You Belong To Me was produced by Act One in association with Showtime Networks Inc., Paramount Network Television, Viacom Productions and Grammnet Productions for *Act One '95: A Festival of New One-Act Plays*, at The Met Theatre in Los Angeles, CA in April 1995. It was directed by W.H. Macy with the following cast:

Joyce ....Kathryn Layng
Georgette ....Lucinda Jenney
Larry...Timothy Carhart
Ted..Lindsey Ginter

You Belong To Me

A bar. Early Evening. Joyce and Georgette.

JOYCE: Where'd you find this place?

GEORGETTE: See the juke box?

JOYCE: Yeah.

GEORGETTE: All Patsy Cline.

JOYCE: The whole juke box.

GEORGETTE: Just Patsy Cline.

JOYCE: Huh.

GEORGETTE: So how long ago did you kill him?

JOYCE: About half an hour.

GEORGETTE: OK. So good. So where's …

JOYCE: On the kitchen floor. With a cleaver sticking out of his head.

GEORGETTE: You wipe off the fingerprints?

JOYCE: Just like you told me.

GEORGETTE: So good. You want another drink?

JOYCE: How do I get away with this?

GEORGETTE: Unless you alert the media, you're okay.

JOYCE: There was so much blood.

GEORGETTE: Well, there would be, wouldn't there. They make good margaritas here.

JOYCE: Very good.

GEORGETTE: Now listen to me, you listening?

JOYCE: Yes.

GEORGETTE: You and I are gonna sit here. We're gonna take my car, I'm gonna drive you home, we both … no okay wait, here's what we do. I drive you, on the way we go off the road, we hit some, have this accident, not a bad accident, but you know, serious enough, they call an …

JOYCE: Who?

GEORGETTE: What?

JOYCE: Who calls?

GEORGETTE: Whoever. Some passing motorist. Somebody.

JOYCE: People don't stop for accidents.

GEORGETTE: Joyce please, somebody will call an ambulance. They take us to the hospital. We wake up, we see the police are in the room. You go, what's going on? One moment you're having a drink with your friend and the cop says, I have terrible news, I'm sorry to tell you, we found your husband murdered. Lying on the kitchen floor we found Larry dead with a …

JOYCE: Meat cleaver.

GEORGETTE: Meat cleaver sticking out of his head.

JOYCE: Who called the police?

GEORGETTE: I don't know.

JOYCE: There's too many people calling other people. We can't get away with this.

GEORGETTE: Who's this we? I didn't kill him.

JOYCE: But you're aiding and abetting.

GEORGETTE: After the fact.

JOYCE: My alibi is that I was out drinking with you?

GEORGETTE: At least I'm coming up with something.

JOYCE: I would never get away with it.

(*Larry enters.*)

LARRY: Sorry that call took so long.

(*He looks at them. Joyce and Georgette look at each other.*)

LARRY: What? What did I miss?

GEORGETTE: Nothing Larry. Nothing at all.

(*Lights fade. The living room. Larry and Joyce. Larry reading a newspaper.*)

LARRY: Huh.

JOYCE: What?

LARRY: That property on Wilshire is on sale.

(*Goes back to reading paper.*)

JOYCE: Larry …

LARRY: Yeah?

JOYCE: You ever think about killing me?

LARRY: What?

JOYCE: I mean did you ever imagine killing me?

LARRY: No.

JOYCE: You ever think of how you would kill a person?

LARRY: You thinking of killing me? (*Pause.*)

JOYCE: No. (*Pause.*)

LARRY: You're talking about like after we have a big fight or something. Like that?

JOYCE: Yes.

LARRY: No, I can't say that I have. (*Thinks.*) Uh no.

JOYCE: Not ever?

LARRY: (*Smiling.*) No, Joyce. Why would I want to kill you?

JOYCE: I mean imagining. Like if I took out a gun. (*She takes out a gun.*)

LARRY: Uh huh.

JOYCE: And I pointed it at you?

LARRY: Hey, where'd you get that gun, Joyce?

JOYCE: You know, we're so close, it'd be kind of impossible to miss you.

LARRY: Is that a real gun?

JOYCE: It's loaded, I checked right after dinner.

LARRY: Okay, I don't get the joke, Joyce.

JOYCE: I want you to beg me not to kill you.

LARRY: Are you still mad at me about yelling at you about the American Express bill, is that what this is about?

JOYCE: Come on, Lar, beg me. Beg for your life.

LARRY: I wasn't really mad.

JOYCE: I want you to crawl on your belly and say, don't kill me, Joyce. Come on, crawl.

LARRY: Okay you don't have to pick me up after squash this week, I'll get Ted to drive.

JOYCE: Oooh, this gun is getting heavy. It's getting so heavy Larry I might have to make it lighter by emptying a few bullets out of it.

LARRY: Joyce …

JOYCE: Shut up, just shut your face.

LARRY: Joyce, stop this. Put the gun down. You don't want to shoot anybody.

JOYCE: Where'd you get that line, Larry, some repeat of T.J. Hooker?

LARRY: I'm your husband.

JOYCE: I bet you wish it was you holding the gun right now. You wish you had me in your sights, just a little pressure on the trigger and you blow me into next week. (*She starts waving the gun.*) Come on, start crawling.

LARRY: No.

JOYCE: I'm serious.

LARRY: I'm not going to crawl.

JOYCE: Now!

LARRY: I don't think you can really do it.

JOYCE: Oh no?

LARRY: I don't think so. Nope. (*Goes back to reading the paper.*)

JOYCE: Put that paper down.

LARRY: I haven't finished.

JOYCE: I said …

LARRY: I heard you.

JOYCE: Okay, you are dead.

> (*She fires the gun at Larry. Pause. Then Joyce sits and puts the gun away. Larry lowers the newspaper.*)

LARRY: Anything the matter?

JOYCE: What?

LARRY: You got all quiet.

JOYCE: I was just thinking. (*Pause.*)

LARRY: I love you, Joyce.

JOYCE: I know.

LARRY: And? And?

JOYCE: (*Softly.*) I love you too.

> (*Larry smiles. Lights fade. The bar. Georgette and Joyce.*)

JOYCE: The whole juke box?

GEORGETTE: Just Patsy Cline.

> (*Larry enters.*)

LARRY: Sorry that call took so long. (*He looks at Joyce and Georgette.*) What? What did I miss?

GEORGETTE: Nothing, Larry. Nothing at all.

LARRY: Ted had to change the squash time again.

JOYCE: Should we order another?

GEORGETTE: Let's go for it.

LARRY: Sure.

JOYCE: I'll be right back.

> (*She leaves. A beat.*)

GEORGETTE: I want to fuck you right now.

LARRY: Georgette.

GEORGETTE: Right now. Right on this table.

LARRY: Stop this.

GEORGETTE: I can't keep going on like this.

LARRY: What do you want me to say?

GEORGETTE: Say you'll do it. Like we planned. Say you'll kill her.

LARRY: I can't.

GEORGETTE: If you want me you have to do it. (*Takes out a gun.*) Here. Use this.

LARRY: Would you put that away?

GEORGETTE: I even got you a gun.

LARRY: People can see …

GEORGETTE: It's her or me, Larry, make up your mind.

LARRY: Georgette ... you know how I feel.

GEORGETTE: Then take the gun and ice her.

LARRY: Ice her?

GEORGETTE: Take the gun. You know this is right. Otherwise you're living a lie. You've wanted to for years. So have I. All those years of pretending I was her friend. Listening to her boring stories. Looking at her disgusting haircut. I swear if you can't, I will. I won't share you with her. You're mine forever and ever. We're so close to making the dream come true. Take the gun. Take it. (*Pause.*)

LARRY: All right. (*He takes the gun.*)

(*Joyce comes back with drinks.*)

JOYCE: What do we drink to?

GEORGETTE: Long life?

LARRY: To long life.

(*They drink.*)

JOYCE: You know, Larry, I've got to tell you. While you were on the phone before ...

LARRY: Yeah?

JOYCE: Georgette and me, we were sort of joking around.

LARRY: What? (*To Georgette.*) What's she talking about?

GEORGETTE: Joyce pretended she'd killed you.

LARRY: Get out of here.

JOYCE: It's true. we pretended we were sitting here and you were dead. In the kitchen.

LARRY: How'd you do it?

JOYCE: With a meat cleaver.

GEORGETTE: In your head.

LARRY: Ouch.

JOYCE: We were just joking around.

LARRY: I see. Well, I'm not sure I find the joke so funny.

JOYCE: I shouldn't have told you.

LARRY: And you two were just having some drinks and laughing?

JOYCE: We were.

LARRY: Did I put up some sort of a fight?

JOYCE: No, I got you when your back was turned.

LARRY: Meat cleaver, huh? Kind of messy.

GEORGETTE: Maybe you should have used a gun.

JOYCE: We don't have a gun.

GEORGETTE: You do have a meat cleaver.

JOYCE: And that's what I imagined I used.

GEORGETTE: I would have used a gun. Wouldn't you use a gun, Larry?

LARRY: I guess I would.

GEORGETTE: See Larry would have used a gun. Show her the gun, Larry.

JOYCE: What?

GEORGETTE: I gave Larry a gun.

JOYCE: You did?

GEORGETTE: Show her the gun.

LARRY: (*Takes out the gun.*) Here.

JOYCE: Why does ... why did you give him a gun?

GEORGETTE: To kill you.

JOYCE: What are you talking about?

LARRY: The gun is to kill you. I'm going to kill you on the drive home. I'm going to pull over and shoot you and throw your body into a ditch and then Georgette and I can fuck our brains out.

GEORGETTE: That's it.

JOYCE: What about Jerry?

GEORGETTE: I'm going to kill Jerry. Larry will kill you. That was the deal.

JOYCE: No.

GEORGETTE: We've wanted this for a long time.

LARRY: So I'll settle up the tab and then I'll shoot you, Joyce.

JOYCE: But ... why?

GEORGETTE: Tell her, Larry.

LARRY: Because we both hate your guts. And because you really bother me when I'm reading the paper.

JOYCE: I won't anymore.

LARRY: Too late. Say goodbye to Georgette ...

JOYCE: But ...

GEORGETTE: Goodbye, Joyce.

JOYCE: But you love me, Larry. You know you do.

LARRY: Don't make it any harder. Let's go.
     (*Pulls her away from the table.*)

JOYCE: I haven't finished my drink yet.

GEORGETTE: Do it quick, Larry. I'll be waiting. I'll play some Patsy Cline on the juke box and think of you shooting her in the head and then kicking her body into a ditch.

LARRY: I won't be long.

JOYCE: Wait ... please ...

LARRY: Don't beg, Joyce. Just get in the car. I promise it won't hurt. Much. (*He laughs.*) Ahahaha.

JOYCE: I thought you were my friend.

GEORGETTE: Bad call.
     (*Larry pulls Joyce off.*)

GEORGETTE: Thank you, Larry.

(*Lights fade. A shot heard in the darkness. Lights up on the living room. Larry in armchair reading paper. Joyce sits in another chair.*)

LARRY: You know what to do when she gets here?

JOYCE: Of course I do, we've gone over it like a thousand times. I still think poison is a bad idea. People don't poison people anymore.

LARRY: Sure they do.

JOYCE: It's so old-fashioned, like some Agatha Christie book. Poison in the drawing room.

LARRY: I don't know, it has a certain something ...

JOYCE: A certain what?

LARRY: It's classy.

JOYCE: You think it's classy.

LARRY: Guns are so messy. Blood all over the walls and carpet. This way she dies and here we are, like those diet pills. Lose weight while you sleep. No mess.

(*Doorbell.*)

JOYCE: Okay, I am going to get the door.

(*She exits. Larry pretends to be engrossed in the newspaper. Joyce and Georgette enter.*)

JOYCE: Look who's here, Larry.

(*Larry lowers his paper.*)

LARRY: Oh hi, Georgette, how are you?

GEORGETTE: Doing fine, Larry.

LARRY: That's good. Can I get you something to drink?

JOYCE: Georgette just got here. You offer her a drink like she's some alcoholic or something.

LARRY: I was just being polite. Being a good host. You weren't offended were you?

GEORGETTE: No. Although I should tell you I have stopped drinking.

JOYCE AND LARRY: You have?

GEORGETTE: Yes, I found I was drinking too much. I would get home from work and the first thing I did was walk in the door, walk straight to the liquor cabinet and pour myself a stiff drink. Then I would have about three or four more before dinner. A couple of times I had a few too many drinks and would pass out and the next thing I knew it was the next morning and Jerry would be shaking me awake and telling me it was time to wake up and get ready for work.

JOYCE: Wow.

GEORGETTE: Jerry would find me lying on the floor and at first he thought I was only pretending to be asleep, he thought it was some sort of game, Jerry and I sometimes pretend that ... anyway he would gradually realize that I wasn't playing around, that I was actually passed out and he would put me on the couch and make dinner and finally he would go to bed. And it got to the point where we decided maybe I needed some help with this problem and I agreed he was right because I would never want the kids to see me like that and then Jerry reminded me that we don't have kids and I remembered that and said IF we ever had kids I would never want them to find their mother like that and so I've stopped drinking.

LARRY: How about a cranberry juice then?

GEORGETTE: No, thank you.

JOYCE: Some coffee? Just made a fresh pot?

GEORGETTE: No, I can't really drink coffee this late, keeps me up all night.

LARRY: Herbal tea then?

GEORGETTE: No, I'm fine.

JOYCE: Mineral water? Diet Coke?

GEORGETTE: Nope.

LARRY: You really don't want anything to drink? Nothing?

GEORGETTE: No, thanks.

JOYCE: Come on, how about some fresh squeezed orange juice?

GEORGETTE: No.

LARRY: I bet you won't say no to a nice cold glass of lowfat milk.

GEORGETTE: I said no, thank you.

JOYCE: Then some tap water?

GEORGETTE: I'm not thirsty.

JOYCE: But you might get thirsty later. I'll just get you a glass of …

GEORGETTE: Hey, I don't want anything to drink. Nothing. No liquids, okay. (*Pause.*)

LARRY: Okay. Just trying to be a good host.

GEORGETTE: Look, maybe I should be going …

JOYCE: Stay a minute, there's something Larry wanted to tell you.

LARRY: There is?

JOYCE: Yes, Larry, there is, you wanted to tell Georgette about that thing while I go into the kitchen and bring out those cookies I baked.

GEORGETTE: Joyce, I'm not really hungry …

JOYCE: You are going to have one of my fucking cookies and that's it so sit there and shut up and listen to Larry and I'll be right back. Make sure she doesn't go anywhere, Larry. (*She exits.*)

LARRY: Those cookies are great. We want you to have one.

GEORGETTE: (*Pause.*) So Larry, what did you want to tell me?

LARRY: Yeah, the think I wanted to tell you. (*Rattle off stage.*) Now you remember that little deal, that stock option thing we told you and Jerry about? (*Rattle.*)

GEORGETTE: The insider trading thing, Larry?

LARRY: If you want to put it in those terms, the information I gave you about the ... Well, we all profited quite nicely from that little transaction.

GEORGETTE: Yes, we did.

LARRY: And we found out that there's going to be an investigation of that ... you know ...

GEORGETTE: Illegal insider trading move.

LARRY: I'd like to use the term pre-emptive non-loss of funds transaction.

GEORGETTE: So what, the SEC is looking into that deal?

LARRY: Yes, they are. And I've already spoken to Jerry and he's happy to keep quiet about it. In fact, he's fine with lying to the commission if necessary. But he says that there might be a problem with you.

GEORGETTE: Me?

LARRY: He told me that you've had this attack of conscience or something, that you kind of feel guilty about making all that money the way we did, he thinks maybe that had something to do with why you were drinking so much, and well, the bottom line is we are all concerned, Jerry, Joyce, and myself, we're concerned if you're gonna play ball with us on this.

GEORGETTE: Play ball?

LARRY: If you're on our team or not.

GEORGETTE: What we did was illegal, Larry.

LARRY: That's a very subjective response that I'm not financially at liberty to accept right now.

GEORGETTE: But it was wrong.

LARRY: Maybe to the losers who didn't make money on the merger it could be construed as morally bankrupt but to the rest of us who profited by it, including yourself, to the tune of that new car and the addition onto your house, it was a good thing.

GEORGETTE: You want me to lie about what I know about the illegal insider trading thing?

LARRY: If asked.

GEORGETTE: Well, I have to be honest and tell you I have a problem with that.

LARRY: (*Yelling into the kitchen.*) Honey?

(*Joyce enters with plate of cookies.*)

JOYCE: Here we are, chocolate chip cookies.

LARRY: We want you to try one.

JOYCE: Go ahead.

(Joyce offers plate, Georgette takes one.)
GEORGETTE: Aren't you two going to have any?
LARRY: We already ate a whole batch.
JOYCE: We're stuffed.
LARRY: But you go ahead.
GEORGETTE: No, I ...
LARRY: Have a cookie.
JOYCE: Now. *(Pause.)*
GEORGETTE: Just one.
   (She bites into the cookie, Joyce and Larry watch intently.)
LARRY: Pretty good, huh?
GEORGETTE: Yes.
JOYCE: Then eat the whole thing! Eat it! Eat the fucking cookie!
GEORGETTE: Okay. *(She eats the cookie.)* Thank you.
LARRY: She ate the whole thing, Joyce.
JOYCE: Yes, she did. Have another. Now.
   (Georgette does.)
GEORGETTE: That was ... whoa I feel a little ...
LARRY: What? You feel what?
JOYCE: *(Very insincere.)* Are you okay, Georgette? Would you like to sit
   down?
GEORGETTE: Maybe I should ... *(She goes toward the chair.)* ... Gosh
   the room is spinning ...
JOYCE: I wonder what the matter is?
LARRY: Maybe she's sick.
JOYCE: Maybe she's going to die.
GEORGETTE: What?
LARRY: Yeah. Maybe she's going to die.
GEORGETTE: Wait a second ...
JOYCE: Die, Georgette, Die.
LARRY: Die, bitch.
   (Larry and Joyce laugh.)
LARRY AND JOYCE: Ahahahaha.
GEORGETTE: What's happening?
LARRY: Bet you thought we'd never do a thing like this.
JOYCE: Bet you thought we weren't capable.
LARRY: Bet you thought we didn't have the guts.
GEORGETTE: I'm your friend!
LARRY AND JOYCE: Bad call.
   (Lights fade. The bar. Joyce, Georgette, and Larry.)
LARRY: Ted had to change his squash time again.
JOYCE: Should we order another?

GEORGETTE: Let's go for it.

LARRY: Sure.

GEORGETTE: I'll be right back. (*She leaves.*)

LARRY: I didn't want to tell you in front of Georgette.

JOYCE: What?

LARRY: It's about Ted.

JOYCE: About your squash game?

LARRY: No, I just made that up. Ted's wife left.

JOYCE: Beth left Ted?

LARRY: That's what he told me over the phone. He gets home from work, there's a note. He goes into the bedroom, her half of the closet is cleared out.

JOYCE: God.

LARRY: I told him to come over.

JOYCE: What here? You told Ted to come here? Larry …

LARRY: His wife just left him, he's destroyed, Joyce. I told him to come over, have a few drinks, we'd listen to …

JOYCE: Oh Christ, just the way I want to spend my …

LARRY: He is my squash partner.

(*Georgette re-enters with drinks.*)

GEORGETTE: Here we go. What happened? What I miss?

LARRY: Nothing.

JOYCE: Everything's fine.

GEORGETTE: Come on, cheer up, people.

JOYCE: You're right.

LARRY: What do we drink to?

(*Ted runs in.*)

TED: I'll kill her. I swear if I ever find her, and I will, I will find her, no matter where she's gone, I don't care if she's moved to the fucking South Pole, I will track her down and I will kill her, I will get a gun and shoot her or I'll stab her, or better yet, I'll strangle her, I'll put my hands around her scrawny neck and squeeze the life out of her, or no, no, I'll stab her, I'll stab her in the microscopic muscle she calls her heart, I'll stab some butcher knife into the middle of her chest, let her bleed to death, then I'll sit in some bar with a friend and have a drink and pretend like nothing's happened, the whole time her blood is pouring out of her, I'll be sitting in a bar like this and laughing, how could she do this, how could she pack her bags, leave some note and leave me, I'll poison her, I'll find her and tell her I just wanted her to know I understand why she had to do this, I'll say we can still be friends and then I'll say, let's have one last drink and part friends but all the time I'll be waiting for her to down her drink which I mixed with poison, and then I'll watch her gag and shake and fall on the floor and I'll watch her die, I'll watch her look up at me and with her last breath ask why? Why did you do that? And I'll say because you can't leave me, nobody leaves me, you're mine you understand, you belong to me, you're mine, how dare you leave me, you left and for that you have to die and I get to watch you die. So there's your answer. What's everybody drinking?

JOYCE: Margarita.

LARRY: Gin and tonic.

GEORGETTE: I was going margaritas, but I think I'd like a scotch.

TED: Okay, rounds on me. Mind if I play a little Patsy Cline? (*Ted exits.*)

JOYCE: I don't think he's taking this well.

LARRY: He was crying on the phone.

GEORGETTE: Well, he had the car ride over here to get mad.

JOYCE: He is really mad.

LARRY: Yeah, I'd say he was really mad.

GEORGETTE: But to say he would kill her ...

LARRY: He's not thinking right now.

JOYCE: He's overreacting.

GEORGETTE: I mean that's not the solution.

JOYCE: No.

LARRY: No, violence doesn't solve anything.

GEORGETTE: I don't know the whole story, but I think we should make sure he cools down, doesn't do anything rash.

JOYCE: I agree.

LARRY: He's not thinking rationally.

JOYCE: He's not.

GEORGETTE: No, he's not ...

(*They look at one another and drink in silence. Lights fade as we hear Patsy Cline singing "You Belong To Me."*)

END OF PLAY

Water and Wine
by Stuart Spencer

BIOGRAPHY

Stuart Spencer is the author of numerous one-act and two-act plays, including *Blue Stars, Sudden Devotion* and *Go To Ground,* which have been produced in New York at EST, where he is a member. He has written one screenplay, *White Gold,* on commission and is currently at work on another. Mr. Spencer teaches playwriting in private classes at Sarah Lawrence College and at the EST Institute for Professional Training. He also teaches dramaturgy at the Playwright's Horizons Theatre School/NYU Program and is a member of the Dramatists Guild.

AUTHOR'S NOTE

Outside Florence there is a small village called Castelfranco that sits at the base of a very large Tuscan hill. Some would call it a mountain. You can drive to the top of the hill by car, though a little more than halfway up the road turns to dirt and rock. It is the same track, one imagines, used by horses and carts for many hundreds of years.

Coming around the last bend of this single lane path, you can see a large stone farmhouse perched on the final plateau of the hill. It is fronted by a great stone wall holding back the hillside. Once you have reached the farmhouse and stand at its front door you can turn around and see the Arno Valley spread out below you like a great Tuscan table loaded with food and flowers. Around to the side of the house is the entrance to the cellar, half buried into the side of the steeply rising hill. Inside are scattered bottles, an ancient wine press, and the miscellaneous leavings of the wine makers who were this farm's occupants for many centuries.

I write the brief description of this place so that the reader will know that it was this highly personal, one could even say sensual, experience that was the inspiration for this play. For while the essential incident with which *Water and Wine* is concerned—the identification of the *Laocoon* by Michelangelo Buonarroti and Giuliano Da Sangallo— is historically accurate, the play is a work of the imagination. There are many factual inaccuracies in the text. Some are glaring (the farm was just outside Rome, not Florence), others more subtle (the farmer was paid an annuity, not a lump sum). Some I was aware of as I was writing the play, others have been brought to my attention since.

The play, in any case, is not a "historical drama" in our modern sense of the term, meaning that its primary attempt is not to portray history. Instead, I have (attempted anyway) to use history to my own purposes. Whatever was historically convenient was used; whatever was not was discarded or changed. I shaped and selected my raw material so that I was free to explore certain ideas about both art, and the mysterious nexus between love (romantic and familial) and the creation of that art.

And also, it now occurs to me, so that I could relive in some shadowy way the beauty and simplicity and grace of an old farmhouse at the top of a very large Tuscan hill.

ORIGINAL PRODUCTION

Water and Wine was produced by Act One in association with Showtime Networks Inc., Paramount Network Television, Viacom Productions and Grammnet Productions for Act One '95: A Festival of New One-Act Plays, at The Met Theatre in Los Angeles, CA in April 1995. It was directed by Harris Yulin with the following cast:

Giovanni	Tom Bower
Enrico	Adam Scott
Giuliano	Michael Mantell
Buonarroti	Elias Koteas/Xander Berkeley

Water and Wine was first produced at The Ensemble Studio Theatre Marathon 1995, 18th Annual One-Act Play Marathon. It was directed by Nicholas Martin (stage manager, Gregg W. Brevoort) with the following cast:

Giovanni	Ed Setrakian
Enrico	Justin Theroux
Giuliano	Frank Biancamano
Buonarroti	Chris Ceraso

CHARACTERS

GIOVANNI
ENRICO
GIULIANO
BUONARROTI

TIME

Late winter, 1506.

SETTING

A farm outside Florence.

WATER AND WINE

The dark interior of a vaulted chamber. It is used as the storage room for a vineyard, so there is a large wooden vat and an array of bottles— some of them full and corked, others empty.

There are two exits, both heavy wooden doors. The first goes to the outside. The second, upstage, leads to a "cellar" which is burrowed into the side of the hill, so you don't have to descend steps to get into it. The cellar door is locked.

It is late afternoon on a winter's day. Outside it is cold and rainy. The light is beginning to fail. A single candle is on the table. It brings a warm glow to the otherwise dank room. But we can hear the wind and the rain whipping against the side of this stone structure, buried half beneath the ground.

The year is 1506. We are on a farm outside Florence.

The door bangs open and a man enters. He is in his sixties, but the farmer's life has made him look much older. He has a beard, and is weathered and grey.

Behind him will follow Enrico, in his early twenties. He's very handsome and energetic, and very earnest.

GIOVANNI: Christ! What a day! *(He sees the door is still open.)* Close the door for God's sake!

(Enrico reaches back and closes the heavy wooden door.)

ENRICO: The rain is good for the grapes, though.

GIOVANNI: It's bad for the old men.

ENRICO: In the summer, you'll by happy we had so much rain. You'll be dancing around the wine press singing songs to the Madonna.

GIOVANNI: If I live that long.

ENRICO: You say that every year.

GIOVANNI: Every year I could die. And I have never danced around any wine presses. Light a candle.

ENRICO: It's lit. Liccia must have come down.

GIOVANNI: That's it? That's the only candle we have?

ENRICO: They're expensive, papa.

GIOVANNI: Well, we've got money now, don't we.

ENRICO: Do we?

GIOVANNI: Well, as soon they get here and take a look at it. I think they'll pay plenty, don't you?

ENRICO: I don't know. I hope so.

GIOVANNI: Ah well, there you go. Hope. You add faith and charity, and you've got yourself a Beatitude.

ENRICO: Faith, hope, and charity are not Beatitudes.

GIOVANNI: No? What are they?

ENRICO: They're just three good things to have. The greatest of them is charity.

GIOVANNI: Oh forgive me, I'm just an ignorant old man.

ENRICO: Just because I go to church and you don't…

GIOVANNI: The last time I went to church that crazy Savanarola got up in the pulpit and scared me half to death.

ENRICO: They say he's not so frightening since they burned him at the stake.

GIOVANNI: And a good thing too.

ENRICO: Savanarola had some good things to say.

GIOVANNI: Why don't you march down into town and say that to the nearest Medici who happens to be walking by? I understand they've got a few stakes left and kindling is cheap.

ENRICO: That's exactly my point. The Family would do just that.

GIOVANNI: So would Savanarola.

(Enrico dismisses him with a wave.)

ENRICO: Oh—you're an old man.

GIOVANNI: You only noticed just now? Where are the candles?

(Giovanni is looking for them in a low cabinet against a wall.)

ENRICO: One is plenty.

GIOVANNI: We're going to have money soon. You wait and see. We'll have candles, some new clothes, maybe a helper for that lovely sister of yours so she doesn't complain all the time about the work she has to do.

ENRICO: Papa...

GIOVANNI: I'm sorry.

ENRICO: We agreed.

GIOVANNI: Yes, yes. I'm sorry.

ENRICO: Liccia works very hard.

GIOVANNI: God knows she works harder than your mother ever did. Now there was a lazy one.

ENRICO: Papa, that's not nice!

GIOVANNI: It's true!

ENRICO: Yes, but you don't say that about the dead.

GIOVANNI: You say what's true about the dead and let the dead take care of themselves. Anyway, they're dead. What do they care?

ENRICO: You're a wicked old man.

GIOVANNI: Yes and you are young and stupid. So when they get here, you let me do the talking. I plan to get our money's worth out of this little artifact we've discovered. *(He has found three candles. He sits at the table, and sets about putting them in holders and lighting them.)*

ENRICO: Little artifact!

GIOVANNI: Yes, exactly.

ENRICO: Oh papa! It's sculpture!

GIOVANNI: I'm not impressed by words, I'm sorry.

ENRICO: Maybe because you don't understand it.

GIOVANNI: Oh! God save us! And you do, I suppose.

ENRICO: No, but I admit it. I'm humble in my ignorance.

GIOVANNI: It's a very pretty piece of stone, I'll give you that. But all this hub-bub about art? That's for the Medici and the Pope and all those city folks who love to stroll around town gasping at all their lovely belongings. Me, I go into the vineyard every day and do my job. And do you know what? When they sit down to their table in the afternoon, they enjoy a very fine wine because of my work. Wine that in my ignorant opinion is every bit a thing of beauty as any of their fancy art.

ENRICO: Our work.

GIOVANNI: You're right—because the one thing you do know how to do is when to pick the grape.

ENRICO: Thank you.

GIOVANNI: No small talent, that. Not just anyone can time it the way you can. We make good wine because of that.

ENRICO: Thank you Papa.

GIOVANNI: A serious, businesslike exchange of cash is all I'm looking for. No elegant talk for me, if you please.

ENRICO: You're a terrible philistine.

GIOVANNI: I don't even know what that is, so it can't possibly bother me that I am one.

ENRICO: It's in the Bible.

GIOVANNI: This explains why I don't know.

ENRICO: Anyway, we'll both do the talking.

GIOVANNI: I don't think we're having this discussion.

ENRICO: Both of us, Papa.

GIOVANNI: You don't know the first thing about business.

ENRICO: And you don't know anything about art.

GIOVANNI: I don't need to know anything.

ENRICO: For this, it wouldn't hurt.

GIOVANNI: I'm the head of this family and I do the business.

ENRICO: You could give something away and not even know it.

GIOVANNI: We've got one item on the block: a statue. We're trying to get two thousand for it, tops. We'll settle for one. I know the difference between 1,000 and 2,000. That much business sense I know I have.

ENRICO: Papa, please. Just don't close any deals without checking with me first.

GIOVANNI: I'll see how it goes. *(He goes to the upstage door and tests it. It's locked.)*

ENRICO: Papa...

GIOVANNI: I said I'll see. Now leave it. When does he get here?

ENRICO: I don't know. And it's they.

GIOVANNI: They?

(Enrico sits at the table.)

ENRICO: There are two of them. Buonarroti and a friend of his.

GIOVANNI: Another artist?

ENRICO: I don't know.

GIOVANNI: Maybe a businessman.

ENRICO: Maybe.

GIOVANNI: Maybe someone from the government.

ENRICO: Maybe, I don't know.

GIOVANNI: Maybe a Medici.

ENRICO: I doubt it.

GIOVANNI: Why?

ENRICO: They don't even know what we have yet. They may not be interested.

GIOVANNI: Not interested?! Are you serious?

ENRICO: They haven't seen it yet, papa.

GIOVANNI: Yes, but you described it to them in your letter, didn't you? You made that little drawing of it.

ENRICO: I'm sure my drawing looked very simple to the likes of Buonarroti.

GIOVANNI: I thought it looked very nice.

ENRICO: You're my father.

GIOVANNI: Yes, but I don't like you enough to compliment you if you don't deserve it. That was a good drawing.

ENRICO: Thank you.

(Giovanni goes to him.)

GIOVANNI: I always thought you had talent.

ENRICO: Thank you.

GIOVANNI: Who knows? With a little instruction, maybe you could be a real artist.

ENRICO: It takes more than a little instruction, Papa. It takes a long time and hard work.

GIOVANNI: Well, you were always lazy.

ENRICO: I am not lazy!

GIOVANNI: Okay, all right.

ENRICO: You know that you need me here, Papa, and that's the end of it.

GIOVANNI: I was only saying…

ENRICO: We've been through this a hundred times.

GIOVANNI: If you'd let me get a word in…

ENRICO: Let's just drop it! *(Enrico gets up and crosses away from Giovanni, though he soon realizes he has nowhere to go and ends up floating on the other side of the room.)*

GIOVANNI: I never heard of anyone finding a piece like this, have you?

ENRICO: Well, no. But we don't get much news up on this mountainside, papa.

GIOVANNI: They're always digging up a piece of this, a chunk of that. But a whole statue? In virtually the same condition as the day it was finished? Now that's a rare thing indeed.

ENRICO: You may be right. I hope you are.

GIOVANNI: You and that hope again.

ENRICO: I'm only saying that I don't know.

GIOVANNI: And not just any old statue, but a great one. I mean, that is one very impressive piece of marble, don't you think? So dramatic. The way they're all tangled up in the snakes like that, struggling to get free. It's pathetic, really, if you think about it. Really, very touching.

ENRICO: You sound like you almost like it.

GIOVANNI: *(Indignantly.)* I do.

ENRICO: I thought you couldn't care less about all that fancy art nonsense.

GIOVANNI: I don't care about all the nonsense. But I like the statue. It's...I don't know. It's good. It's nothing to get excited about it, but it's good. I never said it wasn't good.

ENRICO: You said you weren't impressed by it.

GIOVANNI: I never said such a thing.

ENRICO: You did. You just said it a few minutes ago.

GIOVANNI: You don't listen. I said I wasn't impressed by all the nonsense that goes with it. Of course I'm impressed by the statue. Who wouldn't be? You'd have to be blind. Or stupid. What do you take me for anyway? A philistine?

(Enrico goes to the table with the wine bottles on it.)

ENRICO: I'm going to have a little. How about you?

GIOVANNI: Unlike my son, I try not to drink up the profits.

ENRICO: So you won't have another after this cup.

GIOVANNI: Exactly.

(Enrico hands him a cup of wine.)

GIOVANNI: You're not such a bad son.

(There's a pounding at the door.)

GIOVANNI: It's them.

ENRICO: I'll get it.

GIOVANNI: Don't forget, I do the talking. *(More pounding.)* Come in! Now be obedient for once in your life.

ENRICO: Yes, papa.

(Two men enter. The first, Buonarroti, is about thirty. He is bearded and not very attractive. He is overbearing in his manner, abrupt and arrogant. The second man, Giuliano da Sangallo, is in his forties. He is quite straight-forward, businesslike. They are both very wet and wind-blown.)

GIULIANO: God in heaven! The wind on this mountain!

GIOVANNI: Bad day out there.

GIULIANO: Terrible!

GIOVANNI: Let me take your cloaks. Enrico, some help here.

GIULIANO: Yes, yes, thank you so much.

(Meanwhile, Enrico has stepped in to take Buonarotti's cloak. Buonarotti's eyes fasten on Enrico, who manages—barely—to meet the gaze. Buonarotti's tone is stern and formal.)

BUONARROTI: You didn't tell us it was so far up the hill.

ENRICO: It's a steep climb, yes.

BUONARROTI: Look at this. I'm soaked through.

ENRICO: I'll get you some dry clothes if you like.

BUONARROTI: No, no, don't bother. I'm not staying that long.

GIOVANNI: We thought you might stay for dinner.

BUONARROTI: We have to get back.

GIULIANO: I don't know. Dinner doesn't sound so bad to me.

BUONARROTI: I want to be back in the city tonight.

GIULIANO: We're going to have to eat somewhere.

ENRICO: Yes—please stay. It would be such an honor for us to have you...

BUONARROTI: I'm not staying for dinner!

GIOVANNI: If he doesn't want to stay he doesn't have to.

BUONARROTI: I just want to look at the statue. That's what I came for.

ENRICO: Of course, of course. I only meant that...

BUONARROTI: I know what you meant.

GIOVANNI: We let our guests do what they like.

BUONARROTI: Thank you.

GIOVANNI: You don't want to eat my daughter's delicious cooking, there's nobody here to force you. My name is DeAngelo. This is my son Enrico. He's the friendly one.

BUONARROTI: I'm Buonarroti.

(Giuliano steps forward to shake hands.)

GIULIANO: Giuliano Da Sangallo. It's a pleasure. The Family would like you to know that they are very pleased you told them first of your discovery.

ENRICO: We knew that they'd appreciate the value of a great work like this.

GIOVANNI: And have the money to pay for it.

(Giuliano is a little embarrassed by this.)

GIULIANO: Yes, yes of course.

BUONARROTI: May we see the statue?

GIOVANNI: It's right in there. *(He indicates.)* We put it in the cellar—it's got the only door we can lock.

GIULIANO: Very smart.

BUONARROTI: You didn't tell anyone else about it, did you?

GIOVANNI: We're peasants up here, you know—not idiots.

GIULIANO: Oh he didn't mean that you…

(Giovanni goes to get a candle and a key, lying on the table. He unlocks the cellar door.)

GIOVANNI: *(Interrupting.)* We didn't tell a soul. But you can never be too careful. I didn't want somebody stumbling in here and catching a glimpse of it before you arrived.—Well gentlemen? Care to have a look?

(Giuliano and Buonarroti look at each other.)

BUONARROTI: You go ahead.

GIULIANO: You're not coming?

BUONARROTI: I want to sit for a minute and clear my head. I've got too many thoughts going around in it. I won't be able to look at it properly.

GIULIANO: Well, if you insist.

BUONARROTI: I do.

GIOVANNI: All right, then. Come along. Take that candle with you.

(Giuliano takes a nearby candle. They are gone.)

ENRICO: Please, have a seat.

BUONARROTI: Thank you.

ENRICO: You're sure you don't want some dry clothes.

BUONARROTI: They'll only get wet when I go back into the rain.

ENRICO: You really can spend the night if you like.

BUONARROTI: You're very kind. No thank you.

ENRICO: Whatever you want. But I want you to know that we're not just being polite.

BUONARROTI: I understand.

ENRICO: We have a comfortable house. The beds are warm and dry and they don't have lice. My sister's cooking is really very good— everybody says so, even my father, and he isn't one to give compliments. I don't understand why you'd want to go back tonight in the rain. It'll be dark soon, too.

BUONARROTI: Maybe I like the dark.

(This stops Enrico short. He turns away vaguely until his eye falls on the wine bottles.)

ENRICO: Would you like a glass of wine?

BUONARROTI: Is it your own?

ENRICO: We grow the grapes right out on that hillside.

BUONARROTI: I'll try a cup.

(Enrico pours two cups.)

ENRICO: I think we make a good wine up here. Very light. But with a good body. *(He hands Buonarroti the cup.)* But you tell me.

(Buonarroti drinks it down.)

BUONARROTI: It's fine.

ENRICO: You barely tasted it.

BUONARROTI: I thought it was fine.

ENRICO: You couldn't possibly know, drinking it that fast.

BUONARROTI: I know everything I have to know.

ENRICO: Then you don't really care about good wine.

BUONARROTI: You're right, I don't. Now please, leave me alone for a minute.

ENRICO: To clear your mind.

BUONARROTI: Yes.

ENRICO: The way a wine drinker will clear his palate. So that you're ready to have the experience.

BUONARROTI: That's right.

ENRICO: That's the only thing that's important to you.

BUONARROTI: Yes.

ENRICO: Sometimes, I draw. Papa tells me I'm very good.

BUONARROTI: For a man who doesn't hand out many compliments, he seems to do it rather often.

ENRICO: I might have gone to Florence to study.

BUONARROTI: Why didn't you?

ENRICO: I thought I should stay on the farm. My father needed the help.

BUONARROTI: We all make choices.

ENRICO: The drawing of the statue that we sent you. Did you bring it?

BUONARROTI: Yes.

ENRICO: May I see it?

BUONARROTI: It's in the cloak. Probably soaked through.

(Enrico goes to the cloak, rummages through the pockets, and produces a rolled piece of paper. He spreads it on the table.)

ENRICO: Do you mind?

BUONARROTI: Mind?

ENRICO: Giving me a critique?

BUONARROTI: You drew this?

ENRICO: Yes.

BUONARROTI: It's not bad.

ENRICO: Do you think?

BUONARROTI: You must practice.

ENRICO: Oh yes, in my spare time. In the winter, mostly. When the weather is like this.

BUONARROTI: I meant you *ought* to practice. More.

ENRICO: Oh.

BUONARROTI: The modeling of the flesh is abrupt, here. You see? You can bring out the sense of muscle, of weight. Don't pass over it as though it isn't there. It's there. Acknowledge it.

ENRICO: I see. Anything else?

BUONARROTI: That's all.

ENRICO: That's the only criticism you have?

BUONARROTI: Yes.

ENRICO: You're very kind.

BUONARROTI: No I'm not.

ENRICO: Then you really mean it. You think I have talent.

BUONARROTI: I don't know what talent is. You can draw.

ENRICO: Enough to go to Florence? To study?

BUONARROTI: That I have no idea.

ENRICO: If you don't know, who does?

BUONARROTI: You want to make it a matter of talent. I'm only saying that I don't know if talent is so important. There's a lot that goes into being an artist besides talent. Personality. Luck. Skill…

ENRICO: But you said I had skill.

BUONARROTI: There's skill and there's technique.

ENRICO: But that's what I would learn if I studied, wouldn't I?

BUONARROTI: I suppose so.

ENRICO: Then you do think I have something.

BUONARROTI: Yes.

(There obviously is something else on his mind. Enrico senses it.)

ENRICO: *What.*

BUONARROTI: Don't go to Florence. Don't study painting.

ENRICO: Why not?

BUONARROTI: It would be selfish. Your father needs you.

ENRICO: If I were a successful artist I could support my father. He'd never have to work again.

BUONARROTI: And you might fail miserably. Most artists fail miserably. Even some of the bad ones. Better to stay at home and make wine. *(Enrico lets this sink in for a moment. It's depressing, not the answer he wanted.)*

ENRICO: Did you want some more?

BUONARROTI: I've had enough, actually.

ENRICO: You don't like it?

BUONARROTI: It's all right.

ENRICO: That's what you said about my drawing.

(Buonarroti shrugs.)

ENRICO: Well, maybe you just don't like good wine.

BUONARROTI: I know good wine, believe me. This isn't good. It's heavy and bitter.

ENRICO: You don't know what you're talking about.

BUONARROTI: I know how something tastes.

ENRICO: You may be a great artist, but I am a winemaker. We have the finest wine in the region on this farm. We're small, we're not famous. But the wine is good.

BUONARROTI: Have it your way. My way, it's heavy and bitter.

(A pause.)

ENRICO: Why do you have to be so unkind?

BUONARROTI: Why do you have to be so beautiful?

ENRICO: Excuse me?

BUONARROTI: You heard me.

ENRICO: I don't know what to say…

BUONARROTI: Try answering the question.

ENRICO: I don't know what you mean…

BUONARROTI: I asked you why are you beautiful. It's a simple enough question, isn't it? You answer mine, I'll answer yours. Why. Are. You. Beautiful.

ENRICO: First of all, I don't happen to think I'm so…

BUONARROTI: Just answer the question.

ENRICO: I look the way I am because…because that's who I am. Because that's how God made me. I had nothing to do with it.

BUONARROTI: Good answer.

ENRICO: Now you. You answer mine.

BUONARROTI: Isn't it obvious? The same reason. I'm not a nice person because God made me that way. *(Buonarroti takes a drink of wine.)* Oh come now, don't look so glum. Your wine is not to my taste. What could be simpler.

(Enrico gets up and puts the wine back on the low cabinet.)
ENRICO: Don't bother taking back your words.
BUONARROTI: I'm not taking them back. I'm explaining them. I told you the truth and you didn't want to hear it. That's my business, after all—telling the truth. You probably never thought of it, but what I do isn't about chipping away at blocks of marble and dabbing paint onto plaster. It's about telling the truth. Everything else is just technique. I've gotten very good at it, as you may have heard. And once you get good at something it's hard to break the habit. And if the truth is unkind, well, then so be it. Or Amen, as they say in church.
ENRICO: Do you go to church?
BUONARROTI: My dear, I *build* churches.
ENRICO: You're a liar.
BUONARROTI: No, I really do. I've already built a chapel for the San Lorenzo. I'm going to build a church for the Pope in Rome if they ever get the old one torn down. In the meantime I'm going to paint the ceiling of the Pope's chapel, which I admit isn't the same as actually constructing the building itself, but believe me—after I get done with the ceiling of that chapel nobody's going to think of that building as a building. They're going to think of it as a ceiling and nothing more.
(Enrico has finally gotten furious listening to this.)
ENRICO: Are you done congratulating yourself? Because what I meant was: you're a liar about being unkind. God didn't make you that way. You're unkind because you want to be. To me, in particular. I could see it the moment you walked in.
BUONARROTI: You saw that.
ENRICO: Yes.
BUONARROTI: How observant you must be to see all that with one look.
ENRICO: Yes, because I can see things! I have an eye—just like an artist.
BUONARROTI: Oh, this again.
ENRICO: What is it, jealousy? Are you afraid that I might really be good? Is that it?
BUONARROTI: Now you flatter yourself.
ENRICO: But when you first looked at this—the first thing you said was that I could draw! That it was good!
BUONARROTI: I said it wasn't bad.
ENRICO: That I must practice. But everyone must practice! Everyone

has something to learn! Even you weren't born the way you are! And for someone who grew up on a farm, this isn't bad. Where would you be now if you had grown up on this mountain? The truth is that I could learn. Anyone could learn what they need to be an artist—if they want to badly enough.

BUONARROTI: If that were true, then my donkey could write poetry and the pope would paint his own ceiling.

ENRICO: I am an artist! I know I am!

BUONARROTI: If you're so sure, then why do you keep asking me?

ENRICO: Because you are Buonarroti!

BUONARROTI: And what is that? What is Buonarroti? It's nothing! I am nothing! You are nothing also! We are both nothing! The work is the only thing that is something! More than that I cannot tell you! *(Pause.)*

ENRICO: I think you're the cruelest man I ever met.

BUONARROTI: And *I* think that sometimes, underneath cruelty, there is something very beautiful. And sometimes, in beautiful things, there can be that which is painfully cruel. *(Pause.)* And now if I might have just a glass of water. I understand the water up here in the hills is quite good.

(A noise from within. The others are returning from the cellar.)

ENRICO: *(Suddenly, without warning.)* Take me with you.

BUONARROTI: What?

ENRICO: I want to go to Florence. I don't care if I don't have talent. I want to study art. I want to study with you.

BUONARROTI: Pour me the water.

(Enrico hesitates.)

BUONARROTI: Pour.

(Enrico pours him a glass from a pitcher.)

(Giovanni and Giuliano enter from the cellar, laughing and talking. Giovanni goes to the table and blows out the candle as he talks.)

GIOVANNI: *(Exuberantly.)* No, no—it was completely by accident. Enrico was digging the new well just as I had told him, which was pretty extraordinary in itself now that I think of it, when all of a sudden he's all stooped over, digging away at something in the dirt. The minute I get there I can see from the quality of the marble itself here was something special.

BUONARROTI: *(To Giuliano.)* And is it? Special?

GIULIANO: It's special. Oh yes. It's very special. Just as Pliny describes it.

BUONARROTI: And the…condition?

GIULIANO: Intact. Completely intact.

(Overcome, Buonarroti puts his face into his hands. Enrico makes a move toward him.)

ENRICO: Are you all right?

BUONARROTI: I'm fine. Don't touch me. I'm all right.

GIOVANNI: *(To Enrico.)* Get the man some wine.

BUONARROTI: I don't want any wine.

GIOVANNI: It's very good wine. We make it our…

BUONARROTI: I don't want the wine!

GIOVANNI: I thought I'd ask.

(Buonarroti gets up.)

BUONARROTI: I want to see it now. I'm ready.

GIOVANNI: Enrico, you go with him.

BUONARROTI: No, I'll go alone.

GIOVANNI: Enrico…*(He gestures for Enrico to follow.)*

ENRICO: Here, I'll show you the way.

BUONARROTI: I'd prefer to go alone.

(Enrico takes him by the arm.)

ENRICO: It's very dark in the cellar. You can hit your head…

BUONARROTI: Get your hand off me!

GIOVANNI: Mr. Buonarroti, the statue is still mine and I want you accompanied. I'm not requesting. Understand?

(Buonarroti looks at Enrico, then back at Giovanni. Then to Enrico…)

BUONARROTI: After you.

(Enrico lights the candle, goes to the cellar door and goes inside, followed by Buonarroti.)

GIOVANNI: Some wine?

GIULIANO: I believe I will, thank you.

(Giovanni goes to the low cabinet, brings back the wine and two cups. He will pour them out. He talks through all this.)

GIOVANNI: Quite a charmer, that Buonarroti.

GIULIANO: You must forgive him. He's very decent, really, but very… unhappy.

GIOVANNI: Yes, must be tough. All those dinners with the Pope.

GIULIANO: He doesn't care about that sort of thing.

GIOVANNI: Then we're alike. Neither do I.

GIULIANO: *(Confidentially.)* He enjoys men.

GIOVANNI: Yes…?

GIULIANO: You understand what I mean? Instead of women.

GIOVANNI: You think I never heard of such a thing? I live on a farm, not the moon. *(He assumes a mock-confidential tone.)* We even have men like that around here.

GIULIANO: Well, it's against church teaching.

GIOVANNI: Hm! The church is against church teaching.

GIULIANO: I'd watch what I say! People get burned for less than that.

GIOVANNI: Oh really, who do you think you're fooling? You didn't get where you are with the Medici by being a humble servant of God.

GIULIANO: I am as humble a servant of God as the next man!

GIOVANNI: Tell it to Savanarola.

GIULIANO: I told him—he didn't listen! *(They laugh.)* You know what I wonder? I wonder what you'll do with the money.

GIOVANNI: We haven't discussed money yet.

GIULIANO: No, but we will. If I read you correctly, you want plenty.

GIOVANNI: Something wrong with that? I'll bet the Family asks for plenty when it's making its deals.

GIULIANO: Oh, they do.

GIOVANNI: Well, then.

GIULIANO: I only wonder what you'll do with it, that's all.

GIOVANNI: That depends on how much it is.

GIULIANO: Let's say you get everything you want.

GIOVANNI: I'd go down into the village and hire a couple of men and get them to come up here and tend my vines for me. Then I'd sit in my house and enjoy what's left of my life. That's not so unreasonable, is it?

GIULIANO: Not if you ask me.

GIOVANNI: My son would think so.

GIULIANO: The sculpture doesn't belong to your son.

GIOVANNI: No, but he wants me to let him bargain with you. I don't think that's such a good idea, do you?

GIULIANO: I wouldn't know.

GIOVANNI: He's young and sentimental. He doesn't know about business.

GIULIANO: Well, in that case, if you ask me, you should let him join in the bargaining as much as he wants. *(They laugh.)* I love to bargain with sentimental people!

GIOVANNI: I'll bet you do. He wants to go with you.

GIULIANO: With me?

GIOVANNI: With this Buonarroti fellow, to Florence. He wants to study art.

GIULIANO: Why didn't he just say so?

GIOVANNI: He doesn't want me to know. He's guilty about leaving the old man on the mountaintop. He thinks he's fooling me. He lies about it. "No, papa. I don't want to be an artist. I don't want to be a painter." But I know. I can see it. The more he denies it, the more I know.

GIULIANO: And you won't let him go?

GIOVANNI: I need him here on the farm, don't I.

GIULIANO: Not if you have the money from the statue.

GIOVANNI: He's not very good, though. That's the real problem. He should stay for his own sake.

GIULIANO: Yes, but if the boy wants to go...

GIOVANNI: You saw his drawing of the statue.

GIULIANO: It wasn't so bad. The boy hasn't had any training. He could be very competent if he put his mind to it.

GIOVANNI: I don't believe he's interested in "competent".

GIULIANO: Well, not everyone can be like Mr. Buonarroti here.

GIOVANNI: Tell that to Enrico. He thinks he can be.

GIULIANO: Still, he could have a career of some kind. People do. Thousands of them.

GIOVANNI: He's a dreamer. He imagines things for himself and he thinks they'll come true, but they won't. I couldn't stand him to be so disappointed.

GIULIANO: You know, honestly—and not that this makes much difference to me, one way or the other—but really, I suspect you're a selfish, lonely old man who is afraid he'll be left alone to die up here in the hills.

GIOVANNI: Maybe I am selfish. Then again, maybe selfish is a good thing, if it saves somebody else a lot of heartache and disappointment.

GIULIANO: But you can't keep him here where he doesn't want to be.

GIOVANNI: But it's not me keeping him, don't you see? It's God. Enrico prayed and asked for the gift and God said no. God does that on occasion. Have you noticed? It's God who's keeping him here, or Fate if you prefer. Like the snakes on those men in the statue. It's Fate that's dragging him down and there's nothing to do about it. *(A slight pause.)*

GIULIANO: I have a confession.

GIOVANNI: What's that?

GIULIANO: This wine has given me quite an appetite.

(Giovanni laughs.)

GIOVANNI: Come upstairs, then. We'll have dinner while we wait.

(Giovanni goes to the outside door. Giuliano starts to follow.)

GIULIANO: They won't wonder where we went?

GIOVANNI: Where is there to go? Enrico will know we're upstairs. Come on, don't worry about them. You'll like Liccia. She's very pretty, and not married yet. Tell me, Mr. Da Sangallo, are you married yourself? Because Liccia is very hard working. All day scrubbing and cooking and *(They are gone.)*

(The door to the cellar slams open. Buonarroti stands for a moment, dazed and unsure where to move. Finally he walks into the room. Enrico appears at the door behind him. He blows out the candle. He talks nervously.)

ENRICO: I knew you'd feel this way about it. I did too, the moment I saw it, I knew. Papa doesn't appreciate these things, but I—I know something great when I see it. That's what I want to do. I want to be an artist like that also!

BUONARROTI: For God's sake, just shut up, would you?! *(Pause.)* You don't understand, do you. When God made the world, he *created* something. In the truest sense, the real sense of the word: to bring into being. There was nothing, now there is something. That's what God did. We forget that—there was nothing. *Nothing.* And now…the world. The stars, the sun…*(He runs his fingers along the table top and looks at his fingertips.)*…dust, air, stones. You. I. When an artist paints, or a sculptor hammers the stone—that's not creation. We're just rearranging things. It looks new, it seems as if we've created something, but no—never. It's not possible. Only God can create things and he's long since finished. *But…* sometimes, once in a lifetime, once in a thousand years, there is a work of man that *seems* to be new. That seems to be actually created. The material seems not to have been before, and now it is. *(He gestures behind him, to the inner door.)* That…that creation in your cellar is one of these. Laocoon[1], he's the man, the father, a Trojan priest. He reaches up to escape the serpent's grasp and… *(Unconsciously, he begins to imitate the figures in the statue.)*…his head rears back just at the moment of knowledge, the moment of despair, knowing that the reach is futile. He knows in this instant that he will die in the serpent's terrible grip. And his sons will die too. That all is lost. Yet the moment is about the *struggle,* the agonizing struggle that must go on! Now, and forever. *Now, this precise moment! And forever!* If ever man came close to God, it was in that piece of stone in your cellar. In that marble, man has created something which comes breathlessly close, heartstoppingly close to anything in God's own creation. And you casually stroll out the door and say you'd like to do that too. Well, you can't! It doesn't happen that way! Nobody can! Even *I* can't!

ENRICO: I'm sorry, I...that's not what I meant. I only meant I was inspired, to do great things.

BUONARROTI: It's fake, that kind of inspiration. You don't get inspiration from art, you get it from life. Good art only intimidates you into doing a little better.

ENRICO: I'm sorry.

BUONARROTI: You might as well learn it now. You will never, never create such a thing as that!

ENRICO: All right! I hear you!

BUONARROTI: Yes, but do you understand me?

ENRICO: Yes.

BUONARROTI: And that's the end of it? No more talk of going to Florence.

ENRICO: No, not if you say so. *(Pause.)*

BUONARROTI: I do.

(Enrico nods his head for a moment, accepting this. He picks up the bottle of wine and carries it back to a side cabinet. He pours himself a cup and drinks it before returning it to the shelf.)

ENRICO: I'm sorry if I upset you.

BUONARROTI: You didn't.

ENRICO: I think I did. I apologize.

BUONARROTI: You had to know, that's all. No one around here is able to tell you. But I could and I did. The truth, remember?

ENRICO: I meant that maybe I upset you because I reminded you of your own shortcomings.

BUONARROTI: Mine?

ENRICO: Isn't that really why you're angry? Because I reminded you that even you won't ever make anything like the statue?

(Buonarroti starts to laugh.)

ENRICO: Laugh if you want. But you weren't a minute ago. I guess we all have our limitations. I have mine, but you have yours. You told me why I'll never be an artist. But you said something about yourself at the same time, and when you heard it come out—you didn't like it very much.

BUONARROTI: Wrong! Wrong on both counts! The reason you'll never be an artist? Not because I say so. Because you listened to me when I said it! Because you didn't laugh in my face and say "Ha! Buonarroti! What do you know?!" You'll defend your wine to the death, but your passion for art? I talked you out of it in two minutes.

ENRICO: But even you could not do what that sculptor has done! You said so yourself!

BUONARROTI: No…that's right: I can't. *(He leans forward with enormous conviction.) I can do better.* I'll take what he's done and I'll go farther, I'll be greater, I'll do more. That's why I'm an artist, because I believe that I can. I might be wrong, but I believe. It's all the difference.

(The outside door opens and Giovanni enters, followed by Giuliano.)

GIULIANO: Ah, you're back! Good!

GIOVANNI: We went upstairs for a little something to eat but your lazy sister forgot to make dinner.

GIULIANO: Well? Did you see?

BUONARROTI: Yes.

GIULIANO: Good, excellent. Because we've come to an arrangement, financially speaking.

(Giovanni looks to Enrico.)

GIOVANNI: I think you'll be happy with the amount, Enrico.

GIULIANO: Three thousand, plus an order for a shipment of wine from this fine estate. *(He looks at Buonarroti.)* You don't think it's too much, do you?

BUONARROTI: The sculpture is beyond price.

GIULIANO: Just what I thought. Mr. DeAngelo drives a hard bargain but I believe everyone is pleased now.

BUONARROTI: We're lucky he doesn't want to keep it for himself.

GIULIANO: Yes, indeed. Well. Shall we go then?

BUONARROTI: Everything is done?

GIULIANO: We've signed an agreement. I'll be back up tomorrow with some workmen and a carriage. *(Pointedly, to Giovanni.)* And the money. Nothing to do tonight, but go home and get some sleep.

GIOVANNI: It's not raining so hard. And the wind is stopped.

GIULIANO: Yes, well, there you have it then.

(Buonarroti stands.)

BUONARROTI: Thank you for your hospitality. I apologize if I was abrupt, earlier. I was nervous about seeing it.

GIOVANNI: Well it's all worked out, hasn't it. Everybody's happy.

BUONARROTI: Yes, indeed. *(He goes back to Enrico.)* Do you ever come to Rome?

ENRICO: Rome?! No. Why?

BUONARROTI: I thought you might come see my chapel ceiling when it's finished. I already have ideas for it. It will be very beautiful. Not as beautiful as you, but after all, you are the original, made by God. *(He goes to the outside door.)* Come. *(He exits.)*

GIULIANO: Yes, well, good to meet. See you tomorrow, just after noon, I imagine. *(He hurries after Buonarroti. Giovanni closes the door after him. A slight beat.)*

GIOVANNI: Did he try something with you?

ENRICO: Oh Papa, for God's sake…

GIOVANNI: Listen, you bring your goods to market, sometimes you have to throw in a little something extra to close the deal.

ENRICO: He liked the statue enough all on its own.

GIOVANNI: I closed the deal without you.

ENRICO: It's all right. It doesn't matter.

GIOVANNI: Well I apologize. I said I'd wait for you.

ENRICO: You said nothing of the kind. You told me to mind my own business.

GIOVANNI: Enrico, how can you get things wrong so much? I wonder about you. I promised I'd consult you before I closed the deal. And I didn't—but for three thousand! How could I hesitate? And a shipment of wine, to be drunk by the Medici themselves!

ENRICO: I thought you couldn't care less about the Medici.

GIOVANNI: They drink a lot of wine. I could learn to care about them. *(Enrico moves toward the door.)*

ENRICO: Well you have your money, that's the important thing.

GIOVANNI: It'll be yours soon.

ENRICO: Not so soon, I don't think.

GIOVANNI: I could die anytime.

ENRICO: You've said that for years.

GIOVANNI: It's been true for years.

ENRICO: I'm going up to bed, Papa. *(He again goes to the door.)*

GIOVANNI: I got a thousand more than either of us dreamed of. Don't you want to know what I plan on doing with it?

ENRICO: What, Papa?

GIOVANNI: It's enough to send you to Florence. You could study.

(Enrico doesn't know how to answer.)

GIOVANNI: I know it's what you want. *(Pause.)*

ENRICO: I don't think so.

GIOVANNI: What do you mean? Why not?

ENRICO: A few years ago, maybe. Not anymore.

GIOVANNI: What are you talking about? You're twenty-one years old. People learn to draw when they're twenty-one. Besides, you already know how. You only need to get better.

ENRICO: When I was younger, I think maybe then I might have become an artist. But you change, Papa. A person changes. Then it's not possible anymore.

GIOVANNI: Oh what a bunch of crap!

ENRICO: When the grape is ready to be picked, you pick it. If you wait, the grape is no good for wine. Good for other things, maybe. Not for wine. Not for a great wine. There's nothing you can do to change it. You know that, Papa.

GIOVANNI: You're not a grape.

ENRICO: I'm not an artist.

GIOVANNI: *(Shrugs.)* Well, have it your way.

ENRICO: Thank you, Papa. *(He starts to go, then stops again.)* I do know when to pick the grape, though, don't I.

GIOVANNI: Like no one I ever saw. You have the knack.

ENRICO: It's an honorable profession, winemaking.

GIOVANNI: I always thought so.

ENRICO: I know you did. Good night Papa.

GIOVANNI: Good night.

(Enrico goes out and closes the door. Giovanni goes to cabinet, gets the bottle of wine and a cup, and sits at the table. He pours a little in the cup and drinks. He likes what he tastes. He fills the cup and takes another good drink. He sighs happily. The lights fade to black.)

END OF PLAY

[1]Lay - ahk′ - oh - on′.

The Juiceman Cometh
A One-Act Play
by Peter Spiro

BIOGRAPHY

Mr. Spiro's produced plays include *Howya Doin' Franky Banana* at the Nuyorican Poets Cafe in New York City, a one-act version of *Woman in the Second Floor Window* at BACA downtown, and *The Gift* done by Theater for the Forgotten. Mr. Spiro's poetry has appeared widely in magazines and anthologies nationwide including the recently published anthology, *Aloud: Voices from the Nuyorican Poets Cafe* by Henry Holt. He can be seen reading his poetry in the upcoming film special *The United States of Poetry* due to air on PBS this coming fall.

AUTHOR'S NOTE

For Jay Kordich, The Juiceman.
And for fat, starving people everywhere,
and for Mr. O'Neill, wherever he is.

CHARACTERS

BOB: a health-conscious juice bar customer.
BILL: a health-conscious juice bar customer.
LUCY: Jay's former flame, also a health-conscious juice bar customer.
JAY: the Juiceman.

SETTING:

A juice bar.

ORIGINAL PRODUCTION

The Juiceman Cometh was produced by Act One in association with Showtime Networks Inc., Paramount Network Television, Viacom Productions and Grammnet Productions for *Act One '95: A Festival of New One-Act Plays*, at The Met Theatre in Los Angeles, CA in April 1995. It was directed by James Eckhouse with the following cast:

Bob	Jay Patterson
Bill	Rick Zieff
Lucy	Sandy Martin
Jay	Sherman Howard

The Juiceman Cometh

SCENE ONE
A juice bar.
*Bob and Bill each have shots of wheatgrass in front of them and a large
glass of vegetable juice.*

BOB: To Jay.
BILL: To Jay.
    (*They down shots of wheatgrass, take a slug on their juice.*)
BOB: Oatmeal.
BILL: Absolutely!
BOB: How many whatchacallems …
BILL: Grams.
BOB: … of crude fiber does it have?
BILL: Must be …
BOB: Two, two and a half – what?
BILL: More like … five, or more.
BOB: I'm talking about *crude* fiber.
    I think you're thinking *total dietary fiber.*
BILL: Two grams.
BOB: You sure?
BILL: Total dietary fiber is something like six grams.
BOB: Cheers!
BILL: Crude is two.
BOB: To total dietary fiber.
    (*They drink.*)
BILL: (*Raises his glass.*) *Organic five-grain cereal.*
    (*They drink.*)
BOB: (*Raises his glass.*) Your multi-grain bagels.

(*They drink.*)

BILL: (*Raises his glass.*) Whole wheat hot-dog buns.

(*They drink.*)

BOB: (*Raises his glass.*) Tofu dogs.

(*They drink.*)

BILL: Fill'er up?

BOB: Absolutely.

(*Bill goes to the bar.*)

BOB: Jay said he's coming when?

BILL: What is it now?

BOB: (*Looks at his watch.*) Two, two O four.
He said one.

BILL: He'll be here. (*Returns with the refills.*)

BOB: You think Jay'll want his favorite drink?

BILL: Absolutely.

BOB: I thought he might.

BILL: Carrot apple.

BOB: Nah.

BILL: His favorite drink is carrot apple.

BOB: No way.

BILL: All right, you tell me.

BOB: Triple A – carrot, celery, apple, beet, parsley, and wheatgrass.

BILL: I don't think so.

BOB: Don't tell me that.

BILL: It's what I'm telling you.

BOB: He invented carrot apple.

BILL: He didn't invent it.

BOB: Saved his life.

BILL: It may have saved his life, but I don't think he invented it.

BOB: All right then, who?

BILL: You don't need to invent it. It just is.

BOB: Nothing's just is. Everything is something.

BILL: Squash it.

BOB: It's squashed.

BILL: All right.

BOB: (*Pause.*) I met him once.

BILL: Who?

BOB: Who we talkin about?

BILL: You met Jay?

BOB: Shook his hand.

BILL: Where?

BOB: In the produce section of the Trillium market in Lincoln City, Oregon. (*Pause.*) At first I didn't wanna say nothin because I was carrying with me a pound of smoked salmon and half of beef jerky.

BILL: You ate beef jerky?

BOB: I done a lotta things in my time.

BILL: Beef jerky?

BOB: Hey, we live and learn. Am I right? (*Pause.*) So there I am with the salmon and the jerky, and there's Jay. I go to myself, "Oh shit, oh shit." I'm thinkin, stash the jerky somewhere and go up to the guy. I mean the salmon ain't half as bad as the jerky. I mean the salmon is fish.

But before I can stash the jerky he turns –

BILL: He turns?

BOB: Like this. (*Shows him.*)

He turns like this, see, and he goes – I'll never forget this – he goes, "Nice melons, huh?"

BILL: So what'd you do?

BOB: What do you think I did.

I go, "Sure. Beautiful melons."

And then I say, "Avocados look pretty nice too."

And he goes: "Oh yeah."

BILL: He said, "Oh yeah"?

BOB: Oh yeah.

And then I go, "Hey, ain't that you?"

BILL: What'd he say?

BOB: He says, "Yeah, I'm me."

BILL: "I'm me"?

BOB: This is what he said. (*Pause.*)

So I go, "Lemme shake your hand."

And he shook it. (*Pause.*)

And I helped with a hundred-pound sack of carrots out to his car.

BILL: What'd you do with the beef jerky?

BOB: I'd like to say I got rid of it.

But I can't say that because I did, in fact, eat it.

BILL: You ate the whole half?

BOB: No. I'd say a good quarter though.

BILL: I bet it's still rotting in your intestines.

BOB: This was years ago.

BILL: It takes years sometimes.

BOB: Been clean ever since. (*Pause.*)

BILL: You know who I met once?

BOB: Who?

BILL: Linus Pauling.

BOB: Get the fuck …

BILL: I swear.

BOB: Where?

BILL: In a restaurant.

BOB: You met Linus Pauling in a restaurant?

BILL: I served him. I was his waiter.

BOB: Damn!

BILL: You know what he ate?

BOB: What?

BILL: You know what he ate?

BOB: No.

BILL: You know what he ate?

BOB: How in the fuck should I know what he ate!

BILL: Don't work yourself into a case of high blood pressure.

BOB: Just tell me what he ate.

BILL: Steak.

BOB: No.

BILL: You think I'm making this up? I saw him with my own two eyes.
   He ate steak.

BOB: Whataya know.

BILL: I know he ate the steak.
   And he ate a slice of cheesecake for dessert.

BOB: Wicked.

BILL: I wasn't gonna say nothin.
   I mean we're talking, you know: "How are you tonight, sir?"
   I tell him what the specials are:
   "We have the angel hair pasta with rock lobster sauce."
   But in between his last cup of coffee and collecting the bill, I say to
   him: "Sir, I admire you."

BOB: You told him you admire him?

BILL: Man's won two Nobel prizes for chrissakes.

BOB: This is true.

BILL: Am I lyin?

BOB: Can't argue with the facts.

BILL: You can but you'll lose.

BOB: So what'd he say?

BILL: When?

BOB: After you told him you admire him.

BILL: He goes, "Thank you."
Like that.
And then I walked away.

BOB: "Thank you." Like that.
And then you walked away.

BILL: What should I have done?
Suck on his ring finger, what?

BOB: If it was me, I'da said, at least, somethin about vitamin C.

BILL: That's the obvious thing.

BOB: It's the correct thing.

BILL: What would you know about bein correct. You ate beef jerky for chrissakes.

BOB: Bringin up stuff from the past, huh?
Somethin I told you in confidence.
And you throw it back in my face?

BILL: I'm only sayin ...

BOB: Let's let sleeping dogs rest.

BILL: Fine.

BOB: You see a dead dog layin in the street, don't go kickin him in the side.

BILL: Definitely not.

BOB: Because the dog might just be sleepin.
And when you go to kick him, he'll bite your freakin foot off.
(*Enter Lucy, finishing off a large vegetable juice. She also has a gym-type bag with her.*)

LUCY: Hey! (*She slurps the last bit of juice through a straw.*) So where's Jay?

BOB: I think, I'm sure, he must be on his way.

LUCY: Goddamn! This place smells of carrots.
I love it.
I love the smell of carrots. (*Pause.*)
What'll you have boys?

BILL: Who me?

LUCY: What's your favorite?

BILL: I like – well I like 'em all, but, my favorite, I think, might be plain old carrot, apple, pear.

LUCY: Carrot and apple you can mix. But never with pear.

I'm surprised at you.

BILL: Who told you that?

LUCY: Who do you think?

BILL: I don't know, who?

LUCY: Jay.

BILL: The Jay?

LUCY: You don't believe me, look it up. Page seventeen: "apple juice, a wonderfully versatile juice that bridges the gap between fruits and vegetables, as it is the only one that should be mixed with either."

BOB: Stupid shit.

BILL: Who you callin a stupid shit?

BOB: This is basic, Bill. Apples are the only things that bridge the gap.

I'm surprised at you.

How long you been juicin?

BILL: I don't know: years.

BOB: And you don't remember Jay's cardinal rule? "Only apples bridge the gap." Not pear.

BILL: Did I say pear?

BOB: You said pear.

BILL: I said pear, but I didn't mean pear.

I meant parsley.

My favorite drink is good old carrot, apple, parsley.

LUCY: Good drink. (*To Bob.*) You?

BOB: I like a drink with carrot and green bell pepper.

LUCY: "The Blemish Blaster."

BILL: What's your favorite?

LUCY: "Crimson Song." (*She goes to get the drinks.*)

BOB: (*To Bill.*) Here's a woman knows what she's talkin about.

BILL: (*To Lucy.*) What's in a "Crimson Song?"

BOB: Don't tell him, let him guess.

LUCY: Carrot, beet, lettuce, Swiss chard.

BILL: "Swiss chard."

BOB: You use Romaine, am I right?

LUCY: Absolutely!

BOB: I try to tell this guy: iceberg lettuce is crap lettuce.

You think he listens to me.

BILL: I don't use iceberg lettuce.

BOB: You gonna sit there right in front of me and lie.
I seen you do it.

BILL: Once. I did it once in my life.
Let's let the sleepin dog, or the dead dog, rest.
Okay?

BOB: All right.
(*Lucy returns with a tray full of drinks, and a few shots of wheatgrass.*)

BILL: So tell me lady –

LUCY: Lucy.
(*Raises her glass. They drink.*)

BOB: Bob.
(*Raises his glass. They drink.*)

BILL: Bill.
(*Raises his glass. They drink.*)

BILL: So tell me Lucy: tell this guy how many grams of crude fiber there is in oatmeal.

LUCY: Fuck oatmeal.

BILL: "Fuck oatmeal"?
You hear that Bob: she said "Fuck oatmeal."

BOB: I heard her.

LUCY: The thing to eat is psyllium husks.

BILL: What?

LUCY: Ain't you never heard of psyllium husks?

BOB: You remember Bill: that guy came by selling psyllium husks.

BILL: What guy?

BOB: The husk guy!

BILL: Oh yeah.

BOB: You remember.

BILL: I remember.
I love a few good husks.

BOB: We all do.

BILL: I love to eat 'em raw.

BOB: (*Raises his glass.*) Nothing better than a good raw husk.

BILL: Or mixed with a little wheat gluten.
(*They drink.*)

BOB: 'Nother Crimson Song?

LUCY: Nah. Get me a collard greens.

BOB: Straight?

LUCY: With a medium spinach.

BILL: I'll take a Crimson Song.

And a shot of wheatgrass.

LUCY: Shot of grass for me too.

With a spritz of lime juice.

(*Bob goes.*)

LUCY: So where in the hell is Jay?

BILL: He'll be here.

LUCY: Oh, I know he'll be here. But I'm wondering – well, I used to say to him, I'd say, "Jay, you can't keep them waiting." And he'd say, "Luce, my main squeeze, I won't."

BILL: He called you, "Luce, my main squeeze"?

LUCY: Well, not in front of other people.

BILL: You trying to tell me you and Jay –

LUCY: Me and Jay go way back.

I knew him when he was a meat eater. (*Pause.*)

I was there for the transition.

BILL: You were the transition woman?

LUCY: He made the transition with me.

BILL: You hear this Bob.

BOB: (*Comes back with the drinks.*) I heard it.

BILL: "The transition woman."

LUCY: I'll tell you this boys, but you gotta promise me you won't tell anyone else. (*Pause.*) I gave Jay his first wheatgrass enema.

BILL: No?

LUCY: Eh?

BILL: Yeah.

BOB: Damn!

LUCY: And I tell you boys, it was not a pretty sight.

The kinda crap that flowed outta Jay, well I wouldn't wanna see that again for as long as I live. (*Pause.*)

As I say, he was a meat eater.

He had whole cuts of beef comin out.

Hamburgers still shaped like patties.

A godawful mess.

Which I cleaned up.

BILL: You know, I always wanted to get one of those.

I heard they really clean you out good.

LUCY: Like Roto Rooter for the alimentary canal.

BOB: I had one a' those.

BILL: What?

BOB: Whata we talkin about? A wheatgrass enema.

BILL: You?

BOB: Would I lie about a thing like that.

BILL: You never said nothin about it.

BOB: It's not a thing you go around tellin people.
You do it, you keep it to yourself.
But like I say, I had it.
And let me tell you: the kinda crap that came outta me was
identical to the kinda crap that came outta Jay.

BILL: C'mon.

BOB: I swear.

BILL: Whole cuts of beef? Hamburgers shaped like patties?

BOB: What came outta my butt looked just like a McDonald's Happy
Meal.

BILL: Get the fuck …

BOB: You think I'm lyin?

BILL: I think maybe you're mistaken.

BOB: Lucy, will you tell this schmuck.

BILL: I think you got it wrong.

BOB: I'M NOT WRONG!

LUCY: Boys! Boys! Please! (*Pause.*) Drink up.
(*They drink.*)

BILL: Whata youse drinkin?

LUCY: Tomato Cooler and a shot of grass.

BILL: 'Nother Pancreas Rejuvenator?

BOB: I didn't have a Pancreas Rejuvenator.

BILL: Carrot, beet, spinach?

BOB: Carrot, beet, spinach is a "Popeye's Pop," you asshole.

BILL: Well I know you had one Bunny Hop.

BOB: I had the Bunny Hop.

BILL: A Cauliflower Quaff.

BOB: Yeah, so?

LUCY: Get him a Red Pepper Zinger with garlic juice.

BOB: There you go.

LUCY: Two cloves.
(*Bill goes to get the drinks.*)

LUCY: If Jay came in and saw you two fighting, he'd turn around and leave.

As you know, Jay is a very peaceful man.

He's serene.

Hostility upsets him.

This, of course, was not always the case.

Jay, before he became Jay, he was a very violent man.

I seen him smack a guy on the head with a turkey drumstick.

I seen him spit corn beef hash in another man's face.

I seen him smash two eggs in a fella's ears. (*Pause.*)

What I'm saying now doesn't leave this juice bar. Understood?

BOB: Absolutely!

LUCY: Jay was an animal.

Like a freakin buffalo with a thorn stuck in his foot.

I seen him once eat a frozen steak.

Ripped the thing apart with his teeth.

Then he swallowed it chunk by frozen chunk.

And he goes; "Luce, get me another."

BOB: I don't believe it.

LUCY: I swear: I was there.

BOB: C'mon.

BILL: (*Comes back with the drinks.*) She said she was there; she was there.

LUCY: I seen him steal a kid's Easter basket filled with painted hard boiled eggs; and I seen him eat every last one of the jelly beans, and all the eggs too. (*Pause.*)

Hey, this is nothin.

If we go back even further into Jay's past, we find he used to work on a ranch, where he killed bulls.

This is how he did it: he'd go into the corral, get the bull steamin mad.

Jay'd stand there waitin, and when the bull charged, he punched the bull dead in his head and laid that fucker out.

One punch to the bull's head, and the bull was dead. (*Takes a quick shot of wheatgrass.*)

I shit you not my friends.

I tell you: I was there. (*Takes another quick shot of wheatgrass.*)

But – it's all different now.

Jay's serene.

Jay is cool.

Jay's the Juiceman and he's nobody's fool. (*She lays her head down, goes to sleep.*)

BILL: What happened to her?

BOB: She's sleep.

BILL: I can see that.

(*Examines Lucy.*)

This broad is a guzzler.

Lookit: her lips are all green.

(*He runs his finger along her lips then licks his finger.*)

Spinach. (*Offers Bob a bowl of sprouts.*) Some garbanzo sprouts?

BOB: Those are adzuki sprouts! (*Stretches, yawns.*) God, I'm tired.

BILL: Listen.

BOB: What?

BILL: She's mumblin somethin under her spinach breath.

LUCY: Jay baby, Jay baby – yeah.

Gimme the whole hog, Jay. Gimme the whole hog.

BILL: Whataya think the "whole hog" is?

BOB: Take a guess.

BILL: The whole hog as opposed to the half hog?

BOB: Ssshhhh. Listen:

LUCY: All the way, Jay.

Give it to me. (*Pause.*)

Suck the knuckle big fella.

Lick the rear end.

Oh Jay. Oh Jay. Oh Jay!

(*Pause.*)

BILL: Did she say "O.J."? (*Stretches, yawns.*) God, am I –

BOB: Go back to sleep.

(*They go to sleep. Pause. Enter Jay with a plastic bag.*)

JAY: Hello friends.

(*No answer. Jay sits at the bar, looks at the empty glasses, runs his finger inside one and licks his finger.*) Fennel juice. (*He takes out an order of barbecued Chinese spareribs from his plastic bag and starts eating them. After he's eaten a few, he belches loudly.*)

BILL: (*Stirring.*) What was that?

BOB: What was what?

JAY: Hey gang.

BILL: Jay?

BOB: Hey Jay!

LUCY: Jay?

BOB: He's here.

LUCY: Is that you?

JAY: Hey, Luce.

LUCY: Goddamn! Whataya know! It's Jay!
> (*Pause. A moment of reflection.*)

BOB: Whataya eatin there Jay, tofu spareribs?

JAY: These?

BOB: What are they, like wheat gluten or some sort of brown rice concoction on a simulated rib bone. (*He smells one of the bones.*)

JAY: Pork.
> (*Pause.*)

BOB: Eh?

JAY: Pig. Pig's ribs.

BOB: C'mon. Don't play around Jay.

JAY: You don't believe me, taste one.

BOB: (*Takes a bite out of a rib and spits it out.*) Pork on a pig's rib. (*Pause.*) Holy Jesus!

BILL: Lemme see that.
> (*Bob gives him the rib. Bill holds it up to the light, examines it, smells it.*)

LUCY: Back on the stuff, huh Jay?

JAY: What can I say, Luce.

BILL: Say it ain't so, Jay. Say it ain't so.

JAY: If I could I would. But I can't.

BOB: You know what's in those spareribs.
We're talkin fat content, we're talking nitrates, your hormones. We're talking about a pig fed with pig shit.

JAY: You think I don't know this.

BOB: You "know this" and you eat them?

JAY: "This" is the tip of the meatberg. (*Pause.*)
First it was small stuff like a bite offa somebody's hot dog. Then it was a bowl of chili. Then it was like an orgy of bacon and eggs, corned beef hash and eggs, ham-steak and eggs. Before you know it, I'm swallowin down pounds of luncheon meat: salami, bologna, turkey roll – liverwurst.

BOB: You ate liverwurst?

JAY: I ate it in hunks.

And oh – let's not forget about a few cans of Dinty Moore Beef Stew.

BILL: Holy cow. Holy cow!

LUCY: Jay, what happened, Jay?

Why?

JAY: I'm at the zoo, where they house the farm animals, chewing on a carrot. I lean on the fence and spy a bull. I look at my carrot, I look at the bull. The bull looks at me and I look back at my carrot.

The sight of it, the thought of it –

I musta juiced over a million carrots in my life, and the feel of it in my hand – orange knob of a thing, small cone-shaped root, little stick – (*Pause.*)

Not one more, I said to myself.

Not one.

I threw the carrot to the floor and hopped the fence.

Me and the bull. I clap my hands and flail my arms.

The bull charges.

And when he was on me …

BILL: "Dead in the head."

JAY: I laid that fucker out.

BOB: I can't believe it.

JAY: Believe it. (*Pause.*)

I thought about my old man who turned ninety-two last November, my old man who gets up every morning to ride his bike.

My old man who goes to The Sizzler every Thursday for a rib-eye steak, who eats McDonald's cheeseburgers for lunch, who at night when he's hungry opens up a can of Spam. Who smoked cigars for most of his life. Whose only complaint at ninety-two is it's hard to ride the bicycle uphill against the wind. (*Pause.*)

I heard on the news: Linus Pauling died.

BILL: No.

JAY: From prostate cancer.

BILL: I don't believe it.

Not Linus Pauling, no. From prostrate cancer?

I met him once.

I was his waiter.

You know what he ate?

BOB: We heard this already.

BILL: They didn't hear it.

BOB: Let's not rehash all this. All right?

He met Linus Pauling in a restaurant.

He served him steak and cheesecake.

All right?

Fine. I told them. Now let's forget it.

BILL: I listened to your story.

BOB: I told it once. Do you see me tellin it again.

BILL: You will.

BOB: No I won't.

BILL: I know you.

BOB: You don't know me!

LUCY: Boys, boys! Please.

It doesn't mean anything, Jay.

My mother had the same diet as your father. She died at fifty-four.

So what does it mean? Your father's lucky? He's got a great set of genes, something, and it doesn't matter what he eats.

JAY: I remember when he turned ninety. We had a big bash. Everybody's eatin bratwurst, drinkin beer. Me, I sit there with my portion of buckwheat sprouts and black beans; the next morning I woke up with a hangover.

It was a feast and I turned my back on it.

I refused to feast with other men.

Life's feast.

And what is life if not one long feast? (*Pause.*)

Where are we? Huh? Where are we? (*Pause.*)

I'm asking, where are we?

BILL: We're here.

In this juice bar.

BOB: We're here all right.

We been here, waitin for you.

JAY: We are where the deer and the antelope roam.

Deer and antelope. And why are they here?

LUCY: To roam.

JAY: To eat.

LUCY: To roam.

JAY: The taste buds tell no lies. (*Pause.*)

To sit out in the sun on a wonderful summer day and smell a steak cooking over charcoal. Or to go to a baseball game and eat a ballpark hot dog. Or the aroma of bacon frying in the morning. Ham for Christmas. Thanksgiving turkey.

Pizza for chrissakes. A slice of pizza with pepperoni and extra cheese.

"My country 'tis of thee, sweet land of liberty, of thee I sing."

Baked clams. Raw clams on the half-shell.

Lobster bisque. Lobster claws, cracked crab, and mussels.

Leg of lamb, lamb chops, lamb stew.

Chicken cutlets, chicken gizzards.

Fried chicken. Chicken and dumplings.

Biscuits and gravy!

A cool glass of milk.

Chocolate mousse, cheesecake.

Hot fudge, banana splits. (*An epiphany.*)

Ice cream!

For God's sake, ice cream!

Anything and everything, as long as it tastes good, I'll eat it.

I want to open my mouth wide enough to swallow every four-legged animal on this planet, everything edible that flies or swims.

Fill me, feed me.

Shove it down my gullet.

Tack it to my palate.

I'm an animal. I'm an animal.

Gimme a bone to suck on. Gimme a leg to chew.

I'm an eating machine. All I want to do is eat.

And all I want to eat is meat.

Meat. Meat. Meat.

And a sugar frosted, chocolate fudge dipped, caramel cream filled, fat saturated, cholesterol packing dessert. (*Pause.*)

I've got bull's blood on my hands and pork rinds in my belly. (*He breaks down.*)

BOB: He's down.

BILL: He's out.

BOB: Just a shell of the man he once was.

BILL: Look at him: he's a wreck.

BOB: He's finished.

LUCY: You disgust me.

BILL: Who me?

LUCY: The both of youse.

BOB: What'd we do?

LUCY: Now is not the time to whine.

Now is the time for all good people, to come to the aid of the Juiceman. (*Pause.*) Will you help me?

BOB: Tell us what to do.

LUCY: First, we gotta flush him out.

BILL: Wheatgrass enema.

LUCY: Can you handle it?

BILL: I think I can.

LUCY: And you?

BOB: Count me in.

LUCY: All right boys, help me lift him.

BILL: Got him.

(*Bob and Bill lift Jay and move him toward a table, Bob and Bill under each arm. Jay's arms extend outward, resembling Christ on the cross.*)

JAY: (*As he is being carried to the table.*) Wipe me clean. Make each fragment gleam.

LUCY: (*Pulls an enema kit out of her bag.*) We're going to flush you out and save you.

JAY: Thank you.

Thank you Lord.

LUCY: Jay.

JAY: Thank You for this day.

(*Lights fade to black.*)

END OF PLAY